THE
COMPELLING
COMMUNICATOR

THE
COMPELLING
COMMUNICATOR

MASTERING THE ART AND SCIENCE OF EXCEPTIONAL PRESENTATION DESIGN

TIM POLLARD

CONDER
HOUSE
PRESS

WASHINGTON, DC

Copyright © 2016 Tim Pollard

ISBN: 978-0-9982373-1-2
Library of Congress Control Number: 2016957115

Published by
Conder House Press
Washington, DC

Edited by Don Weise and Stacey Aaronson
Book design by Stacey Aaronson

Photo credits:
Our thanks to Shutterstock for the vomiting pumpkin and mother/child images, and to the Collection Museo Nacional Centro de Arte Reina Sofía, Madrid, for the use of the *Guernica* paintings. And sincere thanks to Sarah Steenland for her original illustrations found on pages 109 and 208.

Printed in the USA

To Ruth, Grace, Angus, Fergus, and Rosie.
Without you, none of this other stuff would mean anything at all.

To the core Oratium team:
Eli, JD, Jerry, Sean, and Sean.
You are the reasons why we really might change the world.

and …

to Eva Kor, my hero, friend,
and the greatest natural communicator I've ever known.

Soli Deo Gloria

CONTENTS

PART TWO

MASTERING PRESENTATION DESIGN

THE
COMPELLING
COMMUNICATOR

PROLOGUE

A TALE OF TWO CITIES

City 1: Orlando, Florida

ABOUT A YEAR AGO, I WAS DOWN IN FLORIDA, WHERE I WAS speaking at a well-known company's leadership conference. I had spoken on the topic of sales messaging for a couple of hours in the early afternoon, and after wrapping up, instead of the normal dash to the airport, I decided to stick around.

The reason I stuck around was that several people had told me I had to stay for the CEO's closing address. People were positively gushing in anticipation of his presentation. "You must hear him—he's incredible." Not surprisingly, this more than piqued my interest. Great communication is so rare that it's worth sticking around for, so I stayed.

This CEO duly took the stage for a tight thirty-minute closing keynote, and I could see what everyone was raving about. By any traditional standard, he was phenomenal. His presentation was unbelievably polished. Flawless, crisp delivery; using no notes, he knew his stuff perfectly. He fully engaged the crowd, pacing about the stage untethered, thanks to his hands-free mic. It was about the best eye contact and body language you could hope to see. He was endearing, witty, and warm. No depressing slide deck; in fact, he had only one slide that stayed up the whole time.

The slide captured his subject well, and it was a terribly important topic: "The Ten Things We've Got to Get Right This Year," and he moved effortlessly and fluently through the list of ten. He then closed on a motivational high, and the crowd went wild. Not quite throwing underwear, but pretty close.

What a treat. Given how much we all struggle as speakers, this was a masterclass in what we all aspire to be. By any traditional standard, he was world-class. Except for one thing I spotted. His ten points weren't organized into any form of narrative flow. There was no real storyline or thread that ran through them. They were ten essentially unrelated things. Important but unrelated.

By design, the conference ended moments after he finished. The emcee thanked him and the crowd and shut the event down, at which point everybody headed for the door. As we were all filing out, I grabbed someone from the audience and asked them a simple question. Sadly, I knew exactly what the answer was going to be.

"Hey, wasn't that great? But do you mind me asking how many of Andy's "Ten Things" you remember?" After a few moments of thought, he named two. *Two!*

Think about that.

+ We were less than five minutes from the close.
+ It was his CEO.
+ The topic was The Ten Things We've Got to Get Right This Year.
+ The speaker's delivery was flawless, witty, effortless, sparkling ...

Surely, if there's any presentation that ought to be fully remembered, it's the CEO speaking on critical issues. Yet a mere five minutes after his presentation, his audience only retained about 20%. That is shocking. I'll explain what went wrong a little later, but for now, hold one thought: This presentation appeared to be world class, and yet there was almost no effective transfer of ideas. Nothing actually stuck.

City 2: Billings, Montana

BY ODD COINCIDENCE, JUST A FEW WEEKS AFTER THE EVENTS described above, I was in an audience of about 2,000 people in a large high school gymnasium, preparing to listen to a visiting speaker who'd been promoted by the school and on local radio.

After a brief introduction from the teacher who'd invited her, a little old lady walks onto the stage. She's rather short, a little stocky, and dressed in a conservative blue in keeping with her 84 years of age. She takes a seat at a trestle table and puts her head down to speak into a table microphone, and apart from looking up from time to time, she basically doesn't change position for the rest of the evening.

While she spent most of her life as a realtor in Indiana, she still speaks in the strong accent of her native Hungary, yet she is easy to understand. She's actually from the former Transylvania, which makes the whole thing eerily reminiscent of a Dracula movie.

She speaks for two full hours, without a break. She never stands, let alone moves around the stage. There is no "body language" to speak of. She never really makes eye contact and uses no visual aids of any kind. She simply talks into the microphone, and in those two hours she communicates three big ideas. Three life lessons, borne from the experience of her childhood.

Today, well over a year later, those three lessons remain indelibly etched in my mind. More importantly, in the intervening months I've spoken to many others who were in attendance that day, including several teenagers, and almost without fail they, too, are able to recall the three lessons with amazing accuracy. Learning truly happened here; indeed, this was one of the most brilliant presentations I've ever witnessed.

The lady in question is Eva Kor, and we'll get back to her story later, but for now, these two cameos present us with a truly perplexing problem.

The CEO checked every box that traditional presentation-skills thinking tells you to check. He had perfect eye contact, body language, humor, delivery polish, and so on. Yet 80% of his message was gone within five minutes. Eva, on the other hand, failed to check any of those traditional boxes, and yet she delivered a presentation superior to virtually anything I've ever seen, and her message stuck perfectly.

What happened here?

The conclusion is unsettling:
We've got the wrong boxes.

PART ONE

Understanding the Skill

We Need to Master

CHAPTER ONE

A PROBLEM WORTH SOLVING

COMMUNICATION SKILLS MATTER. AND I SUSPECT THAT I DON'T need to elaborate on that too much.

One useful principle of presentation design is: "Don't prove what doesn't need proving." Time is the most precious resource in most presentations, yet presenters routinely burn that time hammering a point that the audience is already sold on. (It's a mistake I call "too much club.") That's the danger in this chapter. I'm going to lay out an argument for why it is so critical that we communicate well. You may be thinking, "I get it—that's why I'm reading this book in the first place, move on." So with that said, let me try to burn as little of your mental energy as I can by showing you just how crucial it really is.

The importance of communication as a life skill, and especially as a business skill, has been proven beyond doubt. There are numerous empirical studies correlating communication effectiveness with leadership effectiveness, and it has been discussed in journals from *Forbes* to *Harvard Business Review*. Perhaps more importantly, we all implicitly "get" that communication effectiveness has contributed significantly to the success of many of the world's most admired leaders, from Abraham Lincoln to Winston Churchill to Steve Jobs. Sadly, we also recognize its significance in the rise of some of history's most despised figures. It's been said—rather chillingly—that Adolf Hitler killed twenty million people with his tongue.

∽∾∽

Understanding exactly why communication effectiveness matters so much needs a little more explanation, and a good place to start is the core issue of outcomes. Every presentation is ultimately about getting action. We present for a reason; we want people to do something. We want customers to buy, bosses to back or fund our cherished projects, team members to support a difficult change, donors to give generously, investors to invest, and so forth. Churchill needed a weary people to keep soldiering on in defiance of overwhelming Nazi military might. In the early days of Apple, Steve Jobs wanted the world to migrate from well-entrenched legacy providers and take a risk on the unproven newcomer. We present to drive action.

We are all selling our ideas to others, all the time. In meetings, whether formal or informal, we are trying to get support for our plans and dreams, and at times, the stakes are monumentally high. Perhaps we've worked on a project idea for months or even years, and this is our one chance to pitch it to the divisional president visiting from Paris. **And in that "culminating moment," how well you communicate your ideas plays a pivotal role in whether you get the outcome you're looking for.**

Let's look at one area of business life where this can be clearly demonstrated.

The Curious Case of the Struggle in Sales

AN ESPECIALLY INTERESTING PLACE TO START IS WITH ONE OF THE most important areas where a company must get communications right: sales presentations. The general story of sales is that: A) it's becoming ever-more difficult to even get in to see a customer; B) once you do get in, you may only have that one chance to make your solution truly stand out; and often C) in a normal competitive situation, you don't merely need to be compelling, you need to be more compelling than the other guys waiting out in the lobby. Oh, and by the way, the commercial future of your business unit rests on this communication succeeding, as does your own personal income. This is an incredibly high-stakes communications environment, which is what makes the following data so surprising.

Whenever our company works with a sales messaging client, we conduct a simple, two-question pulse survey that asks them, on a scale from one to ten (ten being stupendous and one being horrible), to assess A) the quality of the core solutions they sell, and B) the quality of the messaging of those same solutions. In other words, how well they are telling their story to the customer.

Great Stories That Aren't Being Told

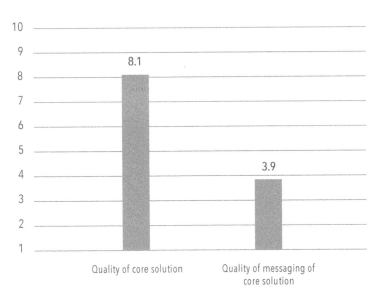

As you can see on the left of the chart, companies self-assess the quality of their solutions pretty highly, at around 8.1/10. That's an impressive grade, but I don't think this is in any way unrealistic. These are mostly Fortune 500 companies, and the quality of what they do for their customers is generally quite high. These are well-engineered solutions that solve important customer problems. But it's the second bar that's so surprising. When you ask about the messaging of these same great solutions, almost without fail, the scores plummet. These companies assess the quality of their messaging at an average of 3.9/10, which is basically less than half the quality of the underlying solution.[1]

This is a consistent pattern we see at almost every organization we talk to; it seems that even the best companies have tremendous difficulty telling their story well. There's nothing more agonizing than battling to finally get that elusive customer meeting . . . and then blowing it with a 3.9/10 conversation. *Truly, a customer conversation is a terrible thing to waste.*

Now, is it possible that these companies are somehow being a little too self-critical? No. When you look at what they're actually doing in these sales presentations, that 3.9 feels about right. In fact, it often feels worse.

When you look at most companies' sales materials, what you typically see are dense slide decks that are wildly overloaded with information. They generally have little or no logical structure and are far too sender-oriented, i.e., the material is much more about

---

[1] This sample includes data from several hundred business units/divisions drawn from over 60 companies. By the way, if you're worrying about sample bias, these aren't only companies who come to us worried about their messaging. We continue to run this survey across a broad spectrum of companies we are not working with—and guess what? The numbers are exactly the same.

the supplier than the customer—and this is the norm across all manner of companies and industries. I have stacks of these in my office. Forty to sixty slides is commonplace. One hundred and forty slides isn't uncommon.

Now, handling these decks definitely gives you the feeling that this probably isn't the best way of communicating with customers, but given that pretty much everyone does it this way, do customers really care? Most companies with poor messaging do want to know how to fix it, but I've met many others who aren't particularly worried. When I ask why, I'm told something like, "We know our messaging isn't great, but we don't think it's really hurting us." Well, as it turns out, that view is dangerously misguided. As we're about to see, audiences in any setting care a lot about how you present to them.

> Tolerating message mediocrity is much more serious than many companies realize.

In an ongoing survey we run with all the executives we work with, we pose a highly revealing question: "When you are in the role of customer and the salesperson makes a poor pitch, to what extent does that affect your perception of the underlying value of the product/solution being sold?"[2]

Essentially we're asking this: When a salesperson makes one of these bad presentations, are you willing to "see beyond" that and try to dig out the value of the underlying solution? Or, conversely, does that bad pitch contaminate your perception of the solution being sold?

---

[2] This question and those that follow form part of the Oratium pre-workshop and pre-keynote diagnostic. The data here spans an exceptionally wide range of executive functions, levels, industries, and geographies. As of this writing, the total sample size of this particular survey is over 2,500.

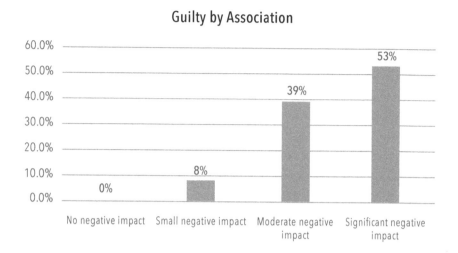

Guilty by Association

When you are in the role of customer and the salesperson makes a poor pitch, how does that affect your perception of the underlying value of the product/solution being sold?

Not only are the results perfectly clear, but the shape of the data is also interesting. In general, survey respondents don't like to choose the ends of a scale, so in most surveys you a get a bell-curve shape with the majority of responses in the middle. But in this case we didn't get that. Respondents, it turns out, were quite willing to express a more extreme, and perhaps more heartfelt, opinion.

As you can see in the left two bars, only 8% said that a poor presentation has little or no effect on them; 39% said it has a moderate effect; and over on the right, a shockingly high 53% said it has a significant negative effect. That's an alarming number, but the more you think about it, the more you realize how perfectly reasonable it is that people would correlate the quality of the message with the quality of the product the message is selling. (Consider how you would have answered that question.) It is completely understandable for someone to say, "If your product/solution is that amazing, then surely you should be able to tell a great story around it"—or the troubling corollary, "If the pitch is lousy, then I have reasonable grounds for thinking the solution might also be lousy."

This chart is telling us something deeply significant. Customers (and as we'll see later, all audiences) form a strong mental association between the quality of the story and the quality of the idea the story is selling. This is why complacency around poor messaging – of any kind – is so dangerous.

Now, given that many people reading this book aren't in sales, and perhaps have little interest in sales, why am I spending time on this particular area, and why should you care? The reason is that there are three lessons we can draw from sales that apply to the much broader world most of us live in.

First, sales presentations rank among the most important that ever get made. Companies and careers hinge on them. As a result, it is telling that most companies can't get them right. And if we can't get the most critical of all presentations right (and these are often carefully crafted by people whose specific job is to build them), do we think the average time-oppressed executive in some other function is doing any better?

Second, I'm sure the problems I described in those sales presentations sound eerily familiar. Dense, overloaded slide decks? Confusing structure? The content all about the presenter? The point is that sales isn't nearly as different from the rest of the presentation world as we might think. Said differently, the mistakes being made in sales presentations are virtually identical to the mistakes you see in all other business presentations you've been subjected to—be they from finance, IT, legal, or any other corporate function. **Sadly, the miserable experience of "Death by PowerPoint" is by no means confined to sales.**

Now, why is it important that the mistakes in sales presentations are the same ones we see elsewhere? Because in sales, unlike any other business function, you get immediate, verifiable data with respect to whether messaging was effective, which means that if you can figure out ways to improve that messaging, you can actually measure the improvement. As such, sales presentations provide a laboratory where innovations in communication design can be tested and their impact quantified.

In this book, I'm going to lay out a systematic process for creating compelling communication on a consistent and scalable basis that can be applied in any communications setting. We have qualitative evidence of its effectiveness everywhere, but through our work in sales, we can prove that the process works, because we can actually quantify the results.

Third, there's a critical insight in the sales story, the implications of which extend far beyond sales. It's that 53% "significant negative effect" number from our bar chart: audiences care how you present.

It's surprising to me how often presenters know they have built a poor presentation, but somehow manage to persuade themselves that it doesn't really matter. The proof of this is how often they decide to simply apologize for the shortcoming rather than taking the time to go back and correct it. "I know you can't read this slide," "I know I'm making you drink from the firehose," "If you don't mind me running long, let me take a few extra minutes to get through this." I always find this utterly bizarre. Rather than actually fix the mistake, which they would do if they felt it was important, they merely acknowledge its existence as though that somehow makes it all OK, subtly putting the obligation on the audience to accept the transgression with no further complaint. It's like saying, "I'm so sorry I just punched you in the face. I hope that's OK."

One of our team members was in a presentation recently where the speaker said, "I'm sorry these slides aren't clear. I just put this together this morning and I didn't have time to tidy it up." That's a troubling statement. At one level, there is a degree of arrogance on display here. When a presenter perceives that their time is more valuable than their audience's, they will never make the time to prepare properly. But I don't think arrogance is generally the issue. The real issue is misguided complacency. As presenters, the real reason we are willing to exchange our convenience for our audience's experience is because we think there's a low price to be paid for that trade. What we fail to realize in those moments is how much audiences care about how we spend their time, and how sharply they may judge us for our decisions.

Audiences do care. As we have just seen, customers make inferences about the quality of the solution from the quality of the presentation. And in the general world of business and leadership, those inferences become even scarier.

The Leadership Scenario

AS WE DID WITH SALES, LET'S START BY UNDERSTANDING HOW WELL we're doing. In our ongoing survey of executives, there's a question that sits right at the center: "Thinking broadly about the presentations you attend, what percentage would you place in each of the following categories?" People sit through a lot of presentations, and this is what they think of them.

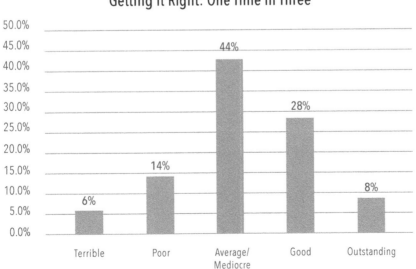

Getting It Right: One Time in Three

Thinking broadly about the presentations you attend, what percentage would you place in each of the following categories?

Looking at the two bars on the right, this data confirms dozens of other studies telling us that only about a third of all presentations are viewed as "good" or better by the audiences that sit through them, which means a whopping two-thirds are mediocre or worse, with a full one in five really "stinking up the joint."

What's easy to forget here is that behind this data, in all those unimpressive presentations on the left, there was a human story. In many of those presentations, someone was trying to accomplish something they cared deeply about. In some cases they still probably got the outcome they were looking for, but in our hearts we know that the farther left they scored, the less likely it was that they actually did.

The data we're reviewing here is revealing, but viewed through the lens of our personal experience, I suspect this isn't actually shocking at all, because these surveys are simply reflecting back the everyday world we all live in: those countless meetings where we were wishing there was some way out, where we were "counting down" to that last slide in the deck in front of us. All those hours of our lives we'll never get back. For many people, and especially those in "meeting-heavy" organizations, this is an almost daily experience.

The more interesting question is, of course, "Why does the data always come out this way and why are most presentations so poor?" The answer is the rather nasty cocktail of mistakes that most presenters keep mixing.

The following is a flip-chart exercise we conduct in our core workshop. The question here is: "What are some of the typical things you see in the business or conference presentations you attend?" The answers we always receive are:

- TMI / crammed / overwhelming
- All about the speaker / sender-oriented
- Boring
- Death by PowerPoint
- Bulleted slides / too many
- Reading the slides
- Irrelevant
- Too long
- Confusing / unclear structure
- Dry
- Too technical
- Predictable

The first remarkable thing you notice is that while we didn't ask only for what was going wrong, the overwhelming bias of the respondents is always toward the problems they see. Although most groups acknowledge that some rare presenters do avoid these pitfalls, the clear consensus of the hundreds of groups that have done this exercise is that most presentations display many of these problems.

The second notable observation is that it's always fundamentally the same list. **The words may change, but essentially, there's agreement that the typical presentation offers too much information, and is confusing, illogical, uninteresting, too slide-driven, and too sender-oriented.** If this is indeed the common pattern, it's no surprise that a paltry one-third are judged as "good" or better.

Now again, as with sales, we need to ask the deeper question. In this general setting of everyday business life, given the typical presentation is pretty mediocre, does a poor showing really matter? As you might expect, the answer is, "Oh, yes. It matters."

A Cautionary Word to Leaders: The Aftershocks of Poor Communication

---

WE'VE ALREADY ESTABLISHED THAT IN ALL PRESENTATIONS WE ARE trying to motivate action—to persuade our audience to do something that's important to us, and in a corporate setting that action frequently matters. We want to get our projects funded, or that headcount (staffing) increase sanctioned. Many times, successful presentations are the springboards of projects and initiatives on which careers are built, which is precisely why rejection of our ideas or proposals is excruciatingly painful. In the executive setting, however, the importance of communicating well goes way beyond the issue of outcomes. What we tend to forget is that we are also being judged when we present, and to a much greater extent than we probably realize.

You Are Being Watched

Let's look at three charts that explore the "ripple effect" of poor communication. The first question considers the extent to which people form opinions about a person's broader leadership ability based on the quality of their communication skills. The question we ask is: "When a leader or senior executive delivers a poor presentation, how does that affect your perception of their overall leadership ability?" Just as we saw in the sales example, we see that the associations are higher than we might have thought.

Leadership Undermined

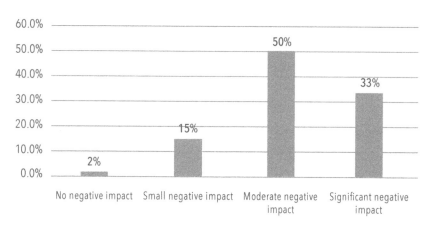

When a leader or senior executive delivers a poor presentation, how does that affect your perception of their overall leadership ability?

Only around 17% say that poor leadership communication has little or no effect on them. Meanwhile 50% report a moderate effect, and 33% cite a significant negative effect—that's a combined 83% forming a notable negative association. This is a significant finding, and distinctly troubling for leaders who struggle in this area. An organization's faith and confidence in its leadership is of paramount importance, and if those leaders don't communicate well, that confidence is undermined at least, it would seem, for 83% of the team.

I recently saw this painfully demonstrated. An old friend of mine is CEO of a successful investment management company. He's smart, visionary, and extremely well qualified to lead. But he presents horribly, routinely going "off script"—which inevitably means he runs long (the product of a highly creative mind that's constantly flying off in all directions). He doesn't distinguish well between his main and supporting points, and thanks to his background in investment analytics, his comments are frequently too technical: perfect for Wall Street, but not ideal for anyone else. Unfortunately, at the company's recent all-staff meeting, each of these habits was on full display.

I was a guest that day with no official responsibilities, so I simply observed from the sidelines. I understood that most of the folks in the room didn't know him that well, and it was fascinating to observe their unfolding reaction. As the presentation proceeded, it was clear that they were sharing opinions, but what was also clear was that they weren't responding to their CEO's message; rather, they were responding to *him*. From the sly smirks and exaggerated puzzled looks exchanged between the largely millennial attendees, I could see the disrespect, and even hostility, brewing in the room. It was sobering.

Will this corrosion of confidence boil over at some point into open rebellion? Probably not, but I saw the damage done.

> However unfairly, his leadership credentials were being seriously questioned, entirely on account of his communication deficiencies.

The second question from our survey only adds to this concern: "When a leader or senior executive delivers a poor presentation, how does that affect your perception of their critical thinking skills?" This question explores an even deeper correlation. Do audiences associate quality of communication with quality of thought?— or essentially, how smart you are?

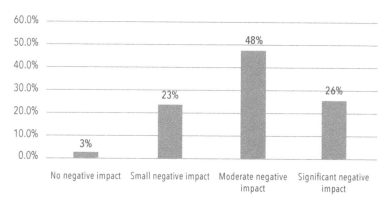

When a leader or senior executive delivers a poor presentation, how does that affect your perception of their critical thinking/analytical skills?

Again, we can see that they do. While it isn't quite as extreme, at 74% (the combination of the two bars on the right), a significant majority see poor communication as having a notable negative impact on their perception of a leader's critical thinking skills. Once again, this association feels completely reasonable. *"If you were smart, you would be able to create a clean, crisp, compelling argument, rather than this dry, mind-numbing PowerPoint."* I've had that thought myself a hundred times.

These two charts combine to make a powerful statement. Everyone wants their leaders to lead well. It's unhelpful to an organization then, if thanks to poor communication, its leaders are undermined by lingering doubts about the quality of their thinking, and by extension, their decision-making.

To this point, we've looked specifically at leadership, but what if you aren't yet a leader, or at least not a senior one? Does communication still matter, or does the more junior person get a free pass? Sadly, there's no such thing. The stakes for them are equally high, and possibly even higher.

Our final chart looks at the "aspiring leader" and examines an intriguing final correlation, which is whether more senior people associate the poor communication performance of less senior people with their future prospects for promotion. It's a pretty high-stakes question that asks, "When a person more junior than yourself (or a direct report) delivers a poor presentation, how does that affect your perception of their future potential/promotion potential?"

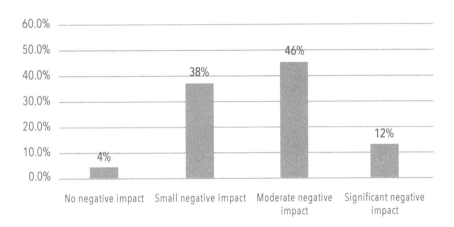

Give the Kid a Break

When a person more junior than yourself (or a direct report) delivers a poor presentation, how does that affect your perception of their future potential/promotion potential?

The first thing you notice is that fortunately, as you would hope, audiences aren't quite as severe in their judgment as they are with senior employees. The more junior presenter is given more leeway when they mess up, with about 40% (the two left bars) saying that it doesn't greatly affect their perception. That's the good news. The bad news, however, is obvious: while these junior team members are cut a little more slack, it's actually not that much more. As good as that 40% is, this means there's a rather alarming 60% in the two bars on the right, with 12% reporting a significant negative impact. It seems that there's some fairly stern judgment awaiting the junior employee who doesn't communicate well.

To this point, I've argued that the responses seen in the survey appear completely reasonable, but in this case, it seems a little harsh that respondents would so severely judge someone who's just coming up. The data, however, makes a noteworthy point regardless of whether we like what it tells us. **We live and work in a highly competitive world. Anytime someone presents, irrespective of how junior they are, they are being evaluated, however unfair, unreasonable, or premature that may seem to be.**

This insight was powerfully reinforced recently when we were preparing to teach our executive communication skills class as one module of a Fortune 50 company's leadership academy. It's one of my favorite standing engagements: a super-smart company with great people and a world-renowned learning culture. As I was reviewing the pre-class diagnostics, one response jumped out at me, being both highly insightful and brutally honest. Here's the question we ask, and the verbatim answer from a mid-level engineer:

> List some words you would associate with the experience of delivering an important presentation.
>
> *"Nervous, inexperienced, very stressful . . . afraid that I'll ruin my career because of one bad presentation. Senior executives form opinions very quickly and they have long memories."*

What a sobering statement—and this is a company legendary for its positive corporate culture where, supposedly at least, mistakes are OK as long as you learn from them. But that's not what this guy is feeling. You can only imagine how this effect multiplies in the more typical "churn and burn" organization.

Taken together, this collection of data strongly reinforces what we instinctively know: that in a general business setting, communication is a competency of the greatest importance. Aside from the question of whether you are compelling enough to secure the outcome you want, perhaps as important is the fact that you are being judged. And when things don't go well, all kinds of unspoken associations are being made, some of which may haunt you for a long time.

Now for the Good News: The Door Swings Both Ways

OF COURSE, BY FOCUSING ONLY ON THE NEGATIVE CORRELATIONS, it's easy to miss the enormous upside that can follow when a presenter hits it out of the park. The associations and repercussions flow both ways, and I'm actually living proof of this. I recall the moment vividly.

Many years ago, at around twenty-five years old, I was holding down a junior consultant job in a well-known consulting firm. It was the weekend, and on the upcoming Monday, my boss—the head of my division—was scheduled to give an important presentation to the Northern European marketing leadership of GlaxoSmithKline (then only Glaxo). It was to be a three-hour seminar on marketing planning in the pharmaceutical industry, and I had been given the vital job of driving the materials to the venue and setting up. I was only too happy to oblige: with a four-year degree in international marketing under my belt, I rocked at carrying the bags of the greater mortals.

Except it didn't go that way. I arrived at the venue early Monday morning to set up, and while I was doing so, my phone rang. It was Terry Collier, my boss and the scheduled presenter. His son had suffered a horrific multiple fracture of his leg in a soccer match the evening before, and Terry was, rightly, on hospital duty. He wasn't going to be able to make it. No problem. I found our main contact, a Dutchman named Ard Renaud (a great but rather twisted guy, as I later discovered), and told him we were going to have to cancel. He looked back at me and, in that dry Dutch way, calmly replied, "I'm sorry, Tim, but no way. We've flown in these people from all over Europe. You're going to have to do it."

OK . . . this wasn't funny. The stakes had just been seriously raised, and I couldn't walk away from the table. Though I didn't recognize it at the time, this truly was one of "those" life moments. If you'll indulge me with a little Shakespeare, the spirit of such moments is famously and beautifully captured in a short speech by the noble Brutus, in the play *Julius Caesar*:

"There is a tide in the affairs of men,
Which taken at the flood, leads on to fortune.
Omitted, all the voyage of their life
is bound in shallows and in miseries.
On such a full sea are we now afloat.
And we must take the current when it serves,
or lose our ventures."

(Julius Caesar: Act 4, Scene 3)

There are times in our lives when presentations are these moments: high tides that, if seized, could lead on to fortune—but if not seized, could lead to misery. And "On such a full sea I was now afloat." I would have done anything to get out of that damned boat, but I truly had no choice. Of course, with over twenty years of hindsight, it's now clear that having no choice in that moment was one of the best things that ever happened to me.

Anyway, there I was. I knew the basic outline of the presentation and had a decent understanding of the content. So I "speed-rehearsed" the opening riff as many times as I could in the hour I had before the nine a.m. start, and then we began. As it turned out, it went pretty well. I rehearsed the after-coffee riff during the coffee break, and prepared the final riff during some impromptu "networking" break that I fabricated.

Now, with Glaxo being our biggest client, news had traveled fast back to the office. This was a big deal, and midway through that final section, our CEO burst through the door like a superhero, fully expecting to rescue the catastrophe that was unfolding, as this spotty kid in a cheap suit lectured senior marketers from one of the world's smartest companies on the subject of marketing planning. But instead, seeing no evidence of a raging fire to be put out, he took his seat at the back while I, admittedly much closer to my notes than I otherwise would have been, brought the meeting to a successful and orderly close. Looking back, I'd love to say I was amazing, but I know I wasn't. I think I was probably pretty good. Solid. But given the calamitous circumstances, it had gone really, really well.

Unbeknownst to me, everyone in the room knew what was going on, which explained the wide smiles and the unprecedented standing ovation I received, while my CEO had a look on his face that was one-third surprised (to say the least), one-third proud, and one-third thoughtful. As I would only understand later, this was one of the most important moments of my career. I received a second ovation when I returned to the office that afternoon, which takes me to the point of the story: within six months, I had risen to lead the majority of that consulting team. Before that fateful Monday I had been a relatively unknown quantity, but thanks to that one soccer match and the onstage opportunity it created, my initial profile—and career trajectory—had completely changed.

I know this could all sound self-serving (I assure you, you will read about several of my many screw-ups as the book progresses), but I'm running that risk because it's crucial to demonstrate the positive side of the "communication correlation." I was far out of my depth, but somehow I delivered on this critical presentation, admittedly under unusually adverse circumstances, and those three hours unquestionably accelerated my career by at least five years (though I think it took more than that off my life).

> For good or ill, people are watching.
> Never underestimate just how much.

(By the way, one amusing postscript. Several months later I was back working with my Dutch friend at Glaxo, when he confessed something to me over lunch. Back on that memorable day, he would have been completely willing to cancel the meeting; this was clearly a case of force majeure, but he wanted to push me to see if I would rise to (or fold under) the challenge. I don't have assault with a soup spoon on my resume, but I came close in that moment. Maybe the real lesson of the story is that as wonderful as the Dutch are, beware their sense of humor.)

SUMMARY

Both the negative and positive examples we've looked at in this chapter point to one simple conclusion. **While most of the work people do is conducted quietly and outside the gaze of the public eye, the uniquely high-profile nature of presentations lends them a significance that is far greater than we tend to appreciate.**

When people see you present clearly, strongly, with a well-crafted argument, they infer—rightly or wrongly—that you possess several valuable competencies, and that perception can benefit you immensely. But likewise, it is quite common for audiences to infer that a person who presents in a confusing, disorganized, and dull way isn't that great a leader, and maybe not that great a thinker either.

We all intuitively understand that communication matters. What I hope I've done through these few pages is provide a window into just how much it matters. Which raises the most fascinating question of all: Why haven't we fixed this? If it's this important, why are the majority of presentations still mired in too much information, illogical in structure, and all wrapped up in mind-numbing, narcoleptic PowerPoints?

There's a variety of shallow reasons why people present poorly, and two of these are worth briefly exploring. But the real reason is far deeper and much more interesting.

CHAPTER TWO

WHY DO WE PRESENT SO POORLY?

I F YOU THINK ABOUT THE DISCUSSION SO FAR, IT PRESENTS A tremendous paradox. I've demonstrated compelling reasons why communication is terribly important, but I've also shown something that we all know from experience: that most presentations aren't very good.

That's a genuine paradox. People and companies tend to be good at the things that truly matter. Can you think of any other area where there's something important to be done, but where it's OK to fail two-thirds of the time? Manufacturing quality? Customer service? Plant safety? Of course not. Organizations don't work that way—except, it seems, when it comes to communication.

So, despite knowing its importance, why do we present so poorly? There are numerous forces in play here, but two are initially worth discussing.

1. I'll Get to It Tomorrow

The first is procrastination. We've all made this mistake, but it's still astounding how many people, even though they have an important presentation to make, leave it to the very last minute to get started. Have you ever been on a plane and someone in your immediate field of view is working on a PowerPoint, throwing a presentation together that they are presumably going to give pretty much right after they land? This kind of procrastination—or laziness—is everywhere, and it's deadly.

As we will discuss in great detail, the quality and structure of the argument in any presentation is of singular importance, and to get to its best, every argument needs at least some time to evolve and be refined. Critical ideas need to be identified, clarified, and separated from the body of secondary material. Illogical sequence needs to be spotted and untangled, and all that unnecessary content and duplication needs to be pulled out. Finally, might it be good to actually rehearse? As radical as it sounds, maybe we should practice the words, in search of that single elegant phrase that perfectly captures our big idea.

But when you leave it all to the last minute, none of this essential thinking can happen. Without realizing it, the folks on those planes have traded thinking for typing; they aren't designing, they're just frantically building, which, besides leading to "half-baked" presentations, is one of the chief reasons why we end up with the all-too-common "drinking from the firehose." Remember the famous Mark Twain quote: "I didn't have time to write a short letter, so I wrote a long one instead"? That's what's happening here.

Paradoxically, not giving yourself enough time is one of the primary causes of massively bloated material. If you look carefully, you've probably noticed that those people on the plane are always adding slides not removing them, adding bullets instead of subtracting. Whatever the presentation you're building, there's really no debating that first drafts tend to be pretty feeble; but because most people start too late, that's what the majority of presenters go to bat with. Remember that earlier quote: "I'm sorry these slides aren't clear. I just put this together this morning and I didn't have time to tidy it up."

This book can't and won't fix that problem. But if procrastination is your tendency, let me offer two thoughts: first, you owe yourself better than this, because there is nothing more frustrating than knowing—and regretting—that you underperformed because you underprepared. And you certainly owe your audience more than this. **Anytime people are giving up their time to listen to you, that time needs to be honored and respected. You owe them more than "Sorry it's bad, I just put this together this morning."**

Second, it may be a little unfair to call this laziness. Clearly, sometimes it is, but much of the time people are simply succumbing to the pressure of all the things that have a claim on their time. In a world of competing priorities, something has to give, and often it's that presentation that doesn't receive the design time it probably deserves. Because this issue of time pressure is very real, it would be condescending to minimize it, or conveniently sideline it by saying, "If you really cared about the presentation, you'd give it the time it deserved." The grown-up answer isn't to say "make the time"; it's to offer people a process that works in today's time-oppressed reality. As such, we need a process that creates exceptional presentations, but that does so within the parameters of today's overloaded schedules.

To foreshadow what's to come, I can promise that the process you are going to learn isn't only incredibly effective, it's also much quicker and more efficient than what you're probably already doing. We can't ignore time constraints; instead, we have to work within them.

2. The Power of the Crowd

The second common mistake presenters make is defaulting to today's depressingly low cultural bar. You may remember the old saying, "No one was ever fired for buying an IBM." The point wasn't that IBM was always the right solution. The point was that you would never be in trouble for going that route. Something similar applies to presentations. I have never heard a single individual say they like being marched through an agonizingly long slide deck, and "Death by PowerPoint" has become a cocktail party joke. It's all quite funny—until you ask a roomful of executives if they do the exact same thing they hate having done to them—serving up those bloated decks—at which point every hand in the room sheepishly goes up. This odd behavior says much about the power of culture, and it's hard to fight.

At many organizations, the deck is simply the accepted way that presentations are made, to such an extent that deviating from this norm can actually brand you as a dangerous heretic. You may think I'm exaggerating, but I've seen this resistance to change at dozens of companies, and it's especially evident in the largest. While there are far more effective presentation approaches, they aren't always initially popular.

I was recently slated to speak at a major company's leadership conference. This conference was a big deal, and with this organization being in the media/entertainment space, the conference had a producer. He was a nice guy, but he was clearly wound pretty tight: this was a multi-million dollar event, and if anything went wrong, his head was on the block.

I vividly recall our first phone conversation, because it was so revealing. He was briefing me on everything I needed to know: what my cues were, what music would introduce me, how to walk onto the stage. It was a pleasant conversation, but he was clearly making sure that I played my part in not blowing up the conference for his overlords.

We were doing fine until the inevitable question came: "Tim, this all sounds wonderful—can you email me your deck? We need to edit it for house style, and get it all loaded up ahead of time." My cheery answer wasn't what he was looking for: "It's OK, I don't have a deck." Silence. To this day, I swear I heard the involuntary accident taking place in his underwear, and then a cautious, "What do you mean you don't have a deck?" His question had the tone of a suddenly unsettled child asking, "What do you mean you're not my real parents?" However well the early conversation had gone, in his mind, I had now become a dangerous lunatic with the obvious potential to take down my own—and far more importantly, his—career. And so the dance began.

I explained how I was going to do things. By demonstrating the software I would use for my few visuals and showing him the audience's non-PowerPoint handout, I eventually got him off the ledge. Months later, after an extremely successful conference, he couldn't have been happier, but he certainly wasn't during that phone call, and that is my point. There are cultural norms that have become far too deeply entrenched. This highly intelligent man couldn't conceive that there existed even a single alternative way of approaching a keynote, which is bizarre if you think about it. But that's where many people are today.

Most of us have been told at some point, "Send me your deck ahead of time." It is simply assumed that this is how we work, and even though most people dislike the approach, organizations doggedly stick to it. You'd think a fresh approach would be welcomed, but often it's not, because however tedious and ineffective the old way is, it's familiar and it's safe. But beyond the security of predictability, the status quo exists for another important reason. People simply aren't aware of any credible alternative. They know "Death by PowerPoint" isn't going to win them any friends, but they do it anyway, not simply because it's acceptable, but because they have nothing to offer in its place. In many ways that is the driving purpose of this book. There really is another way.

3. The Deeper Reason: Rules Aren't Made to Be Broken

We've looked at procrastination and low cultural norms as reasons why people present poorly. Both of these are real, and either one of them will severely limit a person's effectiveness, but they are not the real reason. The real reason is far deeper and much more interesting. And it's best illustrated through an exquisite true story.

A couple of years ago, one of my oldest friends, Mark, had attended a typical financial services industry conference. There were about 400 people in attendance, and it was the usual blend of keynotes, workshops, and vendor-sponsored coffee breaks. He told me this story over a year after it happened, which is worth noting.

On the second morning of the conference, the crowd was settled in for the opening keynote. Following a brief introduction, the speaker took the stage and immediately brought up his first slide, which was the title of his presentation and a few bullets. Here's where things got interesting. There was a typo on the slide, and it wasn't just any typo. Not a forgivable missed apostrophe or comma, but a heinous spelling mistake right there in the presentation title itself. He's barely started talking, and it's hanging out there in foot-high capital letters. What a moment. In fact, it is so bad that someone in the audience actually calls him out on it. Something along the lines of, "Dude, do you not see that typo?" We've all seen speakers mess up, but this is crash and burn on an epic scale. It seems his credibility is gone, that surely this is irretrievable, that he's finished . . . except he's not.

Calm and smiling, he pulls $20 out of his pocket. Locating the guy who called him out, he says, "Thank you—well spotted!" Then he trots quickly out into the crowd and gives the man his $20. At this point, the room is stunned and silent. Every eye is now on him. He calmly walks back to the podium, and retaking his place, he pulls $200 out of his wallet and puts the sheaf of bills on top of the podium, in full view of the room, and announces: "There's one other typo in my slides. Whoever spots that gets the $200." If you're a *Big Bang Theory* fan, then as Sheldon would say, "BAZINGA!!!"

Brilliant! . . . or is it?

At first blush, I'm guessing many of you reading the story thought this was the coolest thing ever. Rising out of the sea of mediocre presentations, this speaker grabbed the audience in a stunningly memorable way. But let's step back and reflect. Was it really a good decision to play this game?

As it turns out, it's a catastrophic decision from a communications effectiveness standpoint. However funny and clever that game appears to be, from this moment on, no one is hearing a single word he's saying. He has self-destructed, and he has no idea that it's happened. And the reason he's failed is because he's broken several critical rules of communication, only he doesn't know he's broken them, because he doesn't know what they are to begin with.

And there it is:

The real reason we present badly is because we don't know what the rules that govern great communication are, and if we don't know what they are, we can never know if we're breaking them.

Whenever you put a presentation together, you are making literally thousands of implicit or explicit decisions. What content do I include? How much detail? What stories? What sequence? Do I use slides? How many? And on and on. But if we don't have a guiding framework telling us what we should and shouldn't do, what happens? **We do what makes sense to us.** We have no choice but to follow our own instincts, and we've seen exactly where those instincts lead: TMI, bulleted slides, confusing structure, sender-oriented content, etc. You've seen the list.

Now, let's go back to our $200 PowerPoint guy. What rules did he break? He broke at least three.

First, he had a bulleted slide as a visual. Don't do that, ever. Not only is your screen far too valuable to waste with words, but more importantly, six bullets presents your audience with five ideas you don't want them thinking about while you are discussing the one that you do. Bullets aren't only a horrible organizing framework for information, but every bullet you *aren't* discussing is an intellectual distraction from the one you are. (We will be devoting a whole section to the proper use of visuals, but for now, this will suffice.)

Second, he got caught in a trap that ensnares most speakers I see today. Instead of creating engagement between the audience and himself, he created engagement between his audience and his screen, and that's a problem.

PowerPoint is not at fault here, but this issue is directly attributable to the way most of us use it. For a variety of reasons, people today have become convinced that they are required to have something on screen for everything they're saying—so much so that they feel naked without something on screen to talk to.

> Indeed, many speakers today reference the "comfort blanket" of their slides so constantly that they seem more to be having a conversation with their screen than they are with their audience.

So deep has the idea of "a bullet for everything" become that I even know of one Fortune 100 company where the CEO does not allow you to make a point in a presentation if you don't have a slide bullet for it. He's on record as saying, "If it's not on a chart, it's not in your heart." This CEO is generally well regarded, but on this matter he's out of his mind. This idea that you should always have the point you're talking about on screen is the absolute opposite of the truth.

Communication is a very human, personal thing. It isn't something that happens between people and screens; it's something that happens between people and other people. In any presentation, you are trying to have a human dialogue with your audience, and even in a room of 5,000, with its inherent limitations of interaction, that is still the goal.

There is nothing wrong with projected visuals; indeed, when done properly these are an essential element of any presentation. But when you make the screen the continuing center of attention (and especially if you actually turn your back on the audience to read your slides!), you lose that essential ingredient of human connection. The screen takes over while you inadvertently relegate yourself to the role of narrator.

Research shows that if given the opportunity, our brains now tend to favor the screen over the auditory narrative because across the last 100 years, we've migrated from an auditory culture (theaters have AUDiences) to a screen-based culture (television has VIEWers). If you have any doubt about that, if you're fortunate enough to have a teenager in your immediate field of view, take a look at what they're doing. If you give people a screen to fixate upon, they will.

We've all seen it. When everything the speaker says is on a slide, audiences quickly identify that pattern of presenting and without realizing it, default to the screen, scanning and reading the bullets, inevitably getting ahead of the speaker. He or she may be discussing bullet two, but the audience is busily engaged guessing the content of bullet four, and by doing so they completely disconnect from the speaker. Because the brain is powerfully driven by curiosity (which is why you watch a terrible movie to the very end), never mind bullet two; bullet four is a puzzle to be solved. And, of course, the audience generally reaches the end of the slide before the speaker does, so they use the dead time to catch up on email until they peripherally notice the slide change, at which point the dance begins again. Total disconnection.

When you succumb to the inner pressure of always having something on screen to talk to, and the audience then defaults to solely reading that screen, you are no longer the star of your own movie. The screen is the star and you've become the disembodied soundtrack. This seems so obvious when it's explained, so how do we miss it? Again, because we don't know the rules.

Now, before we move on, this screen takeover is a problem in the majority of presentations I see, but how much more so was it in the case of my $200 guy? He's made it infinitely worse. His audience is completely fixated on the screen, because they're hunting for that typo! He could be naked and on fire, but no one would notice.

By the way, where do you think he put that second typo? I don't know for sure, but I bet it was on the last slide, because that fulfilled the point of the game. I love the irony of that. The game he designed with the specific intention of holding attention actually managed to destroy it up to the very last moment.

As important as these two rules are, the third and final rule he broke was by far the most serious—and in discussing it, I'm going to introduce the most important insight within this whole book. The single biggest key to extraordinary communication is one simple idea, and all great communication is great precisely because it adheres to this principle, while all lousy communication is lousy expressly because it violates this same principle. And the principle is this. Whenever you communicate, what you are trying to do is:

Powerfully Land
a
Small Number
of
Big Ideas

There it is. I genuinely believe that if you were to close the book now and never open it again, if you went away and simply applied this rule, my job would be done. But if you do choose to read on, everything that follows is going to be about how to apply and operationalize this idea, because doing it is a bit trickier than it might seem.

Now, as cute and "Twitter-esque" as this is, it's not merely a slogan. This insight gets to the very heart of how the brain works, and it is a touchstone that we are going to return to time and time again.

> The human brain doesn't do very well at storing and retrieving facts and data, especially large quantities of facts and data. But the human brain traffics very well in *ideas*.

For example, if you were to finish reading this book and a friend asked you what it was about, you wouldn't give much detailed information, and you certainly wouldn't recount any data. Instead, automatically and without thinking, you would reduce it to the small number of ideas you had taken away.

The key word here is "reduce": the human brain is reductionist. We are already overloaded with information and it's getting worse every day. Our brains would melt if they tried to process and store even a fraction of the information they are exposed to, so as a result, what the brain consistently does is reduce the information it receives to its simplest and most concise form.

One of the most extraordinary examples of this phenomenon comes from a famous episode in recent US history, the O.J. Simpson trial, and is wonderfully described in the book *The Micro-Script Rules*[3] by Bill Shley.

In the Simpson trial, the prosecution laid out an extraordinary amount of data, taking about seven mind-numbing months to do so. But history suggests that this enormous quantity of data was nullified by one simple idea—seven words offered by Simpson's attorney, Johnnie Cochran. Without my even writing it, most of you are already mouthing it. "If it [the glove] doesn't fit, you must acquit." In the workshops we teach, something like 80% of the participants can retrieve that phrase, unaided, the moment I begin to talk about it. That's pretty astonishing when you consider the trial took place back in 1994. And while it's certainly been knocking around popular culture since then, that single idea from over twenty years ago still remains solidly embedded in most people's memory. (Note: interestingly, the phrase is often remembered as "If the glove doesn't fit, you must acquit." I think "glove" is sometimes added to provide context when the phrase is cited outside the context of the trial.)

This example of the stickiness of an idea is far from unique. On August 10, 1940, Churchill spoke at length about the heroic exploits of a remarkable, outnumbered group of fighter pilots in the Battle of Britain. I doubt anyone knows the full text of that speech, but seventy years later almost everyone—certainly in Britain—

---

[3] This is a fabulous book that all communicators should read. Shley argues, correctly in my view, that given the reductionist nature of the brain, the precise linguistic structure of your idea warrants your close attention. Put another way, word your idea very carefully.

knows the phrase "Never in the field of human conflict was so much owed by so many to so few." The whole speech is actually remarkable, but it's that one idea that stuck.

Likewise, President John F. Kennedy's "Ask not what your country can do for you, ask what you can do for your country" is only one idea from a much more developed speech. The speech itself may not be remembered, but the idea survives.

By the way, here's a pop quiz: Do you notice what all three of these sticky ideas have in common? Read them again and see if you can tell.

The answer is that they are all antithetical, meaning they each present two competing thoughts and then challenge you to reconcile them. It's an extremely powerful device for engaging an audience's brain, which we'll explore later.

I could cite example after example, but the point has been made. The human brain is reductionist. It doesn't traffic at the level of facts and data; it traffics at the level of ideas. The big lesson for us is that in presentations, we need to work with that fact and not against it.

> Everything we do as presenters needs to be about finding and nailing those big ideas. When you give an audience the big idea that emerges from your data rather than just the data, it's exactly what the reductionist brain wants. The idea simply snaps into place, as though the audience were saying, "Ah, that's it."

So back to my $200 PowerPoint guy one last time. Did he power-fully land an idea? Absolutely. My friend Mark remembered this story vividly, and you will recall that he had witnessed it over a year earlier. The presenter actually *did* do something incredibly impactful and memorable. So then, what was the problem?

The problem was that what stuck wasn't a big idea or even close to it. What stuck was a silly game: $200 was available for the person who could spot the second typo. He did something memorable, but it didn't matter. How do I know? Because I asked Mark, "What was his subject? What was this guy talking about?" Mark's answer: "I've no idea." In other words, the theatrics of the game stuck, but nothing else was learned. You don't want to be memorable for the wrong reasons. Falling off the stage will get that job done.

The $200 story is by far my favorite poor communication story. At first glance, it's an innocent little game, but as you dig into it, an incredible array of communications lessons flow from it, chief of which is my core premise that great communication hinges on **powerfully landing a small number of big ideas**.

Defaulting to a Deckload of Data

AS YOU BEGIN TO THINK ABOUT THIS CENTRAL THESIS, I HOPE THAT ALL kinds of alarm bells are going off in your brain, because it's probably already struck you that most presentations do the polar opposite—they bombard with details and rarely identify the big ideas they want the audience to take away, let alone land them powerfully.

I'm presently sitting at my desk, leafing through a sales presentation from a well-known software company. It's designed for an initial discussion with a customer, which would typically be a one-hour meeting with a lively discussion. The PowerPoint deck is comprised of a rather depressing sixty-eight slides, every one of them densely packed with information, and with very little discernable organization. It's what I call a "topic-driven" narrative, meaning that topic four follows topic three merely because numbers work that way, not because there's any logical structure.

There's an awful lot of detail about what this company does, and there's even more detail about how they do it. A rough count reveals that within this deck there are over 3,000 individual facts, and most of them seem curiously trivial. What's more, there are eight organization charts, even though the customer couldn't possibly care about, let alone retain, the names and titles of all these people, most of whom they will never meet. There are no big ideas that I can find, and if they are there, they are so deeply buried in this forest of information that no one could reasonably be expected to spot them.

The most charitable defense of this would be that the salespeople presenting this deck *do* know what the big ideas are and are able to do the gymnastics to draw them out of the data as it gets presented. But we all know that's not true. If the conclusions aren't visibly evident anywhere in the deck after a pretty careful search, then it's fair to say that they aren't there at all. This presentation hasn't been built around big ideas; it has been built around facts and data.

Finally, this deck is the document they leave behind in the hope that the "virus" of their message will spread through the customer's organization. It won't. As we'll see later, of all the problems inherent in the "deck full of data" approach, this is one of the most serious. At sixty-eight dense pages, 3,000 data points, and lacking any real insight, this example is perhaps a little worse than the typical, but it's certainly not unusual. Many presentations follow a pattern just like this one—long on fact, but short on insight. **Instead of powerfully landing a small number of big ideas, they weakly land a large number of trivial ones.**

SUMMARY

There's no question that succumbing to time pressures and descending to low cultural norms are genuine reasons why people present poorly. However, the larger reason is that we don't know what the governing rules of great communication really are, and if we don't know the rules, we are destined to break them.

If we want to be effective communicators, we need a framework that will both explain and keep us from breaking those rules—a framework that will help us to identify what the critical ideas in our work are and to make sure these come across in powerful, memorable ways.

And for that, not any framework will do. It has to be the right framework.

(P.S. There's one typo in this book. If you find it, email me at timpollard@oratium.com and you win $20. Of course, now you're wondering if I'm kidding or not.)

CHAPTER THREE

THE HEART OF THE MATTER IS THE BRAIN

'VE MADE THE CASE THAT WE NEED A SET OF GUIDING PRINCIPLES to steer us toward the creation of effective communication, ideally baked into an easy-to-use, time-efficient process. In a little while I'll introduce just such a process, and we're going to spend the rest of the book unpacking how to use it. But I'd like to start by answering the question: How do you know it works?

The reason you can trust this model is that it isn't simply a "do-it-my-way" decree based on some nebulous personal journey, where I am merely documenting what's worked for me over the years. Rather, the model is built on a much more solid foundation: it's based on how the human brain consumes information.

It's All About the Brain

THE HUMAN BRAIN IS ONE OF THE MOST EXTRAORDINARY THINGS IN all creation, and the more we learn about it, the more it surprises and amazes us. Neuroscience has learned more about the inner workings of the brain in the last ten years than was known throughout all of history before that. In fact, thanks to Functional MRI machines (fMRI), researchers can now study the areas of the brain that are active or "lighting up" under various stimuli and experiences in a healthy living person. For example, in an fMRI, researchers can see what your brain is doing as you smell a rose, or view an old photo of your childhood family pet.

This new understanding of brain science has profoundly affected various fields of study, but here we are going to apply it to the veiled and mysterious world of communication.

Our brains are wired in very specific ways, and that wiring has a huge effect on how communication works, or doesn't. The central idea here is simply that your brain *wants* and *needs* to consume information in certain ways.

Hence, the key to communication lies in understanding and aligning with how the brain processes information, especially (though not exclusively) in an oral environment.

Several times already, I've made passing references to how the brain works and tied that into a principle of communication. For example, if the brain is reductionist and trying to boil messages to their core ideas, then it follows that the presenter who is operating at the level of *ideas* is likely to be immeasurably more effective than one who bombards that brain with facts and data that it quickly discards. In other words, when communicators line up with how the brain wants to consume information, amazing effectiveness is possible. But when they violate these "natural laws" of how the brain works, failure inevitably follows.

This can be simply demonstrated with a few examples, and the first is a frustrating moment we've all experienced. Have you ever been to some function or event where you were introduced to someone for the first time? "Hey, I'd like you to meet my friend,

Phil. He was my college roommate." You greet each other politely, exchange some pleasantries, but then you separate, drifting away on the random tides of the cocktail party. Two minutes later, what's happened? You've forgotten his name. And the odd thing is no matter how hard you try to recall it, that name simply isn't there, so you spend the rest of the evening A) worrying about early onset senility, while B) trying to avoid Phil and the social embarrassment that follows. But of course you actually needn't worry because Phil's somewhere out there hiding in a potted plant, avoiding you for exactly the same reasons.

What on earth is wrong with us? At first sight, this is an inexplicable lapse for human beings who otherwise have extraordinary mental capacity. I, for instance, have memorized several lengthy chunks of Shakespeare, and I also know every line from the movie *Dodgeball* (though quite what that tells you about me, I don't know). I can navigate Washington DC and London entirely from memory, and yet if you introduce me to the CEO of a potential customer, a name I know I need to remember, chances are that seconds later, I've forgotten it. We've all done it, and it drives us crazy.

Well, you'll be pleased to know that there's nothing wrong with you. This is merely your brain at work, and this everyday scenario is a wonderful example of how the brain processes information. (By the way, if you want to know how to never forget a name again, it's an easy fix we'll get to in a moment.)

Here's the issue: the brain stores information contextually. **When our brains are exposed to new information, if we can find a context for that information, it will stick in our minds, but if it can't, it won't.** Put another way, in order to store new information, the brain must connect that information to something it already knows, and if that connection isn't there, your brain has a big storage problem. There is no filing drawer called "Stuff for which I have no context" in which your brain can store acontextual information. It simply doesn't work that way.

And that's the problem with cocktail-party Phil. This nugget of new information (Phil) is what I call an intellectual orphan. There's no context for it, so the brain has great difficulty finding somewhere to store it. It's not that your brain is lazy or doesn't want to do it. It's that it *can't* do it. So the name Phil simply rattles around your brain for a few seconds and then rolls out.

A metaphor that's commonly used for this aspect of memory is Velcro. New information is like the hooks, and information previously stored in the brain is like the loops. If the hook finds a loop, then it connects, but if the hook finds no loop, it doesn't. Cocktail-party Phil is a hook looking for a loop, and when it doesn't find one, it's gone.

All this is interesting, but how does it impact us as we build presentations?

It's profoundly important, because this aspect of memory gives rise to one of the most foundational principles of communication. By definition, whenever we present, in some measure we want our material to be remembered, usually so it can later be acted upon. But if you present information without context, then you are virtually guaranteeing that it will be forgotten.

We've already seen this demonstrated in the Prologue, in the story of the CEO with the perfect delivery but whose message was immediately forgotten. In that cameo, I tried to capture the many things he was doing well, and especially the delivery polish that we often aspire to. But I also said I knew that if I asked a random person what he recalled, most of the presentation was going to be forgotten. How did I know that? Because the CEO's ten-point talk had no discernable structure. There was no storyline. Each point, as valid as it was, stood on its own with no connection to what preceded it or what followed it—and that was the fatal flaw. So important is this one facet of human memory that I knew nothing else he did would be able to redeem that mistake.

> The greatest delivery in the world will never overcome a serious "brain violation" in the design.

Consider it this way: on screen, the bullets looked strong. But in reality, they were Phil Phil Phil Phil Phil to the audience. Whenever you're designing a presentation and you simply "organize" your ideas into bullets, but with no other structure, the outcome is guaranteed forgettability. And it happens all the time. Data suggests that only about 20% of a typical PowerPoint presentation is remembered within a few hours, and a lack of structure is frequently the reason why.

Hopefully, when you first read that CEO story, you were at least a little perplexed. "If he was so great, why was 80% of his message instantly forgotten? What am I missing?" It's all about the brain. And this is the reason why our process for presentation design works. It's because it is built to create thoroughly "brain-aligned" communication.

NEVER FORGET A NAME

I said I'd explain how to never forget a name again, and here it is. The answer, as you would expect, lies in giving your brain a helping hand. Because the brain stores information contextually, you need to create the context it needs, meaning you must tie the name to something that's already in your brain. Like Velcro, you need to provide a loop for that hook.

We already do this naturally when the connection is obvious. For example, if I met a man whose name was Angus, I'd think, "Wow, my son's name is Angus." This would come to me without thinking, and I would remember the name. The trick is: when that connection isn't readily apparent, you need to make the same kind of connection intentionally. The way to do this is the next time you're presented with a name you want to remember, take a brief moment as you hear the name and create a context for it, associating it with a mental picture.

A couple of examples:

I know a great guy who works at Rockwell Automation. I first met him at a workshop, and his name is Saumil. When I met him, I simply pictured him sawing wood on the roof of a large . . . you guessed it, sawmill (I got lucky with that one). This image sticks, and when I see him, I see the bigger picture and his name is right there.

An executive we work with at LinkedIn is named Emi. To remember her name, all I did was picture her clutching the famous award (spelled "Emmy," but that doesn't matter), and there it is, locked in. (By the way, research suggests that the weirder and creepier the image, the stickier it becomes. This is why I don't suggest you generally share what you're doing. Name storage is a very private thing.)

Emi, pictured here, kindly consented to let me demonstrate how this works. On the left is the Emi I met, but whose name I would likely have forgotten. On the right, thanks to Photoshop®, is my "mental snapshot." And behold, her name is immortalized.

You get the idea. Whatever the name, there's almost always an association you can find, and it really works. One of our senior team members, Eli, is a really smart guy, and though he's not a mental savant in any particular way, he's mastered this name association method. Now, whenever we teach a workshop, he will generally have most of the thirty-five names memorized by the first coffee break. This method isn't foolproof, but it works most of the time, and it's a lot better than the old trick—asking them to spell it. "Hey, how do you spell your name?" "M-I-K-E."

(Footnote: If you have a particular interest in human memory, much of what I'm discussing here is in the spectacularly good book about memory entitled *Moonwalking with Einstein*.)

SUMMARY

Our brains want and need to consume information in a certain way, and as we saw in the CEO example from the Prologue, when communication fails to align with these natural laws, it goes terribly wrong. Most communication fails precisely because of these brain violations. But here's the good news: the reverse is also true. When you get it right, and truly align with this cognitive wiring, incredible success can follow, as we saw with Johnnie Cochran in the O.J. Simpson trial. Whether he did it instinctively or by careful intention, who can say? But a deeper look reveals he actually connected with his jurors' brains in three critical ways.

First, that single, simple idea met the jury exactly where they were. At this point in the trial, they were swimming in a bewildering sea of data, and their brains were metaphorically crying out for some summary idea that could cut through all that noise, allowing them to make sense of everything they'd seen and heard. They needed that one big idea, and he gave it to them.

Second, the idea he gave them was sticky to their brains because it was poetic ("If it doesn't fit, you must acquit."), and that poetic structure was memorable. But even beyond its poetry, the final way the famous phrase connected to his jurors' brains was by leveraging a powerful but little-known aspect of brain science. As I mentioned earlier, it's the brain's deep attraction to antithesis.

The idea Cochran presented to the jurors set up a contrast of two propositions: "If it (this glove) doesn't fit … then you must acquit (Simpson)," and he implicitly (actually explicitly) asked the jury to examine the relationship between the two contrasting ideas. This was an extremely clever play. As we'll see later, without your even knowing it, your brain finds this particular game utterly irresistible.

Whether by blind luck or intentional design, Cochran created an idea so sticky to his jurors' brains that it likely played a major role in their consideration of his defense. By definition, the jurors discussed the key ideas from the case during their deliberations, and it's hard to imagine that this singular, unifying idea wasn't central to that final debate. And far beyond that jury room, it was an idea so broadly sticky, that over twenty years later, long after Cochran's death, 80% of people can recall it merely from the mention of its existence. That's the power of brain-aligned communication.

Connecting communication to how the brain works gives us the model we will use going forward. But first, in order to understand why the model is focused the way it is, it will help to explore one of the most important questions on this topic: "When it comes to communication, which is more important: design or delivery?"

CHAPTER FOUR

DESIGN VS. DELIVERY

WHEN I TRAVEL, I DON'T TEND TO TALK ABOUT WHAT I DO for a living. In fact, I tend not to talk at all. Hardcore frequent flyers will understand that. But from time to time I get into a discussion about communications, and as sure as night follows day, I usually hear some variant of this remark: "I'd love to be a great communicator, but I just don't have that natural talent." And what people always mean by that is delivery skill. They are talking about their inability to get up there and effortlessly captivate an audience.

Most people have come to associate effective communication with effective delivery, and there are several reasons why. The primary reason is that there's an enormous industry itching to tell you that the keys to great communication are those "twin peaks" of delivery: eye contact and body language. And in parallel with this industry, there's a large number of self-help groups similarly devoted to helping people become better speakers, but as well-meaning and admirable as their mission is, they have pretty much the same emphasis on the physicality of delivery.

Many of you know precisely what I'm talking about. At some point you've been lured (or forced) into a "presentation skills" class where some instructor, armed with 1950s thinking and a video camera, put you on film in an attempt to purge you of the mortal sin of having your hands in your pockets, and told you that riches and fame await those who don't jangle their keys while speaking. And you may be one of those people who dutifully went away and did everything you were told, only to discover it didn't make a blind bit of difference. I don't want to be overly critical of what these groups do, because in general I don't think they do much harm. However, experience suggests it's often a lot of time and energy for little in return.

Based on the innumerable conversations I've had, most people sense that the physicality of delivery can't be the most important thing when it comes to public speaking, and that the real issues must lie somewhere deeper. **Indeed, the overwhelming majority of people I talk to believe that the traditional presentation-skills training they've been through was at best marginally valuable, and at worst, a complete waste of time.** As such, we need to ask the hard question here about whether delivery really merits the lion's share of attention it always receives in typical training. I want to argue that it doesn't, and that when you obsess over delivery, you're shooting at the bullseye of the wrong target.

There are several ways to prove this.

First, you've probably come away from hundreds of presentations, and whether you loved or hated any given one, I'm pretty confident you never said, "That was terrible. Did you see his hands in his pockets?" No. What you say is what we've already seen:

+ TMI / crammed / overwhelming
+ All about the speaker / sender-oriented
+ Boring
+ Death by PowerPoint
+ Bulleted slides / too many
+ Reading the slides
+ Irrelevant
+ Too long
+ Confusing / unclear structure
+ Dry
+ Too technical
+ Predictable

This list from Chapter 1 is foundational, because it reflects what people really care about, and as such it reveals much about what we need to get right. You may not have caught this the first time you saw it, but there's almost nothing here about delivery! In fact, its absence is startling, given that the polishing of your delivery skills is the basic focus of the entire presentation-skills industry. So if the audience isn't focused on delivery, what *is* it focused on? If you look at the common factor on the list, you'll see it quite clearly: it's the design of the content. All these comments address matters of structure and design—and across hundreds of workshops, this is always the case.

> We've never once received feedback that the problem is "not enough eye contact" or "body language lacked confidence."

When you think about presentations you've loved or hated, it's always about the content, and how that content is organized.

A second and more vivid way of proving that we need to worry a lot less about delivery than we've been told is by returning to the Prologue. Only this time, I don't want you to focus on the CEO, but on that eighty-four-year-old Hungarian superstar, Eva Kor.

Eva is a true hero of mine, and I adore her. She is a Holocaust survivor, and more than that, one of the very few surviving "Mengele twins." In 1943 at the age of ten, she arrived in Auschwitz in a cattle car and was immediately "selected" on the platform, along with her twin sister Miriam. She was pulled away from her parents and older sister, none of whom she ever saw again, because they were murdered in the gas chamber hours later, the tragic fate that befell over 438,000 Hungarian Jews.

Eva survived only because she was a twin. It was a bitter moment of reprieve for these two little girls, because she and Miriam were now destined for a future of brutal and inhuman medical experiments performed by Dr. Josef Mengele. Unspeakably evil, Mengele selected twins so he could conduct comparative experiments and specifically, comparative autopsies after one of the twins had succumbed. (In order to do this, of course, he had to casually murder the second twin.)

Eva's presentation details not only her story of struggle and survival against incredible odds, but also the three life lessons she's derived from that experience. Obviously, the fact that she is discussing the Holocaust makes her presentation inherently interesting, but it's not only the subject matter that makes it so extraordinary. **This is the most architecturally brilliant presentation I've ever seen, because her insights, her big ideas, sit solidly at the center of everything she says, and she instinctively teaches toward *them*, rather than simply describing the historical details.**

For example, she unfailingly tells the story of how, early in her confinement, she got up one morning and went to the rudimentary latrine where, if the water was running, she could at least splash some on her face. As she tells the story, she describes stepping over the naked, dead bodies of other children in the washroom in order to get to the faucet. Children would often die in the night, she explained, and such was the harshness of the Auschwitz winter that it was a matter of life or death to recycle their clothes. So the children would be stripped and placed in the latrine until morning when the bodies would be removed by the guards.

As she's telling this story, I'm thinking about my own two daughters. I love both of them dearly, but I know for sure that at ten years old, neither one would have even been functional during this moment Eva describes. I suspect they'd have been curled up in the fetal position, as far away from the dead children as possible. Listening to Eva, I was desperately trying to make sense of the story and understand its meaning. And then Eva answered my unspoken question with these words:

"Why am I telling you this? Because in Auschwitz, dying was easy. Living took every ounce of strength I had."

She goes on to describe that this was the exact moment when she decided that Auschwitz would not take her life, that she would fight and fight and fight, that she would not be found dead on the latrine floor. And from this narrative her first huge insight emerges: "No matter what you are facing in life, never, ever, ever give up."

And that's it. There's the idea, and it lands with tremendous force. That is what this story means. That is how I can make sense of it.

Here Eva is performing the rarest of feats. Instead of merely presenting the audience with historical data or even stories, she is lifting up and teaching them insight. She's providing her audience's reductionist brains with the ideas they're looking for. And this wasn't simply a lucky line; it's quite intentional, and she knows exactly what she's doing. Her presentation is entirely organized around three or four such critical insights. In the Prologue, I said that everyone I have spoken to remembers her talk. This is the reason why.

What is she really doing? She's powerfully landing a small number of big ideas.

By the way, take particular note of her words, "Why am I telling you this?" To me, there are no more important words in any presentation. It means that the presenter is about to go from data to insight, from illustration to application, from what something is to what something means for the audience. It's a rare occurrence and one hallmark of greatness in communication.

> In your own presentations, if you find yourself saying the words, "Why am I telling you this?" or "Why am I showing you this?", that's a great moment. Why? Because it sends a signal that out of the data or illustration you've shown, insight is about to be taught.

But remember the rest of the story in the Prologue. Her delivery skills, as defined by traditional presentation-skills thinking, are almost nonexistent. She fails all the standard tests of eye contact and body language, but it doesn't matter. In fact, it was only later that I realized I hadn't spotted these delivery deficiencies and forgiven them. I hadn't even noticed. That is the power of content.

Traditional thinking has got it all wrong. That's the big idea, and it's why I'm telling you this story. When presented with great content that has been elegantly organized, audiences are shockingly tolerant of so-called delivery deficiencies. The reverse, however, is of course not true. **Great delivery cannot and will not rescue deficient design. Random, confusing, imprecise material does not become great when it's delivered well. It merely becomes well-delivered random material** (as evidenced by our 10-bullet CEO). His presentation may have entertained, but his material wasn't retained. That's the consequence of letting delivery trump design.

Does this mean that delivery isn't important at all? No, it doesn't, and I certainly don't want to suggest that. You do need a certain level of delivery mastery, but what matters is different from what you've been told.

It's an oversimplification, but I believe there is one word that anchors almost everything you need to know about delivery, and that word is *precision*. The idea here is simple: the presentation you deliver needs to be exactly what you designed. This makes complete sense. If design, or architecture, is truly what's critical, then delivery must be about making sure that that exact design, not something else, is what comes across on the day. Dale Carnegie said, "Whenever you present, there are actually three presentations: the one you planned to make, the one you made, and the one you wish you'd made." He was right. There are lots of ways the things you planned to say aren't actually the things that came out of your mouth on game day. (I'll discuss the pursuit of precision in the book's Epilogue on delivery.)

Which brings me back to Eva. I've now seen her speak several times, and while she doesn't check those traditional delivery boxes, she always nails that one element that matters: she is extremely precise in her language. I recently interviewed her for about an hour and she described how, over many years, she has honed some very precise language for presenting her insights, and whether she's presenting to a bunch of Montana high-schoolers or executives from Google, she never misses her mark.

By the way, let me make something clear. While Eva doesn't "do" eye contact or body language, I'm not saying in any way that she's a boring presenter. In fact, nothing could be further from the truth; she's utterly spellbinding. On two occasions I've seen her hold the attention of thousands of high-schoolers for over two hours, keeping them completely captivated, and without a phone in sight. In today's society, that's all but miraculous.

SUMMARY

Whether it's from surveys, experience, or by example, we can prove that when it comes to great communication, it's content that captivates. When we focus on content delivery but neglect content design, we are shooting at the wrong target. That's what I meant about us checking the wrong boxes.

Most of the people I meet say they want to be great communicators, but they don't think they can be, because they don't have that "natural talent." But if what I'm saying is true—that greatness doesn't reside in delivery but rather in skillful content design—then this is inspiring news, because it means that greatness truly lies within the reach of anyone who possesses and uses the right design tools.

I've seen this borne out countless times as we've taken leaders and executives from all functions and fields, most of whom didn't have that natural gifting, and watched them become incredibly effective communicators. Which brings us to the process that got them there.

CHAPTER FIVE

THE CARBON ATOM

THE MODEL WE ARE ABOUT TO EXPLORE IS A PROCESS FOR architecting virtually any piece of communication. It will result in that communication being memorable and impactful, because it will "fit" with the way the brain works, and especially with the way the brain makes decisions. The model is especially effective for designing the traditional presentations that we see every day in professional life, and it is used by many companies to equip mid-level and senior executives in advanced communication skills. It's also the model we use to train and coach TEDx[4] speakers and other leaders in the nonprofit and government sectors.

In addition, the model is highly effective for designing commercial sales messaging. Of course, given that most presentations are trying to persuade someone to take an action—to "buy into" an idea or proposal—I tend to think that all presentations are sales presentations, so it makes sense that the model works in both places. From an architectural standpoint, the traditional business presentation and the sales presentation are surprisingly similar.

---

[4] TED is a nonprofit devoted to spreading ideas, usually in the form of short, powerful talks (18 minutes or less), originally focused on Technology, Entertainment, and Design. Independently run TEDx events help share ideas in communities around the world. TED and TEDx Talks are now seen as a global benchmark for clear, powerful, engaging communications.

As we explore the model, I'm sure your reference points will be evaluating presentations you have made in the past and thinking through how it all affects the presentations you need to make in the future—and those are two great reference points. However, I want to encourage you to be thinking about all the other communications settings in your world where this might be applicable. For example, many of our clients have applied this model to web design, research reports, white papers, and even emails. One company explicitly uses it as the basis for designing all performance reviews, and another Fortune 50 client uses the model to design all their in-house training curricula (what better place to get away from Death by PowerPoint and move to insight-based training).

This model is not simply a business tool either; one of our team members used the approach to persuade his girlfriend's family to approve his request to marry her (and successfully! Eli just cele-brated his first wedding anniversary). Interestingly, a surprising number of people have come back and said that this has helped them communicate more effectively with their teenage children. The following paragraph was in an email I recently received from a client the day after we ran a workshop for her team:

> And to share a moment that touched my heart and will touch yours as well, I asked one of the participants how he enjoyed the class. He told me that he had been struggling with communicating with his teenage daughter for over a year now. He really internalized what he learned from the class about thinking about "what is the problem the audience needs to solve?" He had a deep talk and big breakthrough with his daughter the night after the class.
>
> I love it when we can help people succeed in all aspects of their lives!

Helping parents communicate with their teenage kids may be the most stringent test that the model has passed.

The breadth of application of the model should come as no real surprise. Communication is about getting ideas to land and stick in another person's brain. There's really no difference between the audience of 400 executives in a ballroom, and the teenage boy who needs to understand why it's critical that he not text while driving.

Forget PowerPoint . . . for the Moment

ONE LAST, IMPORTANT THING TO SAY ABOUT THE MODEL IS THAT BEING a model for the design of messaging, it isn't an alternative to PowerPoint; it's doing something completely different. Presentation design is about asking and answering a series of questions that govern everything that follows, such as: What is the action I want from this presentation? What argument will most likely get me to that outcome? What is the right flow of that argument? And perhaps most important of all, what are my big ideas and how am I going to land them in the most compelling way?

There's nothing wrong with PowerPoint as a delivery tool for visuals; in fact, it excels at this task. But it isn't a design tool, because it doesn't ask you a single one of these questions. In fact, the premature use of presentation software, which by definition draws you into slide design, is often why those critical design questions never get asked at all.

Thinking of PowerPoint (or Keynote or Prezi) as a design tool is actually most people's deepest misunderstanding of this type of software. It's an easy mistake to make: in everyday business life, if you want to write a document, you open up Word, because that is what it is built to do. Likewise, if you want to do some complex calculations, you open up Excel, because that is what it is built to do. It seems logical, then, that if you want to design a presentation, you naturally open up PowerPoint, because it is "presentation software" and sits in the same suite as these other helpful business tools. But opening up PowerPoint to design a presentation isn't going to help you at all, because thinking through the design of an argument is not what it was designed to do. You can't design a presentation by clicking to add your first slide title. That is absolutely the wrong way to start—it's like laying bricks on each other as a way to design a new office building.

PowerPoint is a superb delivery tool for those visuals you've decided you want to put on screen to support your big ideas. But it is an extremely unhelpful tool at the design stage because it isn't asking you to think about those crucial questions, and may even prevent you from doing so. This model we are going to work through, however, is that presentation-design tool you've been looking for. It's what you use early in the design of a presentation, ideally while sitting in a coffee shop or some other creative space, and long before you start building slides. It's a model that will gently direct you to think about your audience, the big ideas you want to land, and how you're going to land them in a powerful way. In the process, it will build an architectural blueprint that captures all this thinking— a blueprint, by the way, that will make your later slide design a quick and easy process.

On Paper or Online? Your Decision

IF YOUR PREFERENCE IS TO DESIGN ON PAPER, THE PROCESS WORKS perfectly well that way, and in fact, paper is the preference of many people I know. But paper can get messy quickly and doesn't store well. For this reason, you may prefer working in a software tool called "MAST," or Message Architect Software Tool, which allows for much easier editing, revision, collaboration, and storage of your presentation designs. MAST is not a substitute for PowerPoint, it is complementary. In the same way that PowerPoint is not a design tool, MAST is not a delivery tool. You will design a presentation in MAST (or on paper), and if that design requires visuals, you will likely deliver those in PowerPoint, Keynote, or Prezi.

The best news is that you automatically have access to MAST because you are reading this book. As I am passionate about transforming people into effective communicators, I am committed to closing the legendary learning-to-doing gap that exists with all skills training. As such, I want you to be able to apply everything you learn here, and MAST is key to that, because it lays out the presentation design tools you will use and guides you in how to use them. If you want to take the next step of applying what you are reading here, and I sincerely hope you do, MAST is the tool that enables it.

In fact, spending a bit of time investigating MAST at the relevant sections would be time well spent. It is a web-based tool that you can register for at www.messagearchitectapp.com. (When it asks for payment, simply enter the code TCCBOOK. From the first day you log in, you have six months of access to the tool, and you will find it fun and easy to use. After six months, there is a modest subscription that covers the cost of keeping all your presentations securely stored in the cloud.) I'm not particularly interested in selling software, but I'm very interested in receiving emails about radically transformed presentation outcomes.

So, with that, let's look at the model. Given that the next several chapters unpack each piece in detail, here I'll simply provide an overview.

The Carbon Atom

THE MODEL WE ARE GOING TO WALK THROUGH IS HIGHLY PRACTICAL. This is not the theory of how a presentation should be put together—this is actually *how* to do it. We call it the Carbon Atom[5], because it has a nucleus and six orbiting process steps/tools, just as a carbon atom has six electrons.

The model is the product of well over a decade of thought and practice. For many years and in various consulting settings, my job was building and delivering presentations. And in so doing, I was always striving to push the boundaries of what worked, especially for the design of lengthy and/or technically complex presentations.

When I found something that did work, that was good in itself, but I always wanted to understand *why* it worked. That led me to research into brain science, along with important side trips into areas

---

[5] We work with many engineers, and they are generally a delight. However, if I had a dollar for every chemical engineer who's told me that calling this the Carbon Atom is wholly wrong from a chemical standpoint, I'd be rich. I'm sure they're right, but I also don't care. And if you're a chemical engineer: OK, I've got it.

like the theory of literary structure. Often, when I finally got to the root of why something was working (or not working), it would trigger new lines of investigation. "If the brain works this way . . . maybe this would work?" And sometimes it did. I was fortunate that over several years, I had literally hundreds of presentations through which I was able to keep refining my understanding. I think it's significant that long ago I hit Malcolm Gladwell's "10,000-hour rule" when it came to presentation design.

(For those not familiar with this idea, in his book *Outliers*, Gladwell demonstrates that in certain fields, such as piano playing and software programming, expertise tends to arrive when about 10,000 hours of practice have been performed.)

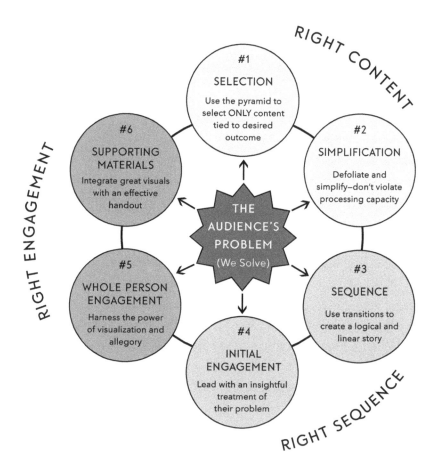

Eventually this model emerged, combining proven practice with underlying brain science (and other) research. It's the core model of our company, Oratium, a training and consulting organization, and it has been tested and proven in a wide range of different environments. If it hadn't worked there, I would have no reason to write about it here.

If this all sounds suspiciously like the personal journey of discovery that I promised not to inflict on you, it's only because I'm asking you to take and apply this model, and I therefore owe you some explanation as to where it came from and why it actually works.

As you look at the model, the first thing to notice is that something sits at the center.

In a fundamental way, every presentation is "about" something. And we've already discussed the fact that presentations are, all too often, more about the presenter, or their organization, or their product, or some pet project than they are about anything else. That needs to change because such sender-centricity really turns people off. We need to place something else at the center, and that something is the audience. As obvious as this seems, it isn't often done in practice. We need to orient around the audience, and specifically the audience's problem that we are proposing to solve. The reasons for this are foundational, all tied to what engages people and what causes them to take action.

Having grounded ourselves in our audience's problem, we then need to get three fundamental things right in the design of the presentation itself, which you see around the perimeter of the model. We need the right content, in the right sequence, with the right engagement (which is the more professionally acceptable word for "stickiness"). And as you see, each of the three has two major sub-components: our six "electrons." We will explore all of these in the chapters to come, so here let me just whet your appetite and orient you to each.

Right Content: Selection

The first step in presentation design is to select the right content, and the key idea here is relevance. It is truly shocking just how much of the material in most presentations is completely irrelevant to that presentation's desired outcome; in fact, it's actually amusing. In the majority of sales presentations, somewhere early on, you always seem to find pictures of the supplier's buildings. I know there's a certain desire to establish credibility with this, but really? Did any customer ever choose a supplier because they had a building? Perhaps a competitive advantage over their competitors who work in caves? It's madness, but almost all companies do it. I actually know a company where a particularly elegant bridge forms a part of their campus, and by rule that bridge needs to be featured in their sales decks. This company is in the food-packaging business.

From our work over the years across the entire corporate and nonprofit landscape, we estimate that around 70% of what's in most presentations simply doesn't need to be there. And setting humor aside, all this irrelevant material is a serious distraction from, and a dilution of, the core argument that you are trying to present. In the finite, confined space within which every presentation operates, irrelevant material is a dangerous consumer of your precious time, and more importantly, your audience's precious mental energy.

However, this pursuit of relevance isn't simply about identifying what's irrelevant. As important as it is to understand what goes out, of far more importance is understanding what goes in, i.e., what is this presentation's true intellectual heart? The most central question you need to answer is: "In this presentation, what are my big ideas?"

> If we are trying to powerfully land a small number of big ideas, then the defining question of any presentation design has to be: What are those ideas and where do they come from?

That's what we're doing in the section called "Selection." Identifying your presentation's key insights and how those insights will be defended and supported. Without that, nothing that follows really matters.

Right Content: Simplification

Having identified the intellectual core of the presentation, and established what material will be relevant to that argument, we need to make sure that A) we focus on only the most relevant material, and that B) this material is kept as simple as possible. As we will see, the issue in view here is the surprisingly limited capacity of even the sharpest human brain when it comes to taking in new information.

Most people have no idea how little of their audience's brain they get to work with, which is why the ubiquitous problem of TMI (too much information) is so damaging. **Bombarding with too much information is one of the more serious violations of a natural law of brain science.** When we don't fully grasp the limitations of the brain's capacity for new information, even if we have only relevant material, we are still perfectly capable of overwhelming the audience with both quantity and complexity. We've already discussed the problem of quantity, but complexity is equally dangerous. Sometimes a single acronym that a speaker uses, but that the audience doesn't understand, is enough to fracture comprehension and derail an otherwise excellent presentation.

Right Sequence: Sequence

Having assembled the right information—and only the right information—we now have to structure it correctly. Think about any great book you've read: when you reached chapter 6, I'm sure it made perfect sense. Why? Because chapter 5 preceded it and set up its context. Imagine reading *The Lord of the Rings* but reading the chapters out of sequence. What on earth is going on? Who is this Gollum? What the heck is his problem? Suddenly, this perfect book makes no sense whatsoever. It's the same wonderful content, and each chapter is still as beautifully written, but it makes no sense because the narrative sequence is gone. How content is organized is critical to comprehension, and it's as true for business communications as it is for books and movies.

Every presentation is an assembly of content objects—individual topics or chapters. Your goal is to take your raw content and create a logical and elegant narrative flow, such that "A" leads to "B" leads to "C" leads to "D" and so on, with the result that every piece makes sense because of the context that was set up by the piece that preceded it. If I've first been told how Gollum was once ensnared and consumed by a mind-controlling ring, I now perfectly understand why he is so bent on recovering it at any cost. Every presentation works the same way.

Right Sequence: Initial Engagement

The second piece of sequence is interesting and it's perfectly set up by what you just read. If, in any presentation, each topic creates the context for what follows, i.e., if "A" leads to "B" leads to "C" and so on, then it sets up a profound question. What is "A"?

"A"—your opening—is unique because it's the only piece of a presentation for which there is no prior context. It's the piece that has to stand on its merit alone, and it uniquely bears the burden of securing your audience's attention, which, as we'll see, is an increasingly daunting task in an ever-more distracted world.

How best to open a presentation is a fascinating discussion, because most presentations today begin with their focus on the speaker, "Thanks for your time today . . . let me start with a little bit of background on myself, our company, the team, this project, our buildings . . ." In the majority of presentations, at the very moment your audience is deciding whether to engage, you give them every reason not to. As such, we need to change our approach. **The presentation must be anchored in your audience's problem, so we need to open with the one thing most likely to secure both the audience's attention and their commitment to the rest of the conversation. That thing is _them_, and more specifically, the problem they have that you're going to solve.**

Right Engagement: Whole-Person Engagement

Up to this point, by following the model, you will have all the right content, organized into a highly logical narrative flow and anchored in the audience or customer problem. But you could still be incredibly dull and boring . . . and hence forgettable.

Even if you've got the shape of the argument fundamentally sound, how you make that argument, at a detailed level, is critical. You will certainly use facts and data, but facts and data are not particularly sticky to the human mind. They are primarily processed in the "left-brain" of the audience, and while there's nothing wrong with this, at the risk of slightly oversimplifying, greater stickiness comes from lighting up the "right-brain." Earlier in this section, we began to explore the brain stickiness of the Johnnie Cochran idea, "If it doesn't fit, you must acquit." I said that it was both poetic and that it employed the critical device of antithesis, and because of these two things, the idea engaged more of the right-brain. And that's what made it so sticky.

Right-brain—or better put, whole-brain engagement—is critical to memorability. In this section, we'll dig into the correct use of the tools of right-brain engagement, such as story and visuals. We'll also explore how and why they work by looking at some of the most recent developments in brain science that reveal what our brains actually do with a well-chosen image or story. Given that "Death by PowerPoint" is essentially a gross misuse of visual aids, this is a highly relevant discussion. The overwhelming majority of presentations today do not use visuals correctly.

Right Engagement: Supporting Materials

Our final section conveniently ties everything together, but what it particularly explores is the idea of enduring stickiness. That is, how your presentation survives after the meeting adjourns. For any presentation to be declared successful, it must live on after the handshakes. Its big ideas need to stick; they need to be remembered, retold, and acted upon in the days and weeks to come.

How does that happen? In every presentation, the speaker uses some blend of the three tools of their narrative or "talk track," their visuals, and the handout they give to the audience. It is actually the correct use of and interaction between these three things that creates long-term stickiness, and of particular importance is the handout or leave-behind.

As we'll see, this discussion inevitably leads to a pretty complete indictment of the traditional slide deck as the tool for creating documents that lead to long-term retention. (That won't surprise you. What do you do with a monster deck after a meeting?) What's really interesting is what you can do in its place.

SUMMARY

Now that we've briefly reviewed the model, here are some final overview thoughts. First, this process is practical and easy to use. Not only does it deliver the exceptional presentation design you want, but it's fully within reach of anyone willing to dig into it and practice it a little bit. And don't forget that there's a software tool that will bear most of the load.

Second, it's almost certainly quicker and more efficient than what you are doing now. As you look at the model and its six elements, you might be tempted to think that it's a lot of extra work, but it's not. What's easy to miss is that this process is getting you to do your important thinking very early on. And if, early in the process, you are identifying critical ideas and placing your focus only on those, you are substantially reducing your workload downstream. You aren't going to burn all that time you traditionally spend building dozens of slides packed with irrelevant material, because that material simply isn't going to be there. In fact, you aren't going to have slide decks at all. You've probably heard the phrase from the world of construction, "Measure twice, cut once." It's exactly the same with presentation design. The right thought up front saves a lot of wasted time later.

Third, it's actually fun. Many people we speak to dread the whole experience of preparing presentations. This stems partly from the laborious workload I just described, but I mostly think it's because they don't have any clear process in their minds. Absent a process to follow, many people are paralyzed by that "blank-sheet-of-paper" moment, not knowing where to start. In contrast, with this new method, the blank sheet of paper is completely stripped of its ability to intimidate, because you will know exactly what to do at each step along the way.

> This is in no way a trivial point; presentation design really should be fun, because it's one of those rare moments where we get to express our creativity and imagination.

Since the process we're learning solves the problem of "how will this message get built?", you are freed up to enjoy pondering the much more interesting question of "what will this message say?"

Finally, where do you do it? You can design a presentation any-where, but research shows that we are significantly more creative in certain environments. Believe it or not, human creativity is opti-mized at exactly the decibel level of the average coffee shop. That's a happy coincidence for the many Starbucks addicts out there. More important, though, is the role the environment plays on helping trigger the synaptic connections that are so important to creative thinking. Even though it's not strictly scientific, I think it's accurate to say, "A dull gray cube leads to dull gray thinking."

Research shows that environments that present unfamiliar and interesting visual cues trigger those synaptic connections. For me personally, art galleries and zoos (especially the monkey or otter enclosures) work really well. Not without reason, I'm actually writing today in a cabin in Montana. The wide variety of dangerous wild animals I can see through my window are keeping my juices flowing wonderfully.

My favorite author, Alain de Botton, in his outstanding book *The Art of Travel*, discusses not how or where to travel, but rather *why* we travel and what it does for us. In one chapter, he specifically discusses the unique way in which journeys stimulate our brains to explore new ideas and make new connections. He coined a phrase that I love and use often: **"Journeys are the midwives of thought."** It's so true, and it's why I'll choose a train over a plane anytime my itinerary makes it possible.

By definition, presentation design is a creative process, so you'll be most productive if you cooperate at least a little bit with how your brain likes to do creativity.

CHAPTER SIX

A VISION OF THE FUTURE

A T THIS POINT, IT WOULD SEEM NATURAL TO MOVE RIGHT INTO unpacking the model itself, but before we do that, I haven't yet answered the obvious question: What is all this going to do for you?

Given that psychology has proven that humans are generally more motivated by avoiding pain than they are by pursuing gain, I could simply say, "You're never again going to make a lousy presentation" and leave it at that. But as true as that is, it's a little more compelling to add some vision of a brighter future.

So, what's in it for you?

Put simply, you are going to look a lot more like Eva Kor than our ten-bullet CEO. Not in the sense of physically resembling a diminutive eighty-four-year-old Hungarian woman, because I'm guessing that's not what you came here for, but definitely in the sense of trading his forgettability for her memorability. **In short, your presentations will increasingly hit that standard of "powerfully landing a small number of big ideas."** They will be memorable, they will be sticky, and you are more likely to get the actions and outcomes you are looking for from your audiences. Further, given the sea of mediocrity that is today's world of presentations, yours will notably stand out from the crowd, and given we are being actively evaluated when we present, it's reasonable to assume that more of those judgments will be more favorable more of the time.

To go one level deeper, how will your presentations actually look different? The easiest way to demonstrate this is through the lens of a particularly interesting "before and after" case study.

Some of you will be familiar with a US company called Graybar. They are primarily an electrical distributor and are about a $6 billion company. Anytime someone is building or refurbishing anything, they need a whole lot of electrical components, and because it would be completely impractical to work with every manufacturer, Graybar sits in the middle, providing everything that an electrician could need. They are a fabulous company and I'm indebted to them for allowing us to share this case study.

One of the solutions they offer is called "PowerSmart," which is a highly advanced lighting solution. Lighting has changed a great deal in recent times, and just as fluorescent lighting swept away incandescent bulbs many years ago, wirelessly controlled, intelligent LEDs are now sweeping away fluorescents in hospitals, warehouses, schools, and so on. The PowerSmart solution is quite compelling; however, in common with most other companies, Graybar's original messaging approach displayed several of the hallmarks I was describing earlier. It was a pretty dense and lengthy slide deck—an awful lot to do with how the solution worked, but much less about the problem it was solving. And perhaps the biggest thing was that while there was a lot of "stuff" in the story, it wasn't well anchored by a set of big ideas.

Finally, because this PowerPoint was often the main "leave-behind," in essence the deck was the tool Graybar used to equip the customer to later discuss the solution and potentially make a decision (an issue we'll get back to in a moment). This messaging approach was working, but it wasn't working as well as they wanted, so they decided to apply the process we are exploring in this book. This is the result.

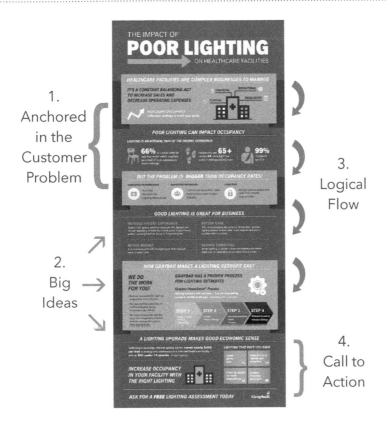

1. Anchored in the Customer Problem

2. Big Ideas

3. Logical Flow

4. Call to Action

This is the new handout—or leave-behind—they have created for the customer, who in this case is a hospital or senior living facility. Obviously this is only one element of their presentation, and you don't see everything else they're doing in the telling of the story. But the structure and content of this document provide some telling insight into what's changed for them, and by extension, what will change for you.

The details of the words on the handout aren't important for this discussion. What *is* important are its big philosophical differences. (The first four numbers that follow tie specifically to the graphic, which should make it a little easier to follow.)

1. It's thoroughly anchored in the customer problem. It doesn't open with Graybar's history or credentials; rather, it opens with an elegant discussion of what can go wrong at a hospital if you get the lighting wrong. Immensely engaging.

2. It contains facts and data, but it doesn't revolve around those. Instead it revolves around a small number of big ideas. Why? Because that's what the customer's brain is looking for and what their brain can ultimately handle. The facts and data do matter, but just like Eva Kor, the facts, data, and stories all point to insights; they don't merely sit there in isolation begging for the customer to figure out what they mean.

3. The big ideas are arranged in a logical narrative flow, meaning that the story unfolds in a way that makes total sense to the listener. One big idea is that it's extremely easy to migrate to the Graybar solution, and that's true. But this idea is only introduced late in the discussion after the value of that solution has been fully established.

4. It naturally leads to and asks for the specific action that Graybar is looking for; in this case, it's an audit of the hospital's current lighting situation that allows them to build the case for a full retrofit.

5. What you don't see here is the interesting script that supports the presentation—there are great stories that illuminate the entire narrative. Grumpy nurses working in dark, unappealing rooms and hallways, suddenly enjoying their jobs more in a brighter, better-lit environment. Frustrated patients unable to do crossword puzzles are suddenly much more satisfied by their surroundings. The whole presentation lights up the right-brain.

6. Overall, it is extremely crisp, clean, and simple. As a result of its sharp focus on big ideas, plus the right amount of data to support those, along with the logical structure, it is incredibly easy for the customer to follow. It's also easy for the salesperson to learn and teach.

7. The handout is simple and follows the exact structure of the conversation. The simplicity of the argument and the quality of the handout accomplishes something remarkable: it makes it easy for the customer to recall and retell the story in the inevitable "meeting after the meeting," which, of course, is where the buying decision is made.

As you consider the before and after here, it is vital that we understand what we're looking at. In no way am I suggesting that the problem is PowerPoint and the solution is moving to infographics. That's the least of what changed; indeed, the medium of the handout document is largely irrelevant. The difference is far more interesting—it's what's going on intellectually between this new handout and the old PowerPoint.

This case study is emblematic of exactly what you can expect to see in your own future presentations. Regardless of your setting, however far away you are from the world of sales, you will see the same seven crucial elements. If you were to apply this model to your next internal presentation, perhaps the legendary "Quarterly Business Review" (QBR), you can expect to deliver a presentation that:

1. Is thoroughly audience-centric

2. Pivots on a small number of big ideas

3. Has a logical narrative flow

4. Is crisp, simple, and easy to understand

5. Is engaging and interesting—rather than simply facts and data, it lights up the right-brain

6. Has a valuable handout, facilitating the story's ability to live on after the meeting

7. Leads naturally to action

You can see why I placed this case, and the vision of the future that it represents, after introducing the model. If you glance back at our model and process, I'm hopeful that you can see exactly how it leads to the creation of presentations that look exactly like this.

In looking at that Graybar transformation, while the new messaging implicitly feels better, you're probably wondering if there was any improvement in actual results—because surely that's the only thing that matters. Well, as I mentioned earlier, sales affords us the unique opportunity to see the quantifiable impact of improving the messaging approach, especially if nothing else changed in that period, as was the situation here.

In this case, the results reveal much about the power of a message transformed. At Graybar, under the old messaging model, conversion rates (the ratio of deals pursued to deals won) were around 15%, which is actually pretty decent. But under the new model, that number is tracking at around 34%. If you don't know sales very well, that's a pretty big deal. The second thing they've seen is that cycle time (how long it takes to close deals and how many meetings are needed to do that) has significantly shortened. Under the old model, they would close in an average of around twelve to twenty-four months, again not bad for a complex solution. Under the new model, however, deals are closing significantly more quickly.

The explanation for this is especially important. The reason why cycle time shortens is this:

> If you think of your message as a benevolent "virus" you are trying to spread, if that message is overly complex and impenetrable, the only way that virus can spread is if you physically come back to do it. But the simpler and more compelling the message is, the more it can be spread – i.e., retold – without your being in the room.

Finally, this message is much easier for salespeople to learn. The great thing about simple, crisp messaging is that it's simple and crisp for everyone—and again, this point is important far beyond sales, because it speaks to any case where you have presentations being given by people who did not design them. For example: If you use communication "cascades" where messaging is passed down and re-presented by descending layers of leaders, it's a big issue, because complex messaging doesn't cascade well. It either doesn't move at all or it gets badly corrupted on its journey down. Similarly, if you have training that's been centrally designed but is delivered by a training team (which is the case in most organizations), and that content is complex and convoluted, the long hours trainers waste learning it create concrete problems of productivity and consistency. In any setting where people have to deliver a presentation they did not create, well-designed messaging transfers far more effectively.

This final point reflects the bigger idea that ultimately, this isn't about sales. Sales simply provides a laboratory where empirical results can be studied. The point is, whenever you deploy the model, results are going to change.

A Significant Reduction in Nerves

ONE OTHER CHANGE YOU ARE GOING TO NOTICE IS THAT IF YOU SUFFER from nerves when you present, these are going to markedly diminish. Everyone gets nervous when they speak in public, and even the greatest speakers, from Lincoln to Churchill, have all described their battle with this old enemy.

However, there are two kinds of nerves. We're all familiar with "opening jitters," and while these do feel a little disconcerting, they are of no concern. Such butterflies simply reveal the adrenaline that's coursing through your body, and they evaporate moments after you begin. Better still, this adrenaline sharpens your senses as you continue to speak, which is invaluable as you seek to be connected to your audience. You can't get rid of these jitters, nor should you try. These nerves are your friends.

More unsettling, however, are those paralyzing nerves that plague some presenters. While these cannot be completely removed, the good news is that there are two things that significantly reduce them.

The first is exceptional presentation design. Many speakers have these deeper nerves because they are not confident in what they are about to serve up. When you know that you have weak, underprepared material, or are about to perpetrate "Death by Power-Point," you will probably be nervous, and with good reason. But when you know your material is interesting, relevant, tight, and provocative, these nerves actually morph into an anticipation of the fun to come as it all unfolds.

The second part of the remedy is effective rehearsal, because it means that in addition to being confident in the material, you will also have confidence that the material is going to come out as planned. (We'll be looking at this in the Epilogue on delivery.)

You will always have jitters, especially on the larger stage, but by following the principles in this book, the serious nerves will significantly diminish. **When you know that A) you have amazing material, and B) the material is going to come out exactly the way you want, then you truly have nothing left to worry about.** When the jitters have come and gone, you can sit back and fully enjoy the ride.

How Will We Know We've Succeeded?
The New Bar of Retellability

AS WE CLOSE OUT THIS VISION OF THE FUTURE, I WANT TO SUGGEST that there's one amazing standard you now have the potential to reach.

When you think about the question, "How do you judge whether communication is successful?", there's a trap to first be aware of. In several settings, such as conference speaking and training, we tend to rely on audience feedback, whether from the informal congratulations, or from more formal tools like evaluation forms ("smile sheets") and surveys. But we need to be careful, because such tools are quite misleading. As gratifying as a perfect score or a standing ovation may be, it's important to understand that audiences generally review speakers based on how entertained they were; they don't review speakers based on what they learned. With our ten-bullet CEO, for example, people were energized and motivated as they came out of the room, which was definitely positive. But while they rated the session highly, they hadn't actually retained much of anything.

So if it's not immediate audience feedback, how does the communicator know if they've succeeded? Obviously, at one level, the ultimate test of communication is whether you got the action you wanted, but what do you need to do to get that action? Is it enough to be understood? Is it enough to be remembered? You do want these things, but I want to argue that this isn't the standard you should be shooting for. I've hinted at it a few times in the preceding pages, but I want to state it clearly here: You want to be so good that your story can be retold.

My wonderful wife, Ruth, is one of many leaders at our church's youth group. This past spring, she came home from one of their meetings raving about how great the evening's message had been. In a rare moment of effective husbanding, I asked her to tell me what it was all about. Sitting at our kitchen table, a couple of hours after having heard it, she was able to perfectly recreate the essence of the message. As you would expect, her summary wasn't especially deep on details, but she absolutely nailed it at the level of the big ideas.

We had a fascinating discussion about the message itself, but somewhere in my mind I filed away what I'd just witnessed, because it was so unusual. That message had done something rare—it had stuck in her brain in such a way that she hadn't simply *remembered* it; she was able to *retell* it.

Recognition Versus Retrieval

Without getting too deep into the science here, there's a difference between recognition and retrieval in the brain that can be illustrated with the "penny test." You've seen pennies tens of thousands of times. If I showed you a penny and asked what it was, you would instantly recognize it. Recognition would unfailingly be 100%. But interestingly, if I asked you to draw the "head" side of a penny, your attempt would likely be horrible. In fact, you can do this test if you like, but most people get almost every detail wrong: Lincoln is facing the wrong way (and did you know it was Lincoln?), the date is in the wrong place, the text is incorrect, and so on.

This is because retrieval, or recall, involves something different happening in the brain. To retell a story, i.e., reconstruct it, requires the engagement of all the neurons connected to that memory, which means it has to have stuck more deeply. In contrast, recognition only requires the brain to "remember" if what it's seeing is something it has seen before. Recognition, therefore, is not the same as recall.

The typical presentation at best gets remembered (and often not very well). What we are shooting for is far beyond that. **The goal of our process is to create messages that can be "retold," and the reason this matters so much is because of the typical time lag between when presentations are made and when decisions are made.**

Earlier we discussed the O.J. Simpson trial and the memorable line, "If it doesn't fit, you must acquit." As with any legal case, the jurors in that instance made their final decision behind closed doors some time after all the testimony had been given. So the question is: What evidence did they go back and discuss to arrive at their verdict?

When the jury went in to deliberate on September 29, it's certain they discussed a range of topics. Jury deliberations aren't recorded, but they invariably focus on identifying the big issues in the case, sorting through the mass of information they've seen in order to isolate the weightiest evidence on which to base their verdict. In this case, it seems highly likely that as the jury was trying to summarize and "boil down" the issues, Johnnie Cochran's powerful idea, captured as it was in that well-crafted phrase, got retold in the jury room.

This example has much to teach us today. In almost all presentations, we are looking for a decision, for some action from the audience. And we face the same challenge—will the decisions typically be made in the moment? Obviously some are, but in most cases, they aren't.

They're Gonna Talk About You When You're Gone

Let's imagine you've presented a project idea for which you need budget and some additional staff. In real life, that decision probably gets made by some group, days or even weeks later. The jury indeed retires to consider their verdict, and in a later meeting, your idea will be discussed. But what if they can't effectively or accurately recreate your argument? As I've already said, with the typical presentation, only about 20% is remembered within a few hours, and only 2–3% within a month. And that's a huge problem anytime there's a deferred decision.

This issue of presentation "retellability" is critical in all settings and is perhaps the single most important issue in sales messaging. One of our clients understands this very well. In fact, during a recent meeting where we were working on some new sales messaging, the head of sales wanted to make sure her team understood why we were focusing on "retellability" so intently. Her insight was brilliant. She simply said, "Guys, you need to understand this—our most important sales presentations happen when we aren't in the room."

As we saw with Graybar, a simple, well-structured message embedded in a great document has an infinitely higher probability of being retold in that decision meeting than a story that's so deeply hidden in a bewildering slide deck that it would take both hands and a flashlight to find it.

Whenever you present, it is good to be understood, and it is good to be remembered. **But only those messages that have penetrated the brain in a special way can be retold.** That's what we should be shooting for, and it's what our process is designed to create. Whether it's at a kitchen table an hour later or in a decision committee a week later, retellability is our goal.

SUMMARY

Any time a presentation meets an audience and asks them to do something differently, the question "What's in it for me?" needs to be addressed. This book is no different. I need to answer your question, "What's in it for me?"

As I hope I've demonstrated through the examples in this chapter, the simple answer is that **the approach outlined in this book will lead to a significant transformation in the effectiveness of your communication.** The reason you can have confidence that you will see these results is that these are results that have been consistently experienced by those who have gone before you.

PART TWO

Mastering Presentation Design

CHAPTER SEVEN

GETTING STARTED:
THE PRESENTATION PROFILE

As we begin the actual process of presentation design, it would be great if the first step was really sexy and exciting. Alas, it isn't.

We naturally want to start thinking about the big, fun aspects of the task at hand, and we will be getting to those shortly, but the foundation we first need to lay is that of the essential preparatory work. This may not be the most fun of all the steps, but think of it like the redecorating jobs you do at home. You may look forward to painting because it's fun, but sanding the walls beforehand isn't so fun. It is, however, a necessary step. In short, whether it's a presentation or a playroom, if you neglect the appropriate initial preparation, you pay a price later: the finished product won't be right.

All that said, I actually find this preparatory work to be pretty stimulating because it motivates me to do some key thinking that is easy to skip. Even better, it's not that burdensome and the exercise rarely takes long.

What we are doing here, right up front, is answering some foundational questions that will have profound implications on the design that follows. The tool we use for this is the "Initial Presentation Profile."

Initial Presentation Profile

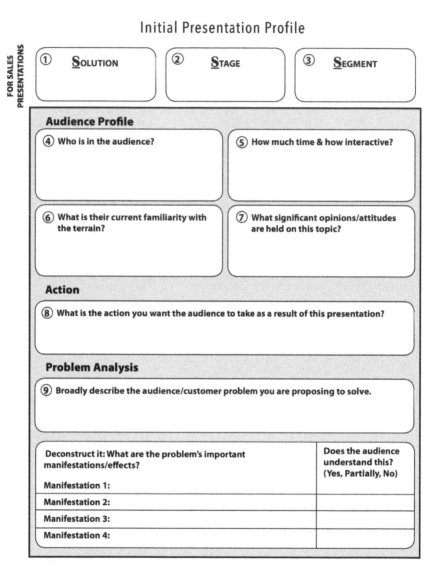

As you can see, the presentation profile contains a set of questions broken into four broad categories. Everyone knows they need to do some initial preparation for any presentation, but they aren't always clear on exactly what questions they should be asking. What's valuable about this tool is that, over a long period of time, we've boiled down the many questions you could ask to the small set that really make a difference. These aren't the only questions you *can* ask, but they are the ones you *have* to ask.

I will quickly go through each, drawing attention to why the question matters and how it influences your design (the numbers in the boxes simply help you see which box my comments are referring to). It's also worth noting that this is the first tool you are going to encounter in the software tool, MAST.

The first section of the profile is only relevant if you are building a specific sales presentation. For a non-sales presentation, you will skip it and jump to question four. The three framing questions here are to make sure you are clear on some key parameters.

For Sales Presentations

1. Solution

   Which product or solution are you selling?

   This is the easy one. A sales presentation is always selling a product, solution, or capability. Ground zero is specifying what this pitch is actually designed to sell.

2. Stage

   At what stage are you in the sales process?

   In most sales pursuits, there will be a series of meetings that take you from the initial sales conversation, which is your first real interaction with the customer, to the final closing meeting. Sales messaging changes in highly significant ways across this journey.

   An early-stage sales message should be heavily about "why." As such, this conversation should focus on the problem the customer has, the importance of solving it, and the basic idea that you can solve it for them, but without great detail. Later-stage messaging will move more into the "how," with a much more detailed treatment of how the solution works and what implementation and adoption look like.

The reason it's worth pinpointing the stage of the process is to avoid one of the most common mistakes we see: almost all sales messaging introduces how a solution works, often in excruciating detail, way too early in the process. Some of you reading my earlier description of those crazy sales decks may have wondered, "How on earth do these things get to a hundred slides?" This is why. It's pretty easy to get to a hundred slides when you are describing the exact flange bolts you use to attach your device.

When you look at this through the audience's eyes, you can see the problem. The customer has absolutely no interest in how something works until they've first understood why they might want to look at it. Recently, the head of sales for one of our clients wryly noted that **"Our problem is that we're selling the car using the owner's manual."** This is a brilliant observation and the perfect articulation of this mistake.

The simple conclusion to draw is this: early-stage messaging should focus more on the "why." Later-stage messaging, when the customer is actually interested in moving forward, then focuses on the "how."

3. Segment

What type of customer are we building this message for?

This final box is by far the most important. Earlier we talked about Graybar and their intelligent lighting solution PowerSmart. Like many companies, they sell this solution into several segments, or "industry verticals," such as healthcare (particularly senior living facilities) and retail. The solution itself is pretty much identical in both applications, so because it involves the same lighting fixtures, sensors, and controls, is it one message?

It's easy to think "yes," because it's the same solution. But that's incorrect. As we said earlier, messaging isn't primarily about the sender or their solution; it's about the customer, and specifically the problem you solve for the customer. So the important question here would be: In the area of lighting, does a senior living facility have the same problem as a retailer? The answer is, not at all. If lighting isn't right in a senior care facility, there are several consequences, including issues of patient satisfaction, low nursing productivity, and even clinical outcomes. But if lighting goes wrong for a retailer, the issues relate to low sales, higher levels of returns (because the sweater didn't look the same at home as it did in the store), and warehousing picking errors.

Because you have two fundamentally different problems, you have two fundamentally different messages. All messaging, especially sales messaging, is grounded in the problem you solve for the customer, and between your segments the problems are usually significantly different. In other words, in designing any sales message, if you aren't clear which customer segment you are building for, you will get completely stuck on one of the questions that's just around the corner in the Presentation Profile: What is the customer's problem you are going to claim you can solve? If the segment isn't clear, you won't be able to answer that.

Audience Profile

In section two of the profile, you'll begin to dig into your specific audience and explore some important boundaries of this specific presentation.

4. Who Is in the Audience?

The most basic audience analysis begins with simply knowing who is in the room and thinking through the implications of that group's particular chemistry. The seniority/juniority mix is important. As some people in the room will be more important in their organization's decision processes, you should consider if those are the people you need to best connect with. If so, be certain to understand and build around their issues and interests. On many occasions I've seen presenters delight the junior members of the audience but completely fail to engage the decision makers.

But the most important question is whether your audience is "homogeneous" or "heterogeneous." A more homogeneous group (say, a group of senior finance executives) will tend to have a similar frame of reference and potentially be wrestling with similar issues and interests. But a more heterogeneous group is by its very definition more diverse. These people don't share the same challenges, so what is extremely interesting to one person might be utterly uninteresting to another. Heterogeneity creates a layer of challenges you need to anticipate and navigate, and the design of any presentation will vary quite significantly based on your understanding of how heterogeneous a group is.

Consider this illustration: Imagine you are designing a presentation pitching a project idea to a senior management committee, comprised of a broad range of functional leaders and where each individual has an important "voice." Thinking through the issues that each faces, and how your presentation interacts with those issues, is a vital exercise. If the project will ultimately boost profitability, that will be a load-bearing issue you will address to the CEO, and if it does so by improving overall margins, that will be highly relevant for the CFO, who is on the hook for those numbers. If it achieves this by improving operational productivity or reducing overtime, that may not be interesting to the CEO or CFO, but it will be extremely important to the head of HR.

What I'm doing here is thinking through how my content relates to the different individuals in the room, rather than the room as a whole. Having done this, I'm going to make sure that the presentation includes coverage of these issues, with each one crafted specifically to address the interest or concern of the relevant "target" executive, the ultimate goal being to win over each of these influencers. (Indeed, this targeting will be evident specifically in my final scripting, e.g., "Finally, I want to talk about how this project will reduce total overtime—and Pete, as head of HR, you'll find this particularly interesting.") As obvious as this "heterogeneous targeting" seems, it rarely happens because presenters don't think through their audience makeup carefully enough.

This particular consideration is one example of what it means to be an "audience-centric" presenter. In a very real way, this presentation isn't "about" a new project at all; it's about an audience.

> In most presentations, your argument will speak to different audience members in different ways. It's your job to know that and to design the argument accordingly.

Case in Point: The CEO Will See You Now

This lesson was embarrassingly reinforced to me not too long ago. Mike Edmonds is the US president of S&C Electric, a billion-dollar Chicago-based company that makes some highly advanced products, helping to make the "smart grid" a reality. He and I had tasked ourselves with taking a presentation that had already been built for the "operating committee" of a typical customer—in this case, a power utility—and redesigning it specifically for the CEO. In other words, we were building a C-level or C-Suite pitch (e.g., CEO, COO, CMO, CFO, etc.) for a product called TripSaver II. (The details aren't important, but this product essentially reduces power outages by making sure the fuse that sits on top of those power poles you see in your neighborhood doesn't blow unless it really needs to.)

As I'd noticed on several occasions, Mike has an uncanny instinct for great messaging. He had done the initial rework and now he was running his revision by me. The message he role-played for me was simple, and it was almost all about return on investment (ROI) and consequently boosting a utility's shareholder value. Secondary to ROI, the message also pointed out that this solution improves safety, because when you have a more reliable grid, you don't have to send as many guys out to remote locations at night, up ladders in thunderstorms, to fix fuses that tripped when they shouldn't have tripped in the first place. That was the pitch. Here was the comical conversation that followed.

Tim: "Mike, I like it, but I think you missed something. You didn't actually tell them about TripSaver."

Mike: "Nope, I know."

Tim: "Maybe I'm not being clear. I don't just mean you didn't tell them how TripSaver works, you didn't actually tell them what it is. I'm not even sure you mentioned it. You didn't tell them what you do."

Mike: "I know I didn't. They don't care."

Tim: "Er, Mike, I'm a trained professional. You have to tell the customer what you actually do."

Mike: (sighing) "Tim, I know these CEOs. They care a lot about shareholder value. A lot. They think about it all day, every day. They also don't like writing cards to wives informing them that their husbands have been injured in the line of duty. They certainly care about whether we can impact those things, but they don't really care how we do it."

And, as a little time and some gratifying (for him) successes would later prove, Mike was absolutely right. The CEO message is proving extremely successful, and while I did win the one concession that he would actually mention the product from time to time, there are no technical details beyond that. I'm exaggerating about 2% for effect, but 98% of this story is completely true and the above conversation happened almost exactly as documented.

It was both funny and humbling for me because mine is usually the most strident voice, telling teams to remove the excessive details of how their widget works, and I constantly admonish people with the line "Don't sell the car by using the owner's manual." But here was Mike suggesting that when it came to the CEO, I wasn't pushing my own logic nearly far enough. The CEO didn't need to know about "the how" at all. (Of course it won't always be true that senior executives don't want any details. In some cases those executives are all about the details, and Mike freely admits that even in his world, sometimes he has to go there.[6])

> Whether it's sales or not, an important rule of messaging is that the more senior the audience, the more the presentation should operate at the level of ideas and not details. And by heavens, if you want to see anyone with a low tolerance for excessively bloated PowerPoints, it's anyone with a "C" in their title.

This story perfectly illustrates the importance of shaping a message to fit the target audience. A different audience, say the technical committee, would care a great deal about what TripSaver is, and exactly how it works and exactly how it gets installed. But the CEO thinks about things in a completely different way.

Bottom line: know who is in the room and how your argument intersects with how they see the world.

---

[6] One benefit of this story is that it is quite illuminating with regard to what any messaging to senior executives should look like. Almost every company I talk to is trying to get into the C-suite, but when they do, because the messaging they have is already too overloaded with details for the operating level, it is horribly ill-fitted to the "C" level.

5. How Much Time and How Interactive Will the Meeting Be?

This question looks innocent, but it's like a land mine waiting to be stepped on. This question raises the issue of your "Quantity Boundary": precisely how much material you can reasonably expect to cover.

When completing the profile, it's easy to fill that box in with "45 minutes with lots of discussion," and then move right along. The problem is that virtually every presenter who ever tried, wildly unrealistically, to fit three hours of content into a one-hour presentation knew that they only had that one hour to work with, but they simply ignored it. This odd willingness to completely ignore the boundaries of "reasonable" quantity is a huge issue in presentation design, which is why the topic of audience bandwidth, and how to stay within it, will occupy us for some time in one of the most important sections of the model—"Simplification."

For now, documenting the amount of time you have to present at least establishes what that boundary is. This question gives you the rope. Later we will discuss exactly how not to hang yourself with it.

6. What Is Their Current Level of Familiarity with the Terrain of the Presentation?

This question logically follows the one above, because this question—also seemingly innocent—establishes your "Complexity Boundary," or how technical you can be. This is a big deal because in the same way we can overwhelm with quantity, we can also overwhelm with complexity, as another mistake of mine demonstrates.

Many years ago, a pastor took one of our open enrollment workshops looking to upgrade his preaching effectiveness. This is fairly common, as pastors will typically preach most Sundays, and if they do so for many years, this repetition often creates patterns and habits that end up calcifying into a tired teaching model. Helping a pastor get unstuck in their preaching is one of the most rewarding things we do.

I had just been teaching on the topic of working within the Quantity Boundary by showing the group how to present only the highest value material (the material with the highest "ROI") when their time is particularly constrained. The pastor came up to me at the break and said, "Tim, this is really good stuff, and I think it's going to transform me. One question, though, what's ROI?" (By the way, for any pastors reading this, ROI means return on investment.)

Ouch! In the very section where a few minutes later I actually taught how not to cross the complexity boundary, I had crossed his complexity boundary! He wasn't a dumb guy by any means, but he's got a seminary degree, not an MBA. It is absolutely logical that he wouldn't have encountered the acronym ROI in his professional life, but I missed it because I hadn't answered this question thoughtfully enough. That's how easy it is to make this mistake.

Thinking through what your audience understands about your specific topic and the general field the topic sits in is crucial, because there's always an information imbalance between presenter and audience—a difference in what each knows and understands, and failing to spot it is deadly.

Again, I'll explain how you solve this later. For now, this question forces you to start thinking about where those information asymmetries lie.

7. Are Any Significant Attitudes or Opinions Held on the Topic?

Final audience question: Where is the audience going to be on your side, and where might they be against you? (My preferred terms here are headwind and tailwind.)

As a presenter you need to know where you will generally have support from your audience (tailwind) and where you might get pushback (headwind), because this changes the way you make your argument. Put simply, you have a much higher burden of proof for an idea when you have a headwind versus when you have a tailwind.

Some years ago, one of the world's largest hotel chains, a well-loved company and brand, launched a vacation timeshare business. As we worked with them to develop their sales messaging, we explored the question, "What is the public's general disposition toward your brand?" The answer from them was, "Overwhelmingly favorable." And it was; this is a decidedly popular company. But when we asked the question, "What is the public's general disposition toward the timeshare business?" the answer was, "Overwhelmingly unfavorable." For good reason, most people have a well-developed loathing of the whole timeshare industry.

Which made for a very interesting messaging question, because these two perceptions are almost polar opposites. Learning that this hotel company was now doing timeshare was like learning that your beloved grandmother just robbed a gas station. As such, it significantly affected the architecture of the message. The positive brand associations were so strong that it was easy to reinforce them; in fact, little time was even spent there (remember, "Don't prove what doesn't need proving"). But much greater thought and time were needed to counteract that prevailing negative perception. The load-bearing idea became, "Timeshare has never been done this way before," deliberately running at the "headwind" they knew was going to show up.

In any presentation setting, these negative perceptions will often be floating around out there in your audience, and they are like little time bombs waiting to go off. "We've tried this before and it didn't work," "This will take up too much time," "Your team hasn't run big projects well in the past," "It's too risky," "We can't afford it." You have to know what they are, and it's almost always best to run right at them, as was done here. In other words, defuse them before they go off.

Asking this final audience question helps flush out where these perceptions might be lurking. And as a general principle, as the following table explains, you should generally "aim left."

POSITIONING YOUR PRESENTATION:
AIM LEFT

Audience members vary in their posture, from outright critic to adoring fan, as seen in this simple chart.

CRITIC	SKEPTIC	NEUTRAL	ALLY	FAN
Poised to fire torpedoes. Looking for opportunity to attack. They are often disruptive, but they can easily alienate the rest of the audience.	Negative and inclined to disagree, though not necessarily hostile. They will be cautiously open to a well-reasoned argument.	Open-minded and balanced in their view. Highly receptive to a well-reasoned argument.	Already on your side. They will be supportive but will not abandon their own position or credibility in the process.	Unreservedly positive. These "groupies" will fully support you, regardless of what you say. Their perceived lack of objectivity sometimes costs credibility.

Most audiences contain a blend of skeptics, neutrals, and allies. Critics and fans tend to be more rare. As you think about how to position your presentation, the general rule we teach is to "aim left," meaning that you want to make an argument that's compelling for the skeptic, specifically by naming and addressing their potential concerns and questions. If you solve that puzzle, the allies and neutrals will take care of themselves.

The previous four questions—Which product or solution are you selling? At what stage are you in the sales process? What type of customer are we building this message for? and

Who is in the audience?—aren't difficult and they don't take long to answer, but they are important because they operate at two levels. First, at a low level, they are forcing you to document some key issues—like the audience's lack of technical knowledge—that can easily be forgotten later, when you are deep in the details of presentation design. Second, at a much higher level, these questions are all leading you away from the swamp of sender-centricity up toward the higher ground of true audience-centricity.

8. What Is the Action?

The next box on the template is the simplest. You need to document the action you want your audience to take as a result of this presentation. There's not a whole lot to say here except to be specific. The more specific you are with the action, the easier everything else becomes. If your goal is for your boss to agree to fund a more detailed study of a project's viability, then say that. This is important, because not only do you now need to build an argument that leads to that, but that action is the exact "ask" you will make at the end.

Note that the action can be mental. Sometimes we aren't looking for a physical "fund this project" outcome, but rather a more intellectual "continue to support what we're doing." This is often the case with a "Quarterly Business Review" or update type of presentation. Thinking there is no action here is a big mistake. You always want your audience to do something, even if it's only mental assent. Since this action is the purpose of the presentation, make sure you know what it is.

9. The Problem Analysis

The final set of questions accomplish something different, because they begin the development of some of the most important content your presentation will ultimately contain. These questions ask you to analyze the audience problem you are going to solve.

If you remember the overall model of the Carbon Atom, you will recall that the audience problem sits at the very center of any presentation as the primary driver of audience engagement. The "problem riff," i.e., your discussion of the problem, will form a major part of your presentation's opening, and a full section of our process ("Initial Engagement") will be devoted to designing that opening. Here you do the thinking and analysis that makes that later work possible.

You begin by identifying and naming the broad problem the audience has that you are proposing to solve. The reason your initial framing must be broad is that you want to be able to show that the problem has many effects, and here's why: as a default, people don't like change. Most people's to-do lists are already plenty long enough, and overburdened people don't want to invest precious money and even more precious time on a new project, unless they truly feel they have no choice.

> In most presentations, most of the time, the "do-nothing" option is what you're competing against.

And the easiest justification for doing nothing is if the audience or customer feels no urgency to act. Or put another way, they don't see their problem as serious enough to justify taking the action to solve it.

You can't always win this battle, but the best weapon for combatting such natural inertia is to make the problem multi-faceted: to show how many different ways it's hurting them, especially if it's hurting them in ways they don't realize or fully understand. People perceive problems as more compelling when they touch or hurt multiple places, and hence, defining the problem broadly allows you to deconstruct it, demonstrating all the different ways the problem shows up.

An example here will bring this point to life. Earlier, we talked about Graybar selling intelligent lighting solutions to a senior living facility. Now, what is the problem that this offering actually solves? Defined narrowly, you might say it's the electricity bill, and that's true. Typically, an older lighting solution will burn about 65% more energy than a modern alternative. But to a busy hospital CEO, that electricity bill isn't necessarily going to get their attention.

But as the presentation designer here, if you ask a broader question, aimed at taking you beyond the electricity bill, such as, "If you don't get lighting right in a senior living facility, how can that hurt you?"[7] Pandora's box opens.

Using a combination of brainstorming and customer research, it turns out that this problem has many serious dimensions.

+ Prospective clients judge the quality of a facility by its appearance. You don't send your aging mother to live in a facility that looks tired and run down. This is a problem of *customer experience*, and also *brand*.

+ Staff don't work well in poorly lit environments, which affects both how they work and their levels of *absenteeism* and *turnover*. This is a problem of *productivity*, with a side order of *employee engagement*. Not good in a tough labor market.

+ Any poorly lit facility has some inherent *safety risks*. Patients and staff can slip on fluid spills or they can

---

[7] Don't miss how powerful this question is—whenever you are doing an audience-problem analysis, this is the best angle of attack. Take the subject of your presentation (in this case, lighting), and ask the question, "If you get this wrong, what are all the problems (pain points) that flow from this?"

break ankles in dark stairwells. These are problems of *safety* and *legal liability*.

✦ Finally, and arguably most important, data exists on how lighting correlates with prescription dispensing errors. When a nurse reads a patient chart in a poorly lit room, transcription errors are quite possible. Now we have a problem of *clinical outcomes* and the reappearance of *legal liability*... and *brand*.

Wow. Do you see the difference? The typical hospital CEO probably doesn't get out of bed for savings on their lighting bill. But there isn't a hospital CEO in the land who doesn't have some degree of cold sweat about the other eight business challenges that could hit you if you got lighting wrong . . . or nine if you include the original electricity bill.

As a result of this problem analysis, this is an infinitely more compelling story, which is one big reason why sales outcomes have improved so much in this case. This amplification of the problem has largely taken the do-nothing option off the table. We often call this the "Root and Fruit" analysis. The root may seem small and innocent. But the fruit is a larger and scarier prospect altogether.

Our template leads you through this thought exercise, first defining the problem broadly, then identifying all its various manifestations, then looking for data and/or case evidence to support them wherever you can. (And given it's generally good if the thing you're talking about is something the audience isn't aware of, the template gives you that box to check.) Graybar is one of the smartest messaging companies you will encounter. They had data or case evidence for every manifestation we identified.

SUMMARY

However much we may want to skip the less exciting preparatory work, it is the essential foundation of every good presentation. The Presentation Profile lays out a series of vital questions, and while these aren't all the questions you could think about, each is critical in its own way. Whether it was fun or not doesn't matter. This is some of the most essential thinking the designer needs to do.

With this foundation stone set, we can now begin the actual process of building the presentation, which is definitely more fun.

CHAPTER EIGHT

⁓⊂⧁⊃⁓

DEVELOPING THE HEART
OF YOUR ARGUMENT

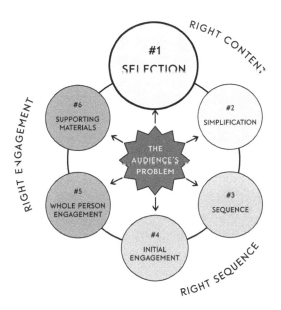

A S WE GET INTO THE MODEL ITSELF, IT'S WORTH NOTING THAT
each of the following chapters is going to be structured in
the same way (a helpful approach that facilitates learning. After the
first section, your brain won't have to waste energy identifying the
structure. This yields more learning for less effort).

We'll start by exploring the specific problem, followed by the
typical mistake or "brain violation" that presenters make, because

that is fundamentally what we're trying to solve for. Having understood the problem, I'll lay out the broad philosophical solution to that problem, and then finish by showing you how to "activate" that solution with a specific tool that will bring you back into alignment with your audience's brain. Each section stands alone and solves a single problem, but taken together the sections combine to form one single design process.

Of course, I could simply show you the tool in each case, but it's both more interesting and more effective to show you the "why" before the "how."

What Is the Problem? The Search for Relevance

THIS FIRST SECTION ADDRESSES ONE OF THE MOST FUNDAMENTAL questions in all presentation design—that of relevance. In a sea of potential content, what is actually relevant? What is the heart of the presentation I'm designing? Put another way, if every presentation is about "powerfully landing a small number of big ideas," what are those big ideas, and where do they come from?

At one level, every section of the model we're going to look at is critical, because as we go through each it will be obvious that you can't afford to get any one of the areas wrong. However, I will argue that this section is the most critical, because if you don't have the right content, it doesn't matter how you then sequence it, illustrate it, etc. It's simply the wrong content, and that can't be redeemed.

The issue in view here is the very first problem we run into when designing any presentation, and which flows from the sad reality that at our core, we humans are simply "sender oriented" by nature.

When Unicorns Paint

STEENLAND 2010

I love this cartoon. It's the perfect illustration of how we see the world – through our own eyes …

At the core, we are all addicted to ourselves. Just like the unicorn, we see the world through our own eyes and are instinctively oriented around our own priorities. When you look at a group photo in which you were present, who do you first look for? Yourself. Indeed, the extraordinary rise of the "selfie" presents the clearest evidence yet of our own natural narcissistic tendencies.

And I'm as self-centered as anyone else. I look for myself in group photos; when I drive, I judge other motorists harshly for their mistakes, but I freely pardon myself for the exact same transgressions. Some time ago I picked up a great quote from a friend at Disney. **"We judge others by their actions, but we judge ourselves by our intentions."** What a brilliant insight. That is the exact loophole I escape through. "You're an idiot for changing lanes like that. I'm not because I didn't intend to cut you off: I just had no choice." However dumb my actions, my intentions were pure, so I'm innocent. How very convenient for me.

This natural self-centeredness shows up in many areas of our lives, and it always shows up in our presentations. As presenters, we frequently tell the story we want to tell, the story that's interesting to us rather than the story the audience needs to hear. In many ways, it's understandable. Very often we are both proud of and interested in what we do and we want to share it with others, which is the root of a great deal of sender-orientation. Most people are also much more comfortable talking about their own world than they are crossing over into someone else's world. **It's easy to talk about the project you've been living with for six months, but it's much harder to see it through the eyes of the executive who lives in a strange, foreign world you've never visited and don't understand very well.**

Whatever the reason, the consequences are serious. As a result of this odd facet of human behavior, presentations are routinely saturated with material that is both unrelated and irrelevant to the desired outcome.

In almost any presentation, you see the same suspects. Unnecessary background and history, tangents and rabbit trails ("Here's something interesting I found"), redundancy and repetition, pet peeves and soapboxes, excessive facts and data. The list goes on.

If I were to sum this up in two words, they would be: **unnecessary details**. Almost all presentations contain a ton of material that the audience doesn't actually need to know. Based on the hundreds of presentations we review every year, we've concluded that somewhere between 50–70% of the material in a typical presentation simply isn't needed. It was probably interesting to the speaker, but it wasn't relevant to the discussion at hand. This can reach comic proportions at times, especially in sales presentations, where it's usually the result of a misguided attempt to establish credibility. Case in point: most sales presentations open with an elaborate run of slides, often a dozen or more, filled with completely irrelevant material—pictures of buildings, staff numbers, world maps, awards won. But the record goes to an ad agency we were working with that really should have known better. Their deck was 102 slides, with the first 52 being "credentials" slides, mostly awards they had won. Sometimes sender-orientation is the polite term for narcissism.

The Brain Violation:
You Can't Get There with the Wrong Content

OF ALL THE NATURAL LAWS THAT PRESENTERS BREAK, THIS ONE SEEMS so obvious that you'd think we'd never break it, but we do. Here it is: People can't get where you need them to go with the wrong information. You have to give them the right information to process. In other words, customers won't choose your solution because you have a nice building. Everyone has a building. And your boss isn't going to back your project because the project team has found a great space, with lots of natural light, to potentially work in.

The Essential Solution: Start with the Action

THE WAY YOU SOLVE THIS PROBLEM IS BY FUNDAMENTALLY CHANGING your start point. Sender-centricity starts with the question: "What do I want to say?", and from that bad question flows all the irrelevance I've just described.

In contrast, relevance comes from a different, and special, place. There's a key that unlocks everything, and that key is this: starting with the action you want your audience to take, and working back from there. Hence, the new first question you want to ask is:

What is the desired outcome of this presentation?

From which naturally flows the second question:

Exactly what argument (content, structure, illustration) will get me to that outcome?

As will become clear in the next few pages, starting with the desired action and working back will guarantee a powerful and relevant argument. This sounds like a promising principle, right? But how do you do it?

The Practical Tool: The Pyramid of Planned Outcome

THE TOOL WE WILL WORK WITH HERE IS CALLED THE "PYRAMID OF planned outcome." It's the most critical of all the tools we are going to explore because it is how you first assemble all the essential intellectual content of your presentation.

Even though this is only one piece of the Oratium model, many of our clients refer to us as the "pyramid guys," because this tool lies at the heart of what we do. In fact, most of the people who become familiar with the tool fall in love with it because it takes something highly complex and makes it extremely simple. Loving a triangle might sound a bit strange to you, but you can be the judge.

The tool makes use of an important flow or sequence in how the brain works, which I can describe as "Know -> Believe -> Do."

As you begin to build any presentation, you start with this question: "As a result of this presentation, what do I want my audience to do?" This is the top of the pyramid, and you fill the action in there (and of course, you've already identified this action in the presentation profile).

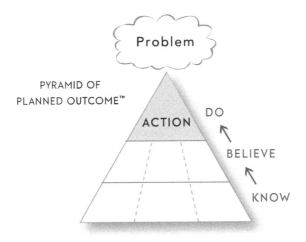

Remember to be specific. The more specific you are with the action, the easier everything else becomes.

Now, specifying the action raises an interesting question. Will your audience do what you want them to do simply because you want them to do it? Of course not. The audience will only take that action if there is some motivation or reason for them to do so. This is why their problem sits above the pyramid. Their desire to solve the problem is the reason why they will take the action. Remember, your audience is also self-interested; they will act because it helps *them*, not because it helps *you*.

This is important to emphasize—the essential axis of every presentation is that the action you are proposing is a solution to a particular problem. If that action ever becomes somehow disconnected from the audience problem, then the presenter has the problem.

We now descend one level in the pyramid to possibly the most important few paragraphs in this book, because I now want to explore what causes people to take action. We all make hundreds of decisions, every day. How do we make those decisions?

Let me illustrate the process by describing a game we play in all of our workshops. Imagine I am holding up an envelope, on which is written the word "congratulations," and I say this: "I want one of you in this room to take a deal I'm offering. I'm going to ask you a simple trivia question. If you get it right, you win this envelope that contains ten dollars. If you get it wrong, you owe me two dollars. And you can 'phone a friend'—meaning that if you don't know the answer, you can ask someone for help."

Inevitably there's a good deal of muttering at this point. Everyone is trying to figure out what the hidden catch is. But there isn't one. Eventually some brave soul volunteers, or is volunteered by the rest of the room. At that point, we proceed to ask the volunteer the trivia question. The question, whatever it may be, is always very simple and the volunteer invariably gets it right. The thirty-four other people in the room kick themselves for being so distrustful of me and losing the easiest $10 they will ever earn.

Yes, the game costs me $10, but it's well worth it because when that person takes the action I want them to take by volunteering, they are proving one of the most important ideas in the world of communication, which is simply this:

> In human beings, action is preceded by belief.

There are several points in this book where we land on a critical thought, and this is one of them. In human beings, action is preceded by belief. In other words, we make a decision when we have established certain beliefs about that decision. What's more, it's easy to demonstrate.

If I ask the room, "What four things did Diana need to believe in order to take my deal?" the group always reasons their way to the correct four things. If you want to pause to figure them out, please do . . . but they are:

1. I have a reasonable chance of getting this question right.

2. There actually is $10 in the envelope.

3. Two dollars is an acceptable risk or cost for this deal.

4. I have help—if I get in trouble, there are thirty-four smart people who can help me out.

Those are the four beliefs that led to this decision, and the exercise proves that it's the establishing of those beliefs that tips the volunteer over into taking the action I want, a fact that I can prove through a simple second "offer," which is: "I want someone in this room to take a new deal. I'm going to ask you a pretty tricky question from particle physics. If you get it right you win $10, if you get it wrong, you owe me $20 and you're on your own."

Naturally the room laughs. No one would ever take that deal (although *Big Bang Theory*'s Sheldon is often mentioned). Why does no one take it? Because this presentation has established an entirely different set of beliefs, these being:

1. I've got no hope of getting it right.

2. I have no help.

3. The risk reward stinks.

Note that those different beliefs still led to a decision: it's unfailingly the "do-nothing" option, or the decision not to act.

Now, over the years, why have we burned tons of time and thousands of dollars on this game? Because, from this exercise emerges the most important question a presentation designer needs to ask and answer, which is: If action is preceded by belief, **"What does my audience need to believe in order to take the action I want them to take?"**

Those beliefs are your presentation's big ideas; this is where they come from. And if you look in the dictionary, what is the definition of a conclusion you draw for the first time when presented with new information? An insight.

Everyone today is talking about insight-based presenting, and especially insight-based selling. And that's great. The problem is, when you ask someone where those insights actually come from, you're usually met with a blank stare. Insights don't come from hope, tequila, or meditative mountain experiences. They come from this question: **"What does my audience need to believe in order to take the action I want them to take?"**

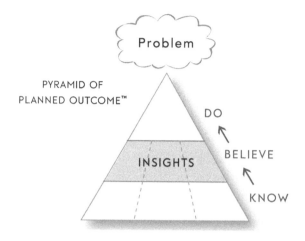

Those big ideas are written in the central layer of the pyramid, which is called the "insight layer." These insights are the intellectual heart of your presentation. They are the big ideas that you are going to powerfully land—and did you notice that they don't flow from your thinking about what you want to say, but rather are derived from what your audience needs to believe? That is how the tool kills sender-orientation and guarantees that your ideas have relevance.

How many insights can you have? In every workshop I ask the group: "How many big ideas can you reasonably fit into any typical business presentation?" and the answer is always the same. Around three or four. And that's right. In fact, I favor three in most presentations because the brain loves concepts structured in threes. I'm not overly dogmatic about whether it's three or four, because the point is: it's not ten. **If you think you have ten big ideas, you don't have any.**

It's funny, everyone who takes our workshop instinctively understands that an audience can only handle three or four big ideas. And yet, despite knowing that, every one of those same people has also tried to pack an insanely large number of ideas into their presentations in the past. They simply never stopped to think about it long enough to realize that it was never going to work.

I'll dig into how insights work much more deeply in a moment, but first let me finish the overview of the pyramid.

Finally, we descend to the bottom level. If insight leads to action, the question that logically follows is: "What leads to insight?" And the answer is simple: knowledge, which comes from data and illustration.

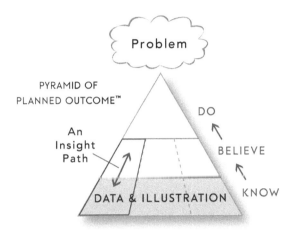

The bottom layer of the pyramid contains the data and illustrations by which you will prove your insights to be true. Big ideas must be supported, because without supporting data, any insight (for example, "The adoption of this new system will be simple and trouble-free") is merely an assertion. As a presenter, you should expect the audience to hear your insight and say: "OK, that's interesting. Prove it." The data and illustration layer is how you do that.

The data and illustration points in each lower box are designed to prove the insight that sits directly above them, and we call this vertical slice of the pyramid an "insight path." Think of it as one run of an argument, or chapter, within your presentation, in which you state and prove an insight. What's interesting here is that we are already beginning to see the essential architecture of your presentation take shape, because any presentation is simply a logical series of insight paths. You address one insight, nail it, and move on to the next. No wonder engineers like this model. There's more process to presentation design than most people think.

Down at the level of data and illustration, always remember that the goal isn't quantity, it's quality. The best arguments are made by focusing on a small number of highly load-bearing proofs, not by assembling every possible data point you can lay your hands on. Audiences quickly become lost if you try to prove an insight with too much data. Your goal is to create the best argument you can, not the biggest.

Which sets up the second huge benefit of the pyramid. In addition to helping you identify your big ideas, the pyramid will not let you reintroduce any of that irrelevant material that keeps trying to get in. The pyramid essentially disqualifies any data point that does not support an insight, no matter how "cherished" that irrelevant nugget is. As beloved as the story of your founder's plucky rise from poverty may be, unless its relevant to an insight (and by extension, relevant to the audience), it doesn't get in. The pyramid is like that scary bouncer at your local nightclub—if you're an irrelevant data point or a picture of a building, you can try to negotiate your way in, but it's not happening.

To give you a feel for a finished pyramid and its inner workings, the following is a simple example. Imagine your city, Metropolis, is trying to be selected as the host city for some future Olympics. To get that outcome, you need the International Olympic Committee (IOC) to take the action of keeping you in the running when they make the cut from twenty-five cities to the final shortlist of ten. You are now going to build a simple pyramid to accomplish that.

Olympic Ambitions

THE PROBLEM THAT THE IOC HAS IS THAT A POORLY EXECUTED Olympics is a catastrophic black eye for them and could even cost committee members their individual jobs.

The desired action we want is for the IOC to keep Metropolis in the running (because we are contending that this will solve their problem—there's that essential connection).

The critical insights, which in real life would be based on a deep understanding of the IOC and their key priorities, might be:

+ Metropolis will have complete, fabulous infrastructure.

+ Everyone will be perfectly safe.

+ The city has great destination appeal.

And laid out in the bottom layer of the pyramid are some key data points or illustrations that might support those insights.

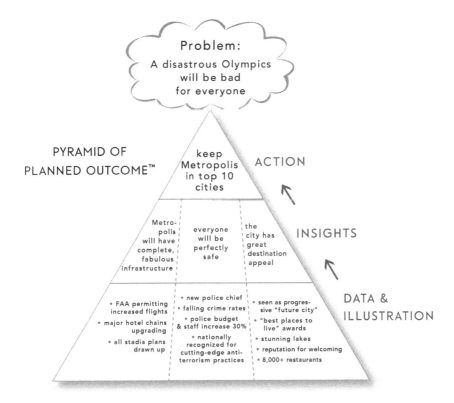

This is a simple orientation to how the pyramid works. And being a straightforward tool to grasp and use, the pyramid will become second nature with only a little practice. Once you're familiar with this tool, you'll find you can build a solid pyramid in under an hour, often less, especially if you know your audience and topic well. The whole purpose of the pyramid is to get you to think, instead of diving into premature slide design. Of course, the work of building those slides and handout is still to come, which is why I often say that once you've built the pyramid, you've done 80% of the thinking but only 20% of the work. However, by doing this design thinking first, you've also drastically cut down the amount of "building" work that's ahead.

Using the Pyramid

AS SIMPLE AS THE PYRAMID IS, MANY PROFOUND QUESTIONS SURROUND it. It's worth dealing with just a few here.

Real Life: Does It Work?

Even though we are now only beginning the full process of presentation design, the pyramid alone can accomplish a great deal.

At one of our recent two-day workshops, one attendee gleefully came up to me at the beginning of day two. He told me that he'd been trying to sell two Harley-Davidson motorcycles, and that when he got home from day one of the class, he had to call back two potential buyers. Before he called them back, he sketched his pyramids (in his right hand in the photo below), and in the process he structured a completely different argument than the one he'd been using before. He sold both bikes.

So, if you use this process, we guarantee $17,000 of incremental income within twenty-four hours. Well, actually we don't, but it's certainly possible.

How Should I Design It: On Paper or in MAST?

It's entirely your call. The Harley guy did it on paper, and we know lots of people who do that. I know one CEO, Larry Tietjan of Experitec, who sketches a pyramid on a cocktail napkin every time he's about to call a customer. Even if it's only a routine check-in, he always wants to think through his desired action (otherwise the call has no real purpose) and the pyramid insights that will drive that action.

However, MAST can be edited much more easily. On paper you often have to crumple it up and start again if you haven't got it right, but changes in the electronic file are faster and easier. You can also build presentations collaboratively in MAST, which is the way a lot of corporate presentations are built. For example, you can design part of it in Louisville and send it over to London for someone else to develop the next insight. We see this happening more and more. MAST is an invaluable tool for teams.

Does Insight Wording Matter?

In presentations, the wording of everything matters, but the wording of big ideas is critical. Remember "If it doesn't fit, you must acquit"? You will want to spend time refining and honing the wording of your big ideas. Don't worry, you don't need to do that now. Because you keep coming back to them, they will always be in your mind, so keep working on wording.

At this early stage, just make certain you are clear what the intellectual idea is. This is one reason why summarizing or abbreviating the insight on the pyramid is a bad idea. Calling an insight "Safety" is simple, but it could end up meaning something quite different when you come back to it later. It's better to be clear: "Everyone will be perfectly safe."

The final question is the most important:

Where Do Insights Come From?

We know that an insight is something your audience or customer needs to believe, but how do you know what that is? Well, in many cases you implicitly know. If you are familiar with your audience, you will know something of what they need to believe. However, here are some helpful tactical guidelines to help you "mine" the insights for your presentations:

1. Insights are frequently answers to implied questions.

Imagine you are proposing a change to an internal system of some kind, and you are aware that the COO in the room, even if she likes the idea, will have one burning question about it, which is: "If we do this, how disruptive will the implementation be?" This question will drive the insight, "The implementation will be remarkably pain-free" (because that's what she needs to believe). **Indeed, there's something magical when a big idea answers a burning question in the room, before it's even been asked.** This is where the presentation profile proves its value, because you've already thought about who is in the room and what they care about.

2. Insights frequently address expected objections.

Earlier I mentioned that one of our team, Eli, used the pyramid to persuade his girlfriend's family to give their blessing to his marriage proposal. As he sheepishly shared with us, this all had to do with an objection that her family, either openly or privately, was likely going to raise. You'll understand enough if I tell you that the load-bearing insight was, "I'm not the guy I used to be." I'll spare you the unsavory details of Eli's checkered past, but suffice to say he's a better man in his thirties than the man they knew in his twenties. The point is, he knew what the objection was and his insight ran right at it.

3. Insights often reflect the competitive battleground.

We have a client who has fully adopted the insight messaging model in sales. At one recent meeting, we were working on a message that was proving tricky. What broke it open was that one member of their team had formerly worked for a competitor. He shared that the main way that competitor was selling against them was with the argument that our client's solution didn't integrate well with the other components it had to be attached to, which was a largely incorrect assertion, but one that was seemingly taking hold in the market. Thus the new insight was born, which was essentially: "Our solution plays well with others." Again, this was something that a skeptical client would need to believe.

Know Your Audience

AS VALUABLE AS THOSE TACTICS ARE, WHEN IT COMES TO DEVELOPING insights, there's really no substitute for the basic doctrine of knowing your audience. I, myself, don't like most traditional teaching on presentation skills—some of it is flat wrong, and where it's not wrong, a lot of what's taught is of such marginal importance that it's never going to make any real difference. But on the issue of knowing your audience, traditional thinking has it exactly right. It's essential, and I can illustrate this with the story of a presentation I gave on a highly delicate topic.

There is a nonprofit organization in my home state of Montana that does fabulous work in caring for the troublingly high population of runaway teens. They have a fundraising banquet every year, and last year I was asked to emcee the event and, more importantly, to do the "ask." This is typically a little uncomfortable, and quite understandably, many banquet speakers prefer not to do this part. But for some reason, I quite like the task. If I believe in the work an organization does, I'm fine getting up there and asking for the support they need and deserve.

This nonprofit has a great daytime center for the kids, but they really needed an overnight shelter for the bitterly cold Montana winter nights. Funding that shelter was the goal of the banquet, and I would have about seven minutes for the ask. Well ahead of the big night, I sat down with the executive director and began building my presentation profile, trying to understand what would be the unique dynamics of this crowd.

In that discussion, she said something that took me completely by surprise. She basically said this: "The thing you need to understand, Tim, is that a lot of the people who are coming won't want to give to this project." I was pretty stunned. "Why not?" I asked. And then I got my education. She told me that most of the invited donors would be fairly wealthy, white, middle-class couples. These are great people, but when that demographic sees a scary-looking teenager with aggressive clothing, a punk hairstyle, and eye-catching tattoos, it's common for their first thought to be that "these are just bad, rebellious kids," closely followed by the conclusion that "if they'd just go home to their families, there wouldn't be a problem and we wouldn't need to build a shelter."

At first blush, this train of logic seems pretty sound. Except that it's not; in fact, it's completely flawed. What I learned that night was the sad reality. It's absolutely true that a runaway teenage girl often looks scary, but the reason is that a girl who's been sexually abused will often intentionally "defeminize" herself, not because she's rebellious, but as a means of future protection against unwanted attention. Masculine clothes, short hair, and tattoos are all part of the defense. If you've seen the movie *The Girl with the Dragon Tattoo*, this was precisely the point they were making. The main character looked exactly the way I've described, and the movie later revealed that prior sexual abuse was the reason.

These kids look the way they do in order to protect themselves. They aren't "bad kids" with a decent home to go back to; in fact, ironically, it's quite the reverse. Most teenage kids run away either *because of* sexual abuse in the home or because of the terrible things they're forced to do to support a parental drug habit. There is no loving family waiting to welcome them home. Kids don't sleep in caves in Montana in February for no reason, but I was one of those middle-class guys who simply didn't understand this world. When this saintly woman took the time to explain it to me (and I'm so glad she did), it all started to make sense.

And from the standpoint of the banquet, that's what I needed. I now understood my audience.

You won't need too many guesses to figure out what the first insight in the pyramid was. It was, simply and precisely: *"These are not bad kids,"* and it was my opening insight, because if I didn't overcome that "headwind," I wasn't getting any further. I opened by running right at the misconception, specifically discussing that these kids do look scary and that perhaps we don't feel motivated to help. But then I landed the insight, "But here's the truth: These are not bad kids ... and let me tell you why," and then presented a few facts and one story about how abused kids will specifically take these measures as a means of self-protection. I think the exact scripting I used to close out that section was, "These kids don't deserve our judgment, they deserve our love and protection." We moved on from there, transitioning into what needed to be done.

The outcome of the banquet isn't the point of the story, but it was a success; the shelter is now built, and our company continues to support this valiant organization. The point here is where insights come from. I had no idea that "these are not bad kids" was the load-bearing insight, and I would never, in a thousand years, have reached that on my own. I only got there because I took a little time to get inside the inner world of my audience.

SUMMARY

This, then, is the pyramid. As you come to work with it, my hope is that you'll find it to be an incredibly valuable tool. At its core it's a tool for thinking, but beyond merely forcing you to think early in the process, it more importantly guides you to the most foundational things you need to think about, namely A) what your big ideas are, and B) how you are going to support them.

Let me close by looping back to the pyramid's true value: the fact that it solves the huge problem of relevance.

In any presentation, the amount of material you could present is always an order of magnitude greater than what you will have time to present, and that creates a problem that most speakers never solve. Too much of that material gets in, and the result is a high percentage of irrelevant content. The essential problem of presentation design is never what to put in; it's always what to leave out. So how do we separate the wheat from the chaff? That's the pyramid. **By refusing to allow the irrelevant information in, the pyramid unerringly holds you to a relevant argument, no matter how tight the presentation constraints get.** If you go back to the Olympics analogy and imagine the IOC asked you to make the pitch in eleven seconds, what would you say?

"Metropolis can guarantee that you won't have a disastrous and personally embarrassing Olympics, because:

+ We will have complete, fabulous infrastructure.

+ Everyone is going to be perfectly safe.

+ The city has great destination appeal."

This "sum it up fast" scenario is not nearly as crazy as it sounds. We've all been called to give an "elevator pitch," to condense our argument into a simple, succinct form. But how do we, in that moment, determine the content that's still worthy of airtime, even when the time slot is only a few minutes? The pyramid, and especially the insight layer, give us the answer.

Now that we have our core intellectual structure and our big ideas, we can start working on how to powerfully land them.

CHAPTER NINE

MAKING IT SIMPLER
(YOUR AUDIENCE HAS LIMITS)

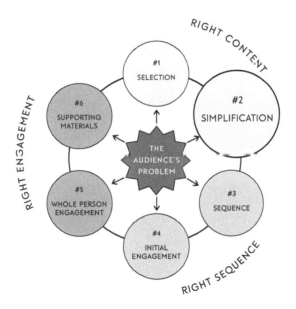

AVING BUILT OUR PYRAMID, WE HAVE THE CORE CONTENT OF our argument established. However, there is a second piece of work that concludes the "right content" exercise, because even if we have established what the relevant material is, we now need to get it down to only the most relevant. And this brings us to the single most common—and most toxic—error that communicators make, and that we have alluded to from the beginning. We call it the fine art of firehosing.

What Is the Problem? The Vomiting Pumpkin

I CAN ALMOST HEAR THE GROANS AS THE TOPIC NOW UNDER DISCUSSION is revealed. **Firehosing can be defined as "utterly overwhelming the audience with a gross excess of material," and there is no more hated mistake in the world of communication.**

We've all been in that room where the speaker has come prepared with a quantity of material that is so wildly unrealistic, it's almost comical that they would even try to get through it. But try they do, to the ruin of all. It's a scenario that can be captured by one simple, if rather tasteless, image.

The "vomiting pumpkin" is a perfect depiction of the problem that, for reasons I don't understand, seems to deeply resonate with most people.

This problem is so well known in sales that it's actually been named either "show up and throw up" or "spray and pray." But sadly, it's not limited to sales; this complete lack of restraint or guardrails shows up in every kind of presentation, and it is so common that if I could somehow reach out and ask everyone reading this, "Who's been firehosed?" every hand would go up.

As we saw earlier on that flipchart list of "What's going wrong in presentations?", almost unfailingly the first item is TMI—too much information, or firehosing. Everyone's been firehosed and they hated it. Which makes a second question rather interesting, because if I could now ask, "Who here has firehosed someone else?", of course, somewhat sheepishly, all the hands would go up again.

There's a peculiar irony there. The practice of firehosing is something we hate when it's done to us and that we know damages the cause of the presenter. Yet despite that, when we become the presenter, faced with the opportunity, most of us commit exactly the same offense.

In every workshop we ask, "Why do we pack too much into our presentations?" It's a simple question, but it opens up several Pandora's boxes.

The list we build inevitably looks something like this:

+ I want to look smart
+ I want to look well prepared
+ I'm passionate
+ To cover my bases (usually expressed as "cover my ***")
+ I need to answer all the possible questions
+ I don't want to finish early
+ This is my only chance with this audience/customer ("One Shot")
+ I don't know what my audience cares about
+ I haven't done my homework
+ The details are important
+ I need to address everyone in the room
+ Insecurity/fear
+ I need to show how I got to my conclusions

What's funny is how the reasons keep on coming as long as we leave the exercise running. There are a lot of forces in play here—and that's the point. It's the breadth of issues on this list that is so profound, and while we see clear echoes of simple sender-orientation (as seen in "I want to look smart"), there are two more significant driving forces worth noting.

The first is the insecurity embedded in the idea "I don't know what my audience cares about," and this issue is its very own, gold-plated, Pandora's box.

> How many presenters, in a desperate attempt to connect with an audience they don't really understand, simply throw all the mud they can at the wall hoping that something will stick?

That's the idea lurking behind "spray and pray": "I see I didn't get you with my first eight points, but this ninth is a doozy."

One client, the head of marketing of a sports company, gave us the best word we've ever fielded on this point. He simply sat back and said, "You know what this is? It's **insurance**." He was absolutely right. If you aren't prepared and don't know your audience well, the temptation to hedge by covering all the bases is overwhelming.

The second big driving force is the "One Shot" problem, and this has notably been rising up in the rankings over the last few years. In an increasingly busy world, it's becoming harder and harder to get in front of crucial decision-makers. So, whether it's an internal VP or a famously elusive customer, when we finally get them in a room, the temptation to give them both barrels is, again, overwhelming. We would never outwardly say this, but the underlying idea is, "It took me six months to finally get this meeting … so buckle up—you're getting all of it." But of course, rather than guaranteeing success, all you're really guaranteeing is that you'll never be allowed in a room with that individual again.

Never Underestimate the Power of the Forces

There's a reason I'm camping out a few moments on the breadth of these forces. If you look at the list again, most of the reasons being given here are quite legitimate. You *do* need to look well prepared, this may actually *be* your one shot, you *do* want to cover all the bases, etc. Precisely because these concerns are real, they are individually powerful enough to make you pack too much in. Which means that when taken together, their effect is all but irresistible.

I firmly believe that the aggregate power of these forces is what drives perfectly sane people into the madness of deliberately doing something that they themselves hate, and that they have never seen succeed. And madness it really is.

Early in the life of our company, there was a business leadership conference where we were doing one of the breakouts. After our session was over, I was looking at the materials from the breakouts I'd missed, and I picked up one handout I have treasured ever since. It's a presentation on the business implications of healthcare reform, which was an important topic at the time and which I'm sure drew many people in. Sadly, for most of them, by the time they realized what they were in for, it was probably too late to escape.

The handout is eighty-eight PowerPoint slides, of which eighty-five are bulleted, with an average of six bullets per slide. If you assume that it took time to settle the group in, do Q&A, and so forth, the speaker had about forty-five minutes of speaking time. You can do the math. It's about thirty seconds per slide, and about five seconds per bullet.

At some level, this is a joke. I'm looking at the handout now, and any description I could come up with simply can't capture the absurdity of what this presenter was trying to do. It's almost beyond belief that someone would seriously try to pack that much in, and yet the cover page reveals that the speaker was an attorney. All attorney jokes aside, this highly educated and intelligent individual created a miserable death-march through 500 bullets, presumably succumbing to the pressure to "cover all the bases." These truly are powerful forces.

What's even sadder is that as bad as this example is, if there was a firehosing Olympics, this presentation wouldn't even get through the qualifying rounds. We show this handout in all our workshops, and the most common reaction is for someone to say: "Oh, that's nothing . . ." and then describe, or better yet, run out and get a presentation of such mammoth proportions that it makes 88 slides look like a note on a cocktail napkin.

A friend recently told me about his company's last annual leadership meeting. After it closed, purely out of masochistic interest, he asked the audio-visual team how many slides had been projected over the previous two days. Their answer was 535. To which he replied: "It felt like more."

Regardless of how common it is, when you bombard an audience in this way, you create three disastrous outcomes:

1. It really irritates the audience. To bring back Mark Twain's quote from Chapter 2: "I didn't have time to write you a short letter, so I wrote you a long one." Audiences feel genuinely disrespected when they see they are getting the long letter because the presenter hasn't put in the time or effort to get their quantity to a manageable level.

   Firehosing has never endeared a speaker to a room full of people, and while we're on the subject, can I just mention: **Apologizing for it isn't the answer.**

   So often I hear presenters say, "I do apologize, you're going to be drinking from the firehose today . . . yuk yuk yuk," as though this fake and insincere apology somehow justifies the offense and makes everything OK. Trust me, it doesn't. This particular phrase drives me to near-murderous rage, because this person isn't sorry at all. If he or she were genuinely sorry, they would have made the effort to correct the problem. In my mind, apologizing makes it worse.

2. The second problem is simple dilution. There's a famous quote from François Fenelon that says, "The more you say, the less people remember." The more you pack in and try to cover, the less chance your big points have of truly standing out. Did any one of this attorney's five hundred bullets have any chance to land powerfully?

    A close cousin to dilution is distraction. When all that extra content contains some interesting nuggets, that causes another common train wreck. It's important to remember that everything you put into a presentation has meeting-derailing potential woven into it, and audiences love to get caught up in some completely trivial backwater, eating away all the time you will need for the meaty topics to come.

    True story: I was in a business presentation once where a major product launch was being discussed. Somewhere in the basket of important issues, a road journey from Chicago to Florida was briefly mentioned in the context of shipping samples to a trade show in Orlando. No kidding, we lost about twenty minutes as the group of senior executives spiritedly discussed what would be the best route.

    When you find yourself in that self-inflicted briar patch, you can't blame your audience. If you toss something out there for their consideration, don't be surprised when they consider it.

3. The third problem dwarfs all others. Yes, it's irritating, and yes, it's distracting; but far more than that, it's a "brain violation" of the highest order. When you overwhelm people with quantity, you create a problem from which you can never recover.

The problem here is as obvious as it is profound. **Your audience has a finite capacity to absorb information, and when you overload that limit, they shut down.** And you can't powerfully land an idea in a brain that is closed for the rest of the day.

The Brain Violation:
The Inviolate Principle of Audience Bandwidth

THE HUMAN BRAIN IS INCREDIBLE IN COUNTLESS WAYS, BUT AS I'VE mentioned before, taking in and processing new information is not its strong suit. The issue in view here is that of capacity. An audience's ability to receive is significantly less than a presenter's ability to transmit. I think we all instinctively understand that at some level this must be true, but what we generally don't understand is just how low that level really is.

In his outstanding book, *Why Don't Students Like School?* (a truly essential read for anyone interested in communications), cognitive scientist Daniel Willingham explores how the brain works when it comes to taking in new information. As he explains, the brain processes new information with "working memory." We can think of working memory as the brain's first port of call for new information, so it's what you use to process what you're seeing, hearing, smelling, and so on. The problem is, working memory is extremely limited.

I came across a wonderful example to demonstrate how limited it actually is. Imagine that the total processing power of your brain were roughly equivalent to the US economy, which today is around 18 trillion dollars. How much of that processing power, in dollars, do you think your brain assigns to working memory?

It's a fun exercise. A trillion? A billion? A million? Keep going. It's about three dollars. If that's true, how on earth do we even get through the day? The short answer is that the brain is incredible at filing stuff away in long-term memory, which is a vast ocean of storage, and which the brain can access in ways still undreamt of in computer science. And it's that access to long-term memory that allows us to function.

Picture a child who's learning to tie his or her shoes. Their early attempts take an agonizingly long time, especially when you're late leaving the house. But any adult can tie their shoes in seconds without any conscious thought whatsoever. What's happening here is that in the adult, this complex series of muscle movements has long been coded in long-term memory, while the child is struggling to have their limited working memory accomplish the same task.

Now, why is this relevant for us as presenters? Because the audience is generally giving us their working memory. As a presenter, you have probably lived with your topic for a long time, but the first-time listener is assimilating the argument, its flow, its visuals, and so on for the first time, while simultaneously trying to relate these new ideas to their world in real time. That takes a tremendous amount of mental energy, and when you overload those circuits, people literally shut down.

> We've all been in that room where it's simply too much coming too fast, and we mentally or literally put our pen down and give up.

The conclusion is unavoidable: You must not exceed the brain's capacity to absorb, and because this is truly a biological limitation, it's not a rule you can bend simply because you feel like it. In fact, this is more of a "law of physics," which is also why you can't get around the problem by firehosing people and then apologizing for it. The audience isn't giving up because it's irritated and doesn't want to follow, it's giving up because it *can't* follow.

At this point we see one of the greatest paradoxes in communication. On the one hand, I've shown that there are immensely powerful forces driving us to pack too much in. And on the other,

I've demonstrated that the capacity of your audience's brain is shockingly limited, and that if you exceed that limit you can't hope to be effective. It's like trying to park a dump truck in a mailbox.

So, is there any hope? Absolutely.

The Essential Solution: Disciplined Defoliation

HERE IS THE GOOD NEWS: AS IRRECONCILABLE AS THIS PARADOX appears, it's not. You are never forced to do this to your audience, because firehosing is not a matter of necessity; it is a matter of self-discipline. This is welcome news, and what makes it true is the liberating fact that **every story can be told within working-memory limitations**. Clearly, in saying this I am not suggesting that every possible detail that could be of interest to every possible audience member can always be covered. But every story can be told in the time and space you have available. You simply need to know how to do it.

Examples of this are out there, and they are often inspiring. The Gettysburg Address is a legendary "presentation." At 272 words, it took Lincoln around two minutes to deliver, yet it stands as one of the most profound, and complete, pieces of communication in history. What many people don't know is that Lincoln wasn't the only speaker on that November day. Edward Everett spoke before him, but his remarks lasted *two hours* and mainstream history has not remembered him. Surely a case of "the more you say, the less people remember."

Perhaps the most poignant example comes from author Ernest Hemingway. He was well known for his extremely economic, almost terse writing style, and reading Hemingway certainly takes some getting used to. There is a story that is often (but sadly, incorrectly) attributed to Hemingway that perfectly illustrates this idea. According to the legend, Hemingway was once bet that he couldn't write a meaningful short story in six words, and after a few minutes' thought, this is what he created:

For Sale
Baby Shoes
Never Worn

Regardless of where it came from, these words are a perfect example of the point I want to make. Within this simple phrase is contained an extraordinary depth of meaning that captures some of the deepest pain of the human experience. It's a story that all too many people, myself included, have some experience with. And it's only six words.

That's the lesson from Lincoln and Hemingway: it's never about the number of words you use. It's about the meaning you pack into those words.

Of course, it's hard to be a Hemingway, but disciplined defoliation is the way we can get there, and it is one of the most important principles of presentation design. **Defoliation is the practical exercise of stripping out everything that isn't necessary, so we can be left with only the most valuable material.** This whole idea is brilliantly captured in one phrase from another author, Antoine de Saint-Exupéry, the French writer, poet, and aviator from the 1930s, who, in addition to writing *The Little Prince*, also wrote:

"The designer has achieved perfection, not when there is nothing more to add, but when there's nothing left to take away."

This is an amazing thought and the rule that needs to guide us, but as I'm sure you realize, it is certainly not what has been modeled for us. Earlier I described those plane rides where you see people working on their presentations, and what are they always doing? They are invariably adding slides and adding bullets, seeking the false perfection of "nothing more to add." Sadly, it's the exact opposite of what they should be doing, which is why we need a tool to help us.

The Practical Tool: The Hundred Pennies Rule

THE HUNDRED PENNIES RULE IS THE TOOL BY WHICH WE DEFOLIATE, and given the pressure on us to always add content, it's particularly valuable to have this in our toolbox. Here is how it works: In preparing any presentation, imagine your audience has 100 pennies of mental energy to burn. It's a fixed quantity, and when they've burned their 100 pennies, they stop working and shut down. Given that this stack of pennies is finite, every penny becomes precious, and hence, the thoughtful designer will burn pennies incredibly sparingly, thinking carefully about how many pennies the audience is burning for a given point.

As you do this, it's important to remember that everything you say or show burns pennies. An odd thing about the brain is that it can't *not* process something you put in front of it. If I say, "Don't picture the Statue of Liberty," you can't help yourself. Everything that's put in front of an audience, every secondary point, every "drive-by," still burns pennies.

What this new mindset does is shift your focus from volume to value, and to a world where each element included is worthy of the pennies it consumes, and where low-value content has been pulled out. Indeed, you will become quite leery of including any secondary material that burns pennies for little value in return. A good example of getting it right would be presenting a point like: "Powerfully land a small number of big ideas." It's a highly valuable phrase, yet easy to comprehend. In short, it's a good "return on pennies." In contrast, getting it wrong would be the lengthy explanation of a research methodology that no one really cares about. Lots of pennies burned, but ultimately for little value. A penny is a terrible thing to waste.

The 100 pennies rule is practical and useful, and it's a liberating exercise to look at your content and for each element ask, "Is this important? Do I really want valuable pennies burned on this?"

Because this is unfamiliar, and the forces driving us to add material are so powerful, I want to give some street-level guidance on how to apply this principle in practice.

Start with Proportion

In the battle to reduce quantity, the place to start is with a word that few people ever think about: proportion—or, how much time each section of your presentation merits. You don't manage down quantity with universal cuts across the board. You want to be more elegant than that. You need to figure out where the deeper cuts need to be.

Lorenzo Ramaciotti is the head of design for Maserati, the Italian sports car manufacturer. Given the way today's Maseratis look, whatever Lorenzo says about design is worth listening to. In a recent interview, he said that the heart of Italian design is "simplicity and *proportion*." It's significant that he would say simplicity, but it's more interesting that he would cite proportion as rising to that same level of importance. But of course he's right. Very often, a car or any other designed object simply looks "ugly" because its proportions are wrong.

It's the same in presentation design. Presenters have a fixed amount of time for their presentation, and when they assign that time poorly between different elements, serious presentational ugliness results. How many presentations have you been in where the introduction droned on, and twenty minutes into the hour there was still no substance in sight? (We call this "too much wind-up.")

Or that seemingly endless description of research methodology, while the research findings that the audience *really* wants to see and discuss get dangerously squeezed into an ever-shrinking back end.

These things happen all the time, and they are simple failures of proportion. Most presentation designers don't think about relative importance nearly enough; they tend to assign time more democratically, or worse, based on what they want to say about that point. In contrast, great communicators design proportion that is Maserati-like. They uncannily linger where the audience wants them to linger, and that gets noticed and appreciated. **There is something highly rewarding to an audience when you breeze through the trivial but dig in on the meaty.**

Getting to that right balance is not particularly hard. It comes from intentionally determining how much emphasis each element should receive, and the way you do it is by looking at your whole argument from end to end through the lens of value. Which pieces are more important? Where will the audience naturally want to linger and discuss? And where will they want me to move on?

Having reached a sense of where in your presentation the value really lies, simply convert that back into minutes. If you know you have sixty minutes to assign, it isn't rocket science to work out that some descriptive point should be kept to around five minutes, but that the critical insight might need fifteen. What you will really notice is how much you end up hacking out of your introductory content.

The whole exercise I just described takes only a few minutes, and it's surprising how easily a little focused thought gets you to roughly the right proportion, which is all you need.

Lorenzo Ramaciotti closed his remarks with an interesting observation that is as true of presentations as it is of cars. He said that "when you get design right, whatever you build will last. But when you don't, whatever you build inevitably fades." Beautifully put.

Having developed your basic proportion, it's time to actually defoliate what remains.

Applying 100 Pennies: Minimize Quantity

There are three specific rules for reducing sheer quantity.

Rule #1: Critical Content Only.

The 100 pennies exercise forces you to sharply focus on your most important ideas, while jettisoning all the secondary content that may be interesting but that you can't afford. There's a wonderful story that illustrates how this works in practice.

A Delicate Discussion of Suicide

Aaron Sironi is a family counselor. As a therapist with an incredible heart for the hurting, and as one of the leading thinkers and practitioners in his field, he is regularly called upon to speak. A couple of years ago he was asked to present at a significant conference, where several thousand counselors would gather to be equipped, and he'd been asked to speak on the tricky subject of "suicide risk diagnosis." Aaron came to us looking for some partnership, because for three reasons, this topic is far trickier than it might initially appear.

First, the stakes are enormous. A family therapist may see hundreds of clients in a month. Some of them may be contemplating suicide, and if the therapist misses it, the consequences can be tragic. It doesn't help that the person with suicidal thoughts generally keeps that information closely guarded, hence "suicidality" is not easy to spot. Second, as important as this subject is, surprisingly little useful research has been done in this field. And third, it's a big topic and somewhat of a labyrinth, and Aaron has been given a one-hour slot. A tricky assignment indeed.

Given that there isn't a substantial body of helpful work in this field, we asked what he had discovered so far in his research. He said that he had found a useful framework for identifying the more important suicide risk factors, namely the acronym:

S.A.D. P.E.R.S.O.N.S.

Each of the ten letters stands for one risk factor. For example:

+ "S" stands for sex. Men are more at risk than women.

+ "A" stands for age. The elderly and adolescents are more at risk.

+ "E" stands for ethanol (alcohol). Risk rises where drinking is involved.

And so on.

The problem, of course, is that even a list of ten things is still a presentation disaster. Given the time he'd need for his intro, housekeeping, Q&A, etc., if he tried to cover every letter in the acronym, he'd only have four minutes for each, and flying through so much so fast would result in everything being immediately forgotten. More importantly, however, is that risk factors generally aren't predictive. They correlate with suicide, meaning they tend to show up in suicide cases, but they don't predict it. For example, a man who is over fifty and drinks alcohol (three risk factors) might have a higher likelihood of having suicidal thoughts, but it doesn't mean all older men who have a glass of wine with dinner are suicidal. Given that this is an almost perfect description of me, that's comforting news.

So we asked this question in search of those elusive critical insights: "Do any of these ten actually predict suicide?" And Aaron answered, "Yes." There were three, and only three, that did. "Build around only those," we said, and he did. A few weeks later he gave the keynote, and it was beyond exceptional. I've listened to it dozens of times, and I'm always struck by its fabulous clarity and focus.

He did do a flyover of the ten, simply because the presence of any one of them is a red flag prompting a counselor to probe further, but he was brief there. He quickly left the seven behind and dug into the three things that a therapist truly needs to understand, and it was simply brilliant. And I've told the story enough times to know that I can't move on without telling you what the three are.

+ "P" stands for Previous suicide attempt. If someone's crossed that line before, it's much easier for them to go there again.

+ "R" stands for Rational thought loss. Mental illness is real, and mentally ill people can easily lose touch with reality. They may hear voices telling them to kill themselves, and they may listen.

+ But the big one, hidden in the ten where you would never find it unaided is "O." Organized plan. People don't commit suicide lightly, and it's rarely spontaneous. They practice and rehearse. They walk out on the bridge and look down, or they hold the gun up to themselves. If you're a therapist looking for clues, the presence of a plan is paramount. In fact, so important was this one predictive indicator that it became the load-bearing insight of Aaron's pyramid and presentation, and he crafted its language carefully. It's a great example of what an insight should look like. The insight was: **"The key to suicidality lies in the inner world of a person's concrete plans to die."**

You could go to a hundred conferences and still never see a presentation like this one. The audience didn't feel entertained; they had truly been equipped. They had been given a message that was tightly focused on the most valuable aspects of a difficult subject, and it was something they could take away and use.

And you see how we got there: somewhere within that "chatter" of ten things (that, by the way, most presenters would have chosen to cover . . . one bullet for each) was a brilliant presentation trying to get out. Critical ideas only.

Rule #2: Ruthlessly Eliminate Repetition.

Most presenters repeat themselves far too much. They will often use multiple stories to illustrate a single point, or lots of data that shows the same thing. It's usually because they want the point to land, and while the motive is understandable, it's generally a big mistake. A second story that teaches the same point as the first is intellectually redundant, and given the extreme limitations of audience capacity, it's burning pennies you simply can't afford to burn.

The exception to this rule is repetition of Insight. Within limits, feel free to keep coming back to your big ideas. It's OK to repeat the big points you want to land.

Rule #3: Be As Brief As Possible.

Finally, within the stories you do tell, be minimalist and concise. Interesting sidebars and intellectual eddies are where presentations go to die. In personal stories especially, we need to be extra vigilant, because when they mean so much to us, we are tempted to discuss every detail. But the more you include, the more you give the audience to process and the more opportunity you give them to get sidetracked. (Remember our twenty-minute rabbit trail, "What is the best way to get to Florida from Chicago?")

Your New Best Friend: The Appendix

In fighting to pull out everything that's secondary, your new best friend is the appendix. In all our training and coaching, we recommend that in addition to a primary handout document, presenters should build an appendix containing all their secondary material. This helps in two ways. Having the appendix keeps all that extraneous material out of the core presentation, and safely off in the appendix, where it can't dilute or distract. But at the same time, it provides all that insurance and "cover my ***" that the presenter might need.

I love it when a presenter is asked a secondary question and replies, "Great question. I don't want to spend a ton of time here, but let's quickly look at page nine of the appendix." They look smart twice because A) they clearly knew what was primary and what was secondary and had separated them, something that an audience will notice and admire, and B) they also knew where the answer was when they needed it. (And their *** was thoroughly covered.)

It's funny. There is absolutely no rule in presentations that you have one single handout, but everyone does. In reality, you almost always want two. The existence of the appendix document fully covers you, but at the same time it allows you to create a beautifully focused core argument, supported by a simple, focused core document, as we'll explore later. It's a neat trick.

If you follow these three rules, as well as provide an appendix, you will never again firehose an audience with too much material. At the core, minimizing quantity can be summarized in one simple principle that we call the Jenga test. You probably know Jenga as the game where you remove blocks from a tower until it falls. That's exactly what you're doing here.

In sum, ask the question, "Do they really need to know this? If I pull it out, does my argument still stand?" And if it does, pull it out.

Applying 100 Pennies: Minimize Complexity

As we strive to simplify, it's vital to get our quantity down to a manageable level. But we need to be aware that there's another side to the firehosing story, which is complexity. And complexity incinerates pennies.

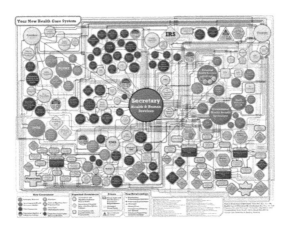

We've all seen charts like this: so monstrously complex that no human could understand them without hours or days of focused effort. This complexity is so obvious that you would think you'd never see graphics like this presented, yet for reasons I will never understand, otherwise rational people put up charts like these all the time. However, the complexity that plagues most presentations isn't nearly this obvious. It's subtler and much harder for presenters to spot because, in a very real way, they are blind to it.

As a general rule, most people present within their own area of expertise, where everything they are talking about is completely familiar to them. But precisely because of their own familiarity, they often fail to spot the complexity that may be as innocent as one acronym, but that nonetheless can derail an audience less fluent with the subject matter. We call this problem "Complexity Blindness." Just because it's simple to you doesn't mean it's simple to everyone else.

This concept is described nicely in another must-read book for communicators. In *Made to Stick* by Chip and Dan Heath, the authors describe an experiment performed by the cognitive psychologist Elizabeth Newton that has come to be known as the "Tappers and Listeners" experiment. Newton took 300 people and broke them into pairs. In each pair, one person was designated the "tapper" and one person the "listener." The tapper's job was to tap out the melody of ten famous songs, and the listener's job was to guess what the songs were.

Based on everything we've said about the brain's limitations when taking in new information, I'm sure you can already sense the train wreck that's coming. The tappers were asked how successful they thought the listeners would be at guessing the songs, and they guessed pretty high at around 50%. But when it was all over, the listeners had only guessed correctly about 2% of the time.

This was simply astonishing to the tappers, and it's an exquisite lesson in how communication works, or in this case, doesn't work. Here you had a group that thought it was communicating effectively 50% of the time, when in fact it was communicating effectively only one in fifty times. And by the way, they generally blamed the listener. (Who hasn't done that? "How did they not get it? That audience was so stupid.")

The cause of this breakdown presents us with a vital lesson, perfectly captured in a phrase I love from the Heaths' book: the problem is that **"You cannot *not* hear the music playing in your own head."** The tappers knew the song title, and once they knew it, they couldn't "un-know" it. They were literally hearing the song playing in their brain as they tapped. But of course the listener didn't have that information, and they floundered amid these seemingly random taps.

All communicators struggle in the same way, and it's a problem that has been well named the "curse of knowledge." That is, it's extremely hard for you to put yourself in the place of the person who doesn't know what you know. In our workshops, we ask people how long they have been in their function, and it's quite common to have people who've worked in their particular field for decades. But even if you've only been in your area of expertise for a few years, it's already difficult to recreate the brain you had on your first day on the job when you didn't know what you now know.

The longer you've spoken the language of your tribe, the harder it is even to notice that this isn't the language of the tribe that's paying you a visit. This is one of the principal reasons why IT (Information Technology) professionals have such great difficulty being understood. Their material clearly makes sense to them, but thanks to their impenetrable insider language, to the average person it might as well be Klingon.

This hidden complexity is like a mild drinking problem. Easy to spot in others, less so in yourself.

So how do we solve for it? Again, there are three essential rules.

Rule #1: Intentionally scrutinize for simplicity.

Even if you don't think your field is especially technical, assume it is. You need to carefully review all your content: your graphics, stories, language, and cases specifically looking for that complexity, and as a general rule, be willing to **sacrifice technical content for teaching**. It's a trade that almost always works in your favor. For many years as a consultant I fought this battle with the researchers whose work I was presenting. The audience doesn't need to know how a conjoint works; they need to know what the conjoint found. (By the way, conjoint is an analysis that simultaneously tests for multiple variables, like the various drivers of employee engagement.)

> The golden rule of technical presentations is this: The conclusions from the data are significantly more important than the details of the data.

To do this scrutiny properly, you must do an **intentional** simplification round, which is one review where you are looking for nothing except potentially confusing terms. Experience has shown me that I will never spot complexity if I'm proofing or editing. Hunting complexity needs to be a highly purposeful act; my brain needs to be focused on that one thing.

Of course, even if I'm looking purposefully, my brain is still already contaminated by its pre-existing "music," so my insider language remains hard for me to spot. A great way to solve this is to run the material by someone with a different technical background. We call this the "untainted eyes" test, and you will be stunned what someone without your specific background will spot.

I know a trial attorney who always runs a closing argument he's designing—before he gets into the courtroom—by the class of eighth graders his wife teaches. I'm not entirely sure how he's allowed to do this, but he does. And he says that it's incredibly effective. He's found that his argument is only simple enough when the eighth graders perfectly understand it. It's a brilliant idea. There aren't many places where ordinary people should act like lawyers, but this is one of them.

Rule #2: Draw the conclusions for the audience.

Tell your audience what your work means for them. Do not ask them to do the highly difficult job of identifying your insights. That's your job.

You may remember the Eva Kor story about stepping over the dead children in the Auschwitz latrine. The first time I heard it, I could have drawn any number of conclusions, but Eva did a brilliant thing by drawing me to the specific point she was trying to make. Left alone I might have inferred a completely different lesson.

This happens to presenters all the time. We present data assuming that the conclusion we have drawn from it is obvious. But it's not, and if we don't "export" the insight, the audience will "import" whatever makes most sense to them, which could be a completely different and even unhelpful idea. Last year, a banking client told us about a major presentation that failed for this reason alone. They had been pitching their services to a young, agile software company. In the deck was a picture of the proposed account team, which in this case was a group of distinguished, older, and mostly white men. They had fully expected to win this account, but to their great surprise, they didn't. And that surprise later became shock when they learned that it was the picture of the account team that had cost them the deal.

Clearly the visual was intended to communicate the insight "Experience." But in the meeting they hadn't made that clear, and by not "exporting the insight," the client was free to import whatever made sense to them. And in this case, what did the young company executives import? "These guys are totally out of touch." Or, as I've heard it described, "stale, male, and pale."

It's a revealing story and an important lesson. **You can never assume that your audience will draw the conclusions you think they will draw, no matter how obvious they seem to you.** You need to draw the conclusion for them, and you are not insulting anyone's intelligence when you do that, in fact quite the reverse: you are respecting the working-memory limitations that make it hard for listeners to interpret information correctly.

Rule #3: Be careful to use audience language and be particularly careful with unexplained terms.

Technical terms and acronyms are probably the worst land mines on the battlefield of hidden complexity. How many three-letter acronyms (TLAs) are in common use in your industry, organization, or function? I can almost see the eyes rolling as I ask the question. Insider language is everywhere, and it's the clearest manifestation of "tappers and listeners," where the communicator understands it while the audience doesn't.

We were recently working with a large real estate company. Now, you would not think of this as an especially technical field, but in their sales pitch to Joe Homeowner, there was a credentials slide containing a bunch of acronyms like "GAR," "DAR," and "NAR," and I was utterly bewildered. What are these guys, pirates? They patiently explained that NAR is the National Association of Realtors. I patiently explained back that none of their customers would know that.

Whenever those terms and acronyms find their way into presentations, it creates a series of fractures in comprehension, and it's the common bane of sales, IT, legal, engineering, and finance. We need to always remember people don't like it when you use terms they don't understand, but they often don't tell you when it's happened. This is why the burden is always on the speaker to root it out.

SUMMARY

Finding and removing both excess quantity and hidden complexity needs to be taken seriously because either one creates real problems of comprehension. There's a sobering principle to be aware of here for anyone selling their ideas to internal stakeholders or external customers: **people don't buy what they don't understand.**

As we draw this section to a close, let me stress that I am not in any way suggesting that we are "dumbing down" our message or shooting for the "lowest common denominator."

What we are doing is aligning our content with the normal, biological limitations of the human brain. Because working memory is so limited, the burden is on us to shoot for a certain, elegant simplicity. We are seeking a clean, uncluttered focus on the intellectual core of our ideas.

Getting to elegant simplicity isn't the easiest thing, because those powerful forces are relentlessly pulling you in the opposite direction. But if you apply these tools under the broad banner of "defoliation," your presentations will increasingly hit that standard of simplicity that is so rare and yet so beloved by audiences on those few occasions when they see them.

Congratulations! We now have the right content.

CHAPTER TEN

⤮

GETTING FROM THE "STUFF" TO THE STORY

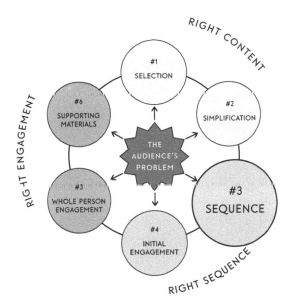

A T THIS POINT, WE'VE ASSEMBLED ALL THE CONTENT OF OUR argument. We've used the pyramid to establish the critical insights and how those insights will be supported, and based on our understanding of the limitations of working memory, we've simplified our argument by both managing down quantity and by "decomplexifying." We have assembled a body of content that is both relevant and elegantly simple.

We now turn to the task of taking this material and finding the overarching storyline that's hidden within it. It's a critical step in the design of any presentation, and it's fun to do. That said, this is a section where the tools are a little more technical, so you'll be seeing examples at different stages of the process.

What Is the Problem? "Next Slide, Please"

THE PROBLEM IN VIEW HERE WAS THE CENTRAL THEME IN THE "failure" story from the Prologue, in which the message of the CEO with the ten bullets was immediately forgotten—despite his sparkling delivery—because he never found the story within his material. And it's a mistake that numerous presenters make.

The problem is randomness. Most presentations do not progress along a logical, linear path, or certainly not one that's clear enough. What we most often see is what we call a "topic-driven" narrative where the speaker moves—or lurches—from topic to topic but without any discernable storyline that holds everything together. The topics may be good, but there's nothing that connects them.

Such a lack of structure leads to two inevitable results. The first is that the presenter loses the audience. Have you ever been in a presentation and turned to a colleague, silently mouthing, "Where are we?" When an audience is unable to track with an argument, they inevitably lose any sense of location and disengage. It's frustrating and exhausting trying to create the narrative that the presenter should have created. What's more, it burns a lot of pennies to try to connect the disconnected.

The second result is that nothing sticks. Random information will not stick in the human mind, and clearly that's the bigger problem. We've seen it all too often: it's the "next slide, please" or "OK, what's next?" syndrome that says there isn't really a storyline here. As interesting as the individual elements of the content might be, absent some clear narrative, we are on a road to forgettability.

I witnessed the bizarre extreme of this recently at a client's sales conference. The final speaker was one of their biggest customers talking about how our client's solution was being deployed, and because he was describing how much his business had improved as a result, the core information was actually fascinating.

But even though he was advancing the slides himself, it was still a "Next slide, please" presentation. There was no discernable structure to his remarks, and as he neared the end, he clicked to advance his slides and the screen went blank. The projector was fine; there was simply no next slide. He stared at the blank screen for a moment and then turned back to the audience and said, "OK, I guess we're done." I didn't laugh out loud, but I came really close. He had built a slide deck, and he was merely narrating his unconnected slides until there were no more slides to narrate. There was no "end," because there was no story here, and as valuable as the information was, I wasn't surprised when I later learned that apart from a few nuggets here and there, nothing had been retained by the audience.

This story illustrates a critical point that's decidedly easy to miss. He had excellent content, just like the "ten-bullet" CEO, but excellent content isn't the issue. If that content isn't properly organized, it's hard to process in the moment—and almost impossible to retain.

The Brain Violation: How Your Brain Stores Information

To understand why the organization of content matters so much, we need to delve a little into how human beings learn. There's no new brain science in play here; this is a principle that has been understood for centuries. The key to human learning is *context*. The brain requires context as it seeks to absorb and retain information, and the following graphic conveys the process quite well.

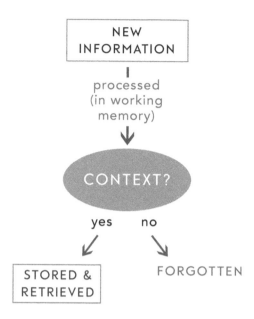

Whenever your brain is exposed to new information, in order to make sense of it, it does something interesting. It goes looking for some relevant context to connect the new information to. As I mentioned earlier, it's like the hooks and loops of Velcro. If your brain finds some context (the loop), then that information (the hook) can be stored and later retrieved. But if it doesn't find context, the brain has nowhere to put it and the information quickly evaporates. Do you remember "Phil" at the cocktail party? When we have no context for the name, we don't have a mechanism for storing it. Your brain doesn't have that filing drawer labeled "stuff for which I have no context." It doesn't work that way. So, absent context, "Phil" is quickly and reliably forgotten.

This process can be demonstrated with a fun two-part experiment.

Part one: Imagine you are in Reno, Nevada, and you want to drive to San Diego, California. In which direction will you drive? We've conducted this exercise in hundreds of workshops and the answer is always the same. The group, in unison, calls out, "Southwest." Except, as you see from the following map, that's wrong. It's actually southeast. Why does everyone get this wrong, and wrong in the same way?

It's because of that process I just described. Most people don't know the precise location of the two cities. So when presented with this question, each brain does the same thing: it reaches back for the nearest available piece of context, and while most people don't know exactly where the cities are located, they know where the states are. And in everyone's "mental map," California is on the coast, which is west of Nevada . . . and knowing San Diego is south, in less than a couple of seconds, their brain plugs that context in and gets them to the answer "southwest." (And with the context being "west coast" and "south," the brain misses how much California hooks back to the east. Hence, everyone gets it wrong.) That's a great example of your brain in action. When presented with new information, it goes looking for context.

Part two: The second exercise shows what happens when the brain does or does not find that context. I came across this exercise in the book I mentioned earlier, *Why Don't Students Like School?* by Daniel Willingham. We use a variant of this exercise in our workshops, as it beautifully demonstrates the role context plays when humans process information.

Take a look at the following list of letters.

XCN

NPH

DFB

ICI

ANC

AAX

Imagine that in a classroom setting I put these letters on the screen and asked you to read them out loud. Then after taking them off the screen, I asked you how many you could remember. How would you fare? You probably guessed that you wouldn't do very well, and you'd be right. It's a random collection of letters, and random information doesn't stick in the mind. After running this exercise hundreds of times, the typical recall is about three to five letters. Not bad actually.

Now imagine that we did the same exercise with this second list of letters.

X

CNN

PHD

FBI

CIA

NCAA

X

How many would you remember this time? I'm sure you know the answer. It's almost all of them. In fact, the typical volunteer correctly recalls about fourteen to sixteen out of the eighteen letters. Why is recall so much greater? Because the brain had prior context, and that context provided the loops the brain needed. When it comes to storing information, context is everything.

Interestingly, in the UK this exercise works quite differently, because ICI was Britain's largest chemical company for decades and the ANC was Nelson Mandela's political party, which tends to be quite well known by the Brits. As a result of their different context, retention of the first list is typically higher, while retention of the second list is usually lower, because America's beloved (or hated) NCAA is almost unknown in the UK. It's fascinating. If you use this particular set of letters, the test works differently between countries because different nationalities have different contexts.

Now, the most important thing in the exercise is this: Look at the two lists again. Do you notice that it's *exactly* the same letters in *exactly* the same sequence? It's the same information, but the point is that it's not about the information; it's about how that information is organized.

We can now see why the "topic-driven" approach is so dangerous. Individual slides like "Five Benefits of Our Solution" or whole presentations like "Seven Top Priorities for Our Department" are exceedingly common, **but what their designers haven't realized is that this approach to organizing content all but guarantees they will be forgotten.** Such frameworks are easy and simple for the presenter to create, but to the audience's brain they stick about as well as that first list of purely random letters.

By the way, this raises a point that's worth pausing on. Numbering your points does not create an actual narrative structure; it merely creates the illusion of structure, which in turn can fool the presenter into thinking he or she has an acceptable organizing framework. Yes, three certainly follows two mathematically but not in any intellectual sense.

For hundreds of years, learning theory has known that humans learn sequentially. We absorb a piece of information, which then becomes the context for, and the basis of, processing all the information to follow. Context creates comprehension. Which raises a question: If context creates comprehension, how do we create that context in our presentations?

The Essential Solution: Sequence Creates Context

FOR THE PRESENTATION DESIGNER IT BOILS DOWN TO ONE VITAL IDEA: **Sequence creates context.** It's the structure of any story that creates the essential context that the brain needs. We instinctively know this because we see it every day: all great books, films, and plays have a structural narrative. In any well-written book, for example, chapter six makes perfect sense because of the context created for it by chapter five. The story develops and flows through a logical arc, ultimately culminating in some great crescendo where the story is resolved. I watch many of my favorite films over and over again, drawn in by the way the story builds to its final act, whether it's *Armageddon*, *Hamlet*, or *The Shawshank Redemption*.

But when a movie or book loses us because that structure isn't there, it defeats us. "I'm so lost" is a sure indicator that this is the first and last time a movie will have our attention. This doesn't mean that some element of mystery isn't valuable. It's OK if the structure takes time to reveal itself, but reveal itself it must.

The goal of every presentation designer is to find that structure. To create an elegant, easy-to-follow run of argument where each piece creates the context for the next. Simply put, the argument needs to be logical. But logical to whom? At first sight the answer is obvious. It needs to be logical to the audience. But unfortunately, as obvious as that seems, all too often that's not what presenters build.

Imagine your CEO has invited you, along with the rest of the company, to an impromptu meeting on a Friday afternoon. There are fifty people waiting expectantly in a conference room, and she opens with these words: "Hello, everybody. Thanks for coming on such short notice. I want to make an exciting announcement. As of Monday we're embarking on a radical change in strategy and direction. We're going to be moving into some major new markets, in some new geographies, and we're going to be developing some significant new products to do that."

She continues, very logically, to talk about the driving forces behind this decision, the economics that will follow, and the promise of greater profitability. She then discusses the timeline of the migration project and talks about the team that will be handling it, and as the hour draws to a close, she ends with something like this: "Obviously, tactically, there are some organizational changes, so in the handouts at the back we have the new org charts . . . I hope you're as excited about this change as I am."

Here's my first question: Does her presentation have a logical structure? Absolutely it does. If you go back and look at it, that presentation structure is perfectly reasonable and logical from the point of view of the CEO (What is the change? ⇨ Where did it come from? ⇨ What will it achieve? ⇨ How will we get there?). The challenge is in my second question: Does that logic work for the audience? Absolutely not! If you're sitting in the audience, what's the first thing that goes through your mind when you hear the words "radical change in strategy and direction?" We've done this exercise hundreds of times in the classroom, and the answer the whole group shouts out is:

"Do I still have a job?"

You can see the problem that's been created. At the opening, the CEO has raised an enormous question in the minds of her listeners, and it's like a cattle prod to the assembled group. From this moment, fifty brains are racing away with thoughts like: "How will I tell my family?" "That was a bad time to refinance the house," "I wonder if that job my brother mentioned is still open?"

So, how helpful is it that the CEO doesn't answer the job security question until the very end? It's a disaster. In fact, brain science suggests that from the moment that question hits the mind of the audience, they are hearing almost nothing that's being said, except that one small part of their brain is listening—specifically—for the answer to that one burning question: "Do I have a job?"

The problem here is competing logic. In any presentation, the presenter has a logic and the audience has a logic. And they're almost always different. When it comes to sequence, having no structure (randomness) is a problem. But a presenter-centric structure can be just as big of a problem.

The Answer: Audience-Centric Sequence

THE POINT OF THIS ILLUSTRATION IS TO DEMONSTRATE THAT WHILE WE do need sequence, it must be sequence of a particular type. The logic must be the audience's logic, not the presenter's. And the key to achieving this is one simple concept:

> Your presentation should arrive at a question the exact moment that question arrives in the audience's mind.

Let's look at how the CEO could and should have done it. It's still Friday afternoon, but now she opens this way: "Hey everybody. Thanks for coming on such short notice. I want to make an exciting announcement. As of Monday we are embarking on a radical change in strategy and direction. Now, I know what you're all thinking! 'Do I still have a job?' Let me tell you, if you're in this room, not only do you still have a job, but that job is about to get a whole lot more rewarding both professionally and personally. Let me tell you what we're doing and how we got here . . ."

And she moves on. But in this case she's carrying a completely comfortable audience with her, because by anticipating their question and answering it, she's built a structure that maps perfectly with her audience's logic. Do you "feel" the difference? It's strange:

when we run these two scenarios in the classroom, even though this is a completely fictitious illustration, people feel a genuine discomfort in the first example, while there's a palpable level of comfort in the second scenario. Maybe too many of us have been in that room at some point in our life.

So, the goal is to be "CEO version two." To find that audience-centric storyline and to track with the questions in their heads. How do we do that?

The Practical Tool: Transition-Driven Storyboarding

The tool that accomplishes this has two intellectual elements. Transitions and storyboarding. Let's start with transitions.

You've probably heard this term before. A transition is essentially a "bridge" between two points. But it's much more than simply closing off one point and introducing the next. A true transition is explaining the intellectual connection between those two points.

Perhaps the best way to describe a true transition is: "A statement of why the next point follows." Let's look at some examples:

+ "Now, you heard me say 'brand new strategy'. . . I know what you're thinking: 'Do I still have a job?' Well, let me tell you . . ."

+ "Given this new system will bring so much benefit, you're probably wondering how easy the migration will be. Let's look at that."

+ "If we agree these are not bad kids, then you may be wondering, 'OK, what is the help they need?' Let's talk about the overnight shelter."

Did you notice that each of these transitions essentially explains *why* you are moving to the next point? In fact, if you look carefully, in each case do you see the implicit question in the audience's mind being referenced?

I often describe presentations as an "imagined conversation" in the sense that the presenter is anticipating the reaction of the audience to what they've said, and then responding to that point accordingly. In the second "new strategy" announcement, the CEO anticipates that the room will be concerned by her announcement, and that they would ask the "Do I have a job" question if they could (and of course audiences often do!). So she names the question and answers it. This idea of the presenter actually stating the audience's question is worth noting, because in many cases the best transition is simply that audience question articulated (as in, "You're probably wondering: How easy will the migration be?"). The signal phrase here is any variant of: **"You're probably wondering . . ."**

> In any presentation I witness, I love hearing the phrase "You're probably wondering," because it tells me that the presenter has thought about, and is explicitly tracking with, the audience's logic.

If that phrase occurs regularly in your presentations, your structure is probably good.

At this point you may be thinking(!) that figuring out what's in your audience's head sounds like voodoo or some Jedi mind trick. In fact, it's not that hard as long as you keep the basic idea straight in your head.

+ You are going to present a point.

+ That point will naturally raise a thought or question in the audience's mind.

+ Think about what that question might be. We call it the "natural question," or "the question in the room."

✦ Having identified it, name it, and make sure the next thing you do is answer it.

And here's the really good news. Clearly any point you make might trigger a range of possible questions in the audience. As long as you've identified a **reasonable** question and run at that, the flow will make total sense and the audience will still track with you. Let me demonstrate.

If I run marketing for a bank, and in a presentation I'm planning to make the point, "I believe we have a serious problem with the way we're onboarding new customers," what are the possible "natural questions" this statement might raise in my audience? (Pause here and think about the question you might want to ask.)

There are probably two leading contenders:

1. How serious is the problem?

or

2. What is causing the problem?

Both of these are reasonable and you could build a transition and a sequence off either one. My instinct says that because business people are pragmatic, if the problem isn't that serious, the audience probably doesn't care about exploring the causes. Thus, to me, the first question creates the more logical flow. Hence, I would go with: "I believe we have a serious problem in the way we're onboarding new customers. Now, as I say that, you're probably wondering, 'How serious is it and does this really merit our attention?' Well, the answer to that is yes. Let me show you what we've found here . . ." That's a perfectly logical flow, because it was built off a reasonable "natural question."

Do you see how this works? It's not a Jedi mind trick; in fact, it's not a modern invention at all. This approach to structuring an argument is an ancient and well-understood literary device, known in scholarly circles as the "diatribe," in which authors play out just such an imagined conversation. It's evident in the earliest Greco-Roman writings of Plato and Socrates, and Ernest Hemingway used this device in several books. In the New Testament, the Apostle Paul structures the book of Romans almost entirely as an imagined dialogue, even to the point of stating the questions he expects his readers to be asking.

When transitions are built this way, their real value becomes clear. They are central to presentation design, because: **transitions reveal structure**.

By far the greatest thing about transitions is that they reveal the structure of an argument. They first reveal it to the presentation designer, because if you can't create a transition between two sections, or the transition "clunks," then you haven't found the right structure yet. That feedback is invaluable during the design process. But more importantly, transitions reveal and explain the structure to the audience. By "roadmapping" your structure, they enable the audience to track with your argument.

If you care to, you can look back in this book and find dozens of transitions that are serving that exact purpose. As a writer, I want to make sure you know exactly where you are in the argument. You may not agree with everything you're reading, but hopefully you're never lost. For example, a few minutes ago, you read this paragraph:

> "For hundreds of years, learning theory has known that humans learn sequentially. We absorb a piece of information, which then becomes the context for, and the basis of, processing all the information to follow. Context creates comprehension. Which raises a question: If context creates comprehension, how do we create that context in our presentations?"

That transition, which I simply stated as a natural question, created the intellectual bridge between: A) the importance of context, and B) how that context gets created in a presentation, which took us into the discussion of sequence. Hopefully that made the argument extremely easy to follow.

So, now we know what transitions are, why they matter, and how to build them. The next question is, if they operate between individual ideas, how do I build the overall presentation flow? (That's the transition ...) And the answer to that is storyboarding.

Storyboard the End-to-End Argument

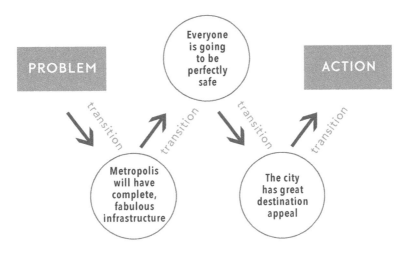

The storyboard containing all the presentation's key elements

The final piece of this is simple. Storyboarding is a well-known tool from the movie industry, and it simply means laying out the whole story from end to end, looking at each scene and seeing how everything fits together. Storyboarding works exactly the same way for us.

It helps that we already have all our story elements. Back in the pyramid, we created a set of insights, each with its key supporting data. We also had an audience problem and a call to action. For reasons that will become obvious in the next chapter, we logically start a presentation with the audience's problem, and we logically end with the call to action. So the job at hand is to storyboard, or sequence, the interior structure.

Sequencing your insights is the first step, and it's like arranging the chapters of a book. This creates your high-level ("macro") sequence, or overall story arc. Then, once you have developed the macro-sequence, you go into each insight—each chapter—and develop the sequence within that specific element. We call these "microsequences."

MACRO SEQUENCE

It's important to develop your macro sequence before your micro sequences. The way you discuss an insight is going to depend on what the audience already knows, so you first need to know where the insight fits in the overall argument. Put another way, you couldn't design the chapter of a book without knowing what ideas the previous chapters had introduced.

The way you do this is fairly simple. Lay out all your main points (doing this on file cards helps), look across the argument, and for each piece ask, "What natural questions are raised by this point?" Then identify the point that most naturally answers that question. As you do this, your points will begin to organically place themselves either "upstream" or "downstream" in your argument.

Let me bring this to life. Imagine you had to sequence that pitch for Metropolis to the International Olympic Committee that we described earlier (and that is on the previous page). We said that there were three insights, which were:

+ "Metropolis will have the infrastructure."

+ "Everyone will be perfectly safe."

+ "The city has great destination appeal."

How would you sequence these insights (i.e., your macro sequence)?

Given that you are making the argument that you can guarantee a fantastic Olympic experience, the most likely first question in the IOC's mind is, "Can you actually get everything built that you need? Can you pull this off?" That's the question you'd state as your transition leading to what is now your first insight, "We will be ready with amazing infrastructure."

A logical next question that flows from that (and remember, it only has to be reasonable) might be: "Now, having the infrastructure is great, but there have been some scary incidents in the past, so you're probably wondering, within all these facilities and as people move between them, will everyone be safe?" There is the transition to your second insight: Safety.

Which leads to your final natural question/transition. "So it's going to be safe, but of course people want to be more than just safe. Are they actually going to love being here . . . ?" And there's your transition to the final insight.

Storyboarding isn't difficult; you simply need to be clear on the process. And as you storyboard, identifying the audience questions naturally creates your transitions.

Write Your Transitions Down

This is an essential practice, for two reasons:

+ If you can't write the transition down, the logic/sequence of the argument isn't there yet. Thinking it all fits together isn't enough—you won't know for sure until you write the transition.

✦ You must remember to deliver them. For the audience to benefit from the transition, they must hear it. But if you haven't written it down, it's quite likely that you won't deliver it. **And a great presentation with all the right content, in the right sequence, will still make no sense at all if the transitions aren't delivered.**

At first reading, that may sound surprising or even flat wrong. Surely the important thing is that you have the right sequence. Actually, no. Having the right sequence is not of itself enough, because people can't always "see" that sequence without help.

At a recent "kickoff the year" event at a technology company, a senior executive opened with a story. He's an ultra-fit guy and a serious triathlete, and his story described a recent triathlon that he had completed, but in which his bike had suffered a serious failure. He explained that as a result of the extremely careful preparation he had done, he was able to fix the problem, get back on the bike, and as a result, break the magical "ten-hours" barrier he had wanted so much to break.

It's a great story, and in rehearsal, the transition he had designed to bridge out of the story was key. "And it's the same for you this year. How you prepare for the unexpected will determine how you perform in the turbulent year to come. Let's look at 2017." It was a great transition out of a well-chosen illustration. The problem was, he forgot to deliver it.

In the heat of the moment, as so often happens, he lost the thread in his own mind, so he came out of the story and simply said, "And thanks to that preparation, I finally broke ten hours. OK ... let's look at 2017."

As you would expect, the audience was totally baffled. It was an odd moment. Their unspoken thought was, "Sure ... you're the boss, we can look at whatever you want," but it made no sense. They had no idea how those two things fit together.

This example demonstrates a vital point. There was nothing whatsoever wrong with his flow of content. There was an absolute connection between the two ideas, but no one could see it: **it was the right content in the right sequence, but without the transition delivered, it made no sense at all.**

Hence, *write them down.* If they don't find their way into your notes, chances are you will never deliver them.

A Quick Postscript on Lists

By definition, if we're looking for a good intellectual structure that turns a collection of points into a story, then lists are a big problem. Even though lists are a common structure for presenters to use (they appear in virtually every presentation), they create two real issues.

+ **Forgettability:** They are completely forgettable because, however valid individually, the points are intellectually orphaned. This was our ten-bullet CEO.

+ **The Toxic Mathematics of Lists:** For reasons I can't explain, people with absolutely no talent for mental arithmetic suddenly become math savants when presented with a list. They see you have nine things to cover and that you took seven minutes on the first item, and they immediately calculate they are going to be there sixty-three minutes. And then they become thoroughly depressed.

> It's strange, but we've all done it. Lists create some kind of countdown clock in the mind. The moment you put up a list, the audience starts counting down the points.

Solving the List Problem

Given these problems, you should avoid lists wherever possible. Find the story in your material. Where you truly can't, then keep the list as short as you can. Covering three important things is immeasurably better than seven important and not-so-important things. This requires discipline because our natural "more is better" or "be complete" instinct tells us otherwise. **Most people, once they start building a list, keep developing it until it's as long as possible. Why? Because we value being thorough and complete. But that's not the way to present.** Remember our suicide-risk diagnosis story: ten was a disaster, three was a dream. Dump the seven or put them in an appendix.

Finally, here's a great rule: Always organize your (now short) list from the least to the greatest. If you make your biggest point first, you've emasculated everything that follows. Lists are like a firework display. You put the big firework at the end.

SUMMARY

In any presentation, comprehension is critical. In the last section we discussed how excess quantity and complexity destroy that comprehension. It's the same when you have a structure problem. If your presentation takes an unannounced and wildly inexplicable left turn—or if the flow works for you, but leaves the audience's burning question unanswered until the end—you lose and frustrate them.

In contrast, a great sequence is immensely rewarding to an audience. While your hearers won't necessarily see what is happening on a conscious level, it not only feels good to never be lost, but they will also feel respected as they see the speaker is identifying and answering their questions as they go. What they will also be totally unaware of is the thing you most care about—which is that their retention of the presentation is skyrocketing.

Context creates comprehension, which is why sequence is one of the most critical things to get right. In that true story of the CEO with ten forgotten bullets, it was the lack of intellectual structure *alone* that destroyed an otherwise brilliant presentation. And I close with this because the sad postscript to that example is that there actually was a great story trying to be told. Certainly his ten points were too many, and he'd have been better with four or five, but all his points related to the lifecycle of their customers—acquiring them, serving them, managing their data, and so on. There was a wonderful story staring him in the face, but he never saw it, most likely because he never even thought to look for it. He didn't know he needed to because the importance of having a clear narrative flow is one of those rules that most people don't understand.

In sum, in any presentation, there's always a storyline to be found. It's your job to find it.

CHAPTER ELEVEN

ANCHORING IT ALL IN YOUR AUDIENCE

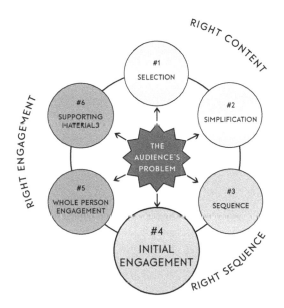

THE NAME JACOB VAN ZANTEN IS NOT FAMILIAR TO MOST people. He was a pilot for KLM, and not just any pilot. He was one of legendary ability, so much so that he actually wrote KLM's pilot safety manual. However, on March 27, 1977, on a densely foggy runway on Tenerife Island, and without permission from the tower, he brought the engines of his 747 up to full power and set his plane thundering down the runway.

Moments later his fully laden Jumbo struck a Pan Am Jumbo that was on that same runway, hidden by the fog. Both planes exploded, and in that tragic moment, 583 people died, including Van Zanten. It was the worst loss of life in aviation history.

As disconnected as it seems, this story, as we will see, is of great importance to presentation designers, because the strange thing that happened in Van Zanten's otherwise sane and rational brain is happening in your audience's brains all the time, and it must be prevented.

In the previous section, we discussed the importance of a presentation's structure. Context is key to human learning and retention, and it's a presentation's logical structure that creates that context. Simply put, each piece of an argument creates the context for the piece that follows it.

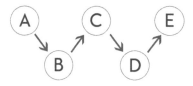

But if A creates the context for B, B creates the context for C, and so on, then a huge question looms: What is A? Or put another way, how should a presentation begin? This brings us to the second part of "right sequence." Your presentation opening bears a huge load: it has to secure attention and interest, and it both anchors and sets the context for everything else that's to come. It has a difficult job to do, and it has to do it at a decidedly challenging moment.

What Is the Problem? A Disengaging Opening

HOW BEST TO OPEN YOUR PRESENTATION IS A HIGH-STAKES DECISION. You have an almost infinite range of options, but if the option you choose doesn't work, your presentation could be over almost before it's begun. **Unfortunately, most presenters do get their opening wrong because they don't understand the rather peculiar rules that govern the first five minutes of every presentation.**

In order to solve the puzzle of the presentation opening, I want to back up and explore the broader question of how information flows in society today, and how our relationship with that information has changed. I'll do this through the lens of four simple questions. These questions will take us down a specific line of reasoning and lead to a profound conclusion for how to make communication engaging in an increasingly "noisy" society.

Question #1: In today's world, do you feel "over-communicated" with?

Answer: Yes.

When we ask this question in a workshop setting, as you would expect, there's widespread groaning. However, while the explosion of information in today's society is something everyone understands from their own experience, I think the incredible scale of this explosion often escapes us.

Back in the early 1980s, the generally accepted wisdom was that the average Westerner was exposed to something like 500 advertising or marketing messages every day. Sadly, I'm old enough to remember discussing those numbers at the time, and even then the number was alarming. Preceding generations, especially those working before the rise of electronic media, had never seen anything like this. From an information explosion standpoint, the early '80s were exciting and uncharted waters. Five hundred messages was a radical number, and as a young marketer, I distinctly remember thinking, "How would I ever get a message through?"

Little did we know. Fast-forward thirty years to a world of social media and ubiquitous mobile devices, and the number that's most commonly floated around has climbed to something like 5,000 messages in a day. Every single day. Admittedly this number has been contested, but the research agencies who look at this all agree that some number in the low thousands is absolutely verifiable.

Anecdotally, it certainly feels true. Skipping from my email in-box to all the news articles available on my Reuters homepage to all the posts and banner ads on Facebook, it doesn't surprise me at all.

It's actually been said that we are now exposed to more information in a day than someone in the Middle Ages was exposed to in their lifetime. Now, admittedly there wasn't a whole lot going on in the Middle Ages: milking the cow and a bout of dysentery amounted to a pretty busy day, but even so, this indicates just how staggering the scale of the communications explosion really is. The day my gas pump started talking to me was when I finally reached my own personal "stop the world, I want to get off" moment.

(Just to put all this in context, can you guess when the following quote was penned? "Advertisements are now so numerous that they are very negligently perused." This was written by Samuel Johnson in 1759. So, actually, it wasn't even penned; it was "quilled." Maybe our modern world isn't quite so modern as we like to think it is.)

Question #2: Faced with this information overload, what have we had to become really good at doing?

Answer: Filtering.

The actual number of messages that bombard us is largely irrelevant, because whether it's 3,000 or 30,000, it's already utterly overwhelming. We are long past the point where we can engage with anything but a tiny fraction of the total quantity. We've had to learn to filter, both quickly and aggressively, in a way our parents' generation never had to.

Think about your day today. Thousands of messages are vying for your attention, a number that is completely beyond your capability to deal with. **The way you protect yourself from being altogether overwhelmed by this onslaught is that you have essentially created a barrier around yourself. It is a screen or filter by which you quickly judge inbound information, and decide whether to engage with it or not. By definition, the vast majority of the messages coming your way are rejected, by which I mean you actively choose to ignore or disregard it.**

The following graphic captures this well.

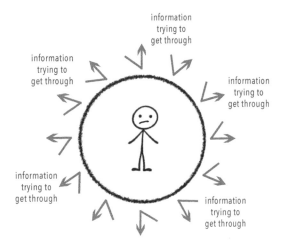

A graphical depiction of how we filter out information in a world of overload

You may be thinking that the purpose of this filter is simply to make your life a bit more manageable, but in fact, it's a lot more serious than that, because if you did let any more than a tiny fraction of this information through, you wouldn't be able to function at all. New medical research suggests that one reason schizophrenic people have so much trouble dealing with life is that their filters aren't working properly. They are unable to distinguish between different types of information, and as a result they find it difficult to reject anything. The resulting ocean that washes over them is utterly paralyzing. I think we've all felt that way from time to time.

It's important to note that based on simple math alone, the default decision today has to be to reject. If I surmise that we engage with perhaps a few dozen or even a few hundred "messages" a day, out of the several thousand, then by definition, the overwhelming majority of information gets rejected. We've built a barrier to keep most information out.

Here's the twist: it isn't just you. Every audience you present to is just as overwhelmed as you are, and they've erected exactly the same barrier to do exactly the same thing. They are trying to keep you out.

Question #3: Not everything is screened out. Some of it gets through. What does information have to be in order for you to let it in?

Answer: Relevant.

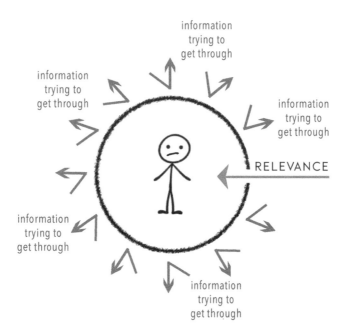

The barrier we've all created is quite efficient, but it isn't designed to be impenetrable. Every day, we all let some information pass through. As you can see on the graphic, it's as though there's one little door. Somewhere within all the ads and postings and articles you evaluate, there's a tiny minority of them that you choose to engage with, and what causes you to engage is critical for us to understand. There's a category here, and it doesn't matter if you call it "relevant" or "valuable" or "important"; the point is that some information has a particular quality that made you willing to engage with it. The most useful umbrella term here is *relevant*.

In order to penetrate your audience's defenses, your presentation must be relevant, but before we explore what makes information "relevant," let's look at our fourth question.

Question #4: You are making a presentation and somehow, early on, you blow it. The audience does not see this presentation as relevant. What chance do you have of getting them back?

Answer: Almost none.

It's not at all surprising that we filter both aggressively and early. But what you might find surprising is how unwilling we are to revisit our decisions. Not only do you have a short space of time in which to secure your audience's engagement, but if you don't do that, your chances of recovering them are extremely slim. I know that statement seems a bit more sensationalist than scientific, but it's not there to shock. The science behind it is very real.

There's an outstanding book by Ori and Rom Brafman called *Sway*. It's a fun read, and it deals with the question of why we knowingly make irrational decisions. Sure, we make dumb decisions all the time, but to knowingly do something that doesn't make sense seems odd, doesn't it? Several reasons why we make irrational decisions are discussed in the book, one of which is a psychological phenomenon called "diagnosis bias."[8]

> Diagnosis bias basically says that when we are exposed to new situations, we tend to make an initial judgment of that situation and are unwilling, even unable, to revisit that judgment later, even if subsequent information shows that our initial evaluation was wrong.

As strange as this first seems, this behavior makes total sense in a world where information is out of control. If I decide not to click on an article, I can't then go back and revisit that decision endlessly. I need to make it and move on.

---

[8] In my view, *Sway* is another Top 5 read. Understanding the irrational elements of human decision-making is essential to every presenter.

In the business world, diagnosis bias is generally not a matter of life or death. But it is life or death in at least two other worlds—those of doctors and pilots. In both arenas, there are many documented cases where an individual made an initial judgment of a situation, but that judgment was wrong. And despite the fact that plenty of evidence later emerged that clearly revealed the mistake, in many cases they did not modify their judgment, and tragedy followed.

Which brings us back to my opening story about the pilot Jacob Van Zanten. The details aren't terribly important here, but as *Sway* clearly explains, "diagnosis bias" is what happened to him. Prior to that fateful attempted takeoff, he had made a decision that he had to leave the island by a certain moment, which was fast approaching. There were several reasons, including the fact that there was not enough hotel space for all his passengers on the small island he'd been diverted to. And despite overwhelming evidence that leaving was the wrong thing to do, he couldn't modify his initial decision. His brain had locked him into a course of action from which a great tragedy resulted.

Now, clearly I'm not suggesting the stakes for the typical presenter come close to the stakes for a doctor or pilot. However, the issue is still real for us because our audiences are making the same quick judgments. **As presenters, we have a short window of time during which the audience is deciding if we are worthy of their limited attention. If we fail to engage them in that time, we will lose them—and it's going to be very difficult to get them back.**

To demonstrate this working in practice, one additional chart will be helpful. How does an audience's attention flow across a presentation?

The Typical Presentation's Bathtub Curve

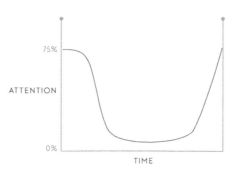

On this chart you have attention on the vertical axis and time on the horizontal, and the typical pattern is quite revealing. As you can see on the left, at the beginning of a presentation, audiences will be giving quite high levels of attention, at around 75%. This is the moment they are getting settled and beginning to focus on the speaker.[9]

Then something curious happens. In the typical presentation, attention and interest rapidly drop to a much lower level, presumably because the foundation for engagement wasn't properly laid in those vital first minutes. Once the attention drops, it tends to stay low for the rest of the presentation, until the very end, when something odd happens. As the presentation nears its close, attention spikes back up to a pretty high level. I call this the "shuffling papers" syndrome, and what I mean is there are signs that the meeting is closing, and as those signs get spotted, everyone suddenly snaps back to attention, bright-eyed and bushy-tailed. Perhaps it's because it's rather rude to be texting as the speaker is thanking everyone. Perhaps it's because the end of the meeting is when tasks get handed out, and people are definitely interested in that. Either way, there's a marked spike at the end.

Looking at the overall patterns, statisticians call this shape a "bathtub" curve and that's an apt term in this case, because lots of presentations slip and drown in the bathtub. I suspect that everyone reading this can empathize with the pattern, because we've all ridden this curve a hundred times. How often have you been in an audience, pretty attentive early on, deciding whether this is worth your valuable time? And when you discover it's not, do you not drift off in exactly this way, succumbing to the siren call of the sixty-three unanswered emails on your iPhone?

The exact numbers on the vertical axis aren't especially important; indeed, I'm not sure it's even possible to quantify "attention" in

---

[9] I've actually seen this data shown in two ways. Here it's the percentage of full attention people are giving you. Elsewhere, and in more academic journals, I've seen it presented as the number of people giving their full attention. Interestingly, the shape of the curve is identical in both cases. At the beginning of a presentation, Initial Engagement is high—with about 75% of the people giving their full attention, followed by a very rapid drop-off.

a legitimate mathematical sense. What is important is the pattern of behavior it represents, which I'm quite certain is correct. Audiences typically start with a high degree of focus, but based on what happens in those vital first few minutes, that attention often rapidly drops off and does not return until—from the speaker's perspective—it is too late.

But here's the good news: while this curve is *typical*, it is not *inevitable*. It is perfectly possible for a presentation to secure the full attention of the audience at the beginning and to hold that attention at a high level throughout, roughly as we see here:

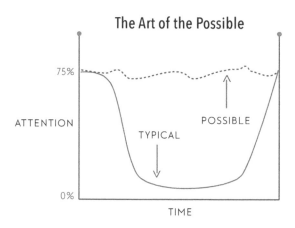

a legitimate mathematical sense. What is important is the pattern of behavior it represents, which I'm quite certain is correct. Audiences typically start with a high degree of focus, but based on what happens in those vital first few minutes, that attention often rapidly drops off and does not return until—from the speaker's perspective—it is too late.

Maintaining engagement is absolutely possible. But only if you have first secured it with the right opening, in those critical early moments when scrutiny is at its highest. Some books say you have seven seconds to make that first impression. I think that's nonsense, but you probably do have only a few minutes. And if you blow it, diagnosis bias says you're not getting that audience back.

I can sum up the argument thus far in four simple ideas.

1. People are overwhelmed with information.
2. As a result, they filter aggressively, rejecting as much as they can.
3. The filter will tend to let in information based on its relevance.

4. If you lose them at the beginning, you're probably not getting them back. They judge quickly and move on.

As you consider how the typical presentation begins, here is where we see two trains collide. Train one is the audience's tendency to engage based on relevance. Train two is the typical presentation opening, and specifically, the horrible habit of **leading with credentials**.

How many times have you seen an opening slide of credentials that looks something like this:

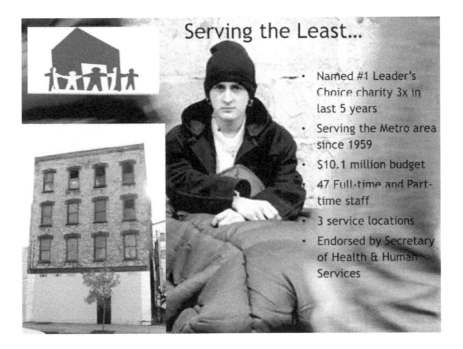

In fact, it's rarely only one slide. By our count, six to twelve slides of history and credentials are the norm in sales presentations, and it's the same with most internal corporate presentations that lead with background, history, and credentials in just the same way.

You see the problem. The credentials-based opening is handing the audience the very reasons they are looking for to justify disengaging.

> At the precise moment when your value is being most carefully evaluated, if you're talking entirely about yourself, you've defined yourself as irrelevant and put yourself outside the barrier. The audience disengages. Grab the soap, you're heading into the bathtub.

What's the answer? As you would expect, it all hinges on that one word—**relevance**. So in an over-communicated world, what is relevant?

Exploring Relevance in an Over-Communicated World

AS I'VE SHOWN, GIVEN ITS SHEER VOLUME IN TODAY'S SOCIETY, WE no longer value information for its own sake. And while we will engage with some content that is purely entertaining, in order to get our attention, information needs to actually be valuable to us. And the most valuable of all information is that which can help make our life easier. We are attracted to information that solves problems. This is true in general, but it is especially true in a business setting. **Business audiences will most deeply engage with information that helps them with a particular problem**, and this point can be proved.

The Google Test

The next time you are at your computer, go back into your search engine history and look at your most recent dozen searches. If you strip out entertainment, what you will find is an uncanny correlation with problems you were trying to solve. Just for fun, here were five recent searches of mine.

+ What are my options traveling from Pamplona to Madrid?

+ Why does a furnace fire up then immediately shut down?

+ What foods lower cholesterol?

+ What's a good Dim Sum restaurant in downtown San Francisco?

+ How often should you feed a thin cat? (We have just adopted an adorable but malnourished stray.)

I've edited these a little, simply for clarity, but in all of these searches, the problem I was trying to solve is clearly evident. Take note that in each case I took the time and energy to deliberately seek the information out. I have a busy schedule, but I still made time to go looking for these pieces of information. Such is the power of the problem.

This all leads to a conclusion that is simple, but of great importance to all presenters. If people reliably engage with, and even seek out, information that solves their problems, it follows logically that a presentation grounded in the audience's problem is likely to be seen as highly engaging, and infinitely more so than a presentation grounded in its speaker's credentials. That's how you penetrate those defenses.

There's a wonderful quote, attributed to the ancient philosopher Philo of Alexandria, though it's not actually found in his writings: "Be kind, for everyone you meet is fighting a great battle." You've got to find that battle your audience is fighting and connect with it. But how do you do that?

The Practical Tool: The Problem-Centric Opening

The tool here is a simple and disciplined approach for designing a presentation's opening. We call it "the problem-centric opening" and it's a discussion of the audience's problem, which has three components—a three-part harmony, if you like. It's good to remember that you've already done the hard work here; in your presentation profile, you performed a diagnosis of the audience's problem and its various manifestations. This tool allows you to convert that research into your presentation opening.

Obviously, every presentation opens with some basic greeting and introduction, giving thanks for the audience's time. Their time is valuable, and it should always be honored. But this should be kept to a minimum. You quickly want to move on to part one.

Part 1: Name the problem.

PRESENTER ACTION	AUDIENCE EFFECT

1. Set up their problem as early as you can.

"Good morning. Today we're going to be talking about an incredibly thorny problem ..."

Reaction:
"Wow! This is about me."

It's a great discipline to get the problem "on the table" as soon as you can. Though I'm certain you have more than seven seconds, the clock of audience evaluation is definitely ticking. They want to know if this is relevant to them, and you only have a few minutes to demonstrate that it is. It might seem a bit geeky, but my personal rule is that I want the problem out on the table within the first minute. You don't want to take any chances. It might sound like:

> "Good morning, thanks for your time. I really appreciate you being here. Time is precious and I don't want to waste any of it, so let's jump right in. I want to talk today about a serious problem. Our growth has stalled and we need to reignite it, but we need to do that in a way that doesn't crush our profit margins."

As simple as this example seems to be, think about the enormous signal these opening lines are sending to the audience. Imagine the presenter here wants to get buy-in for a project that is intended to spark growth. Ninety-nine percent of the time, he or she would open by saying that they are here to talk about the project, not the problem the project solves. As small as it seems, this reorientation is enormous. Make no mistake—the presenter is still there to talk about the project; that hasn't changed. But the project is now being positioned through the lens of solving the audience's problem, and that matters. An executive team is not particularly interested in yet another project, but it is certainly interested in reigniting growth. This reorientation can have a dramatic effect on an audience, which is often some degree of surprise.

We have a client named Sue Graham who's a CEO in the chemicals industry. She's smart, funny, and down to earth. Last year we worked with her and her team to change the orientation of her company's sales messaging, moving it away from the dense and technical approach they've historically taken and making it thoroughly customer problem-centric.

Armed with the new message for one particular solution, she flew to Germany to meet with one of the biggest potential customers in her industry, an organization they've had difficulty gaining traction with in the past. I didn't know this trip was even happening, so I was surprised when she called me from Atlanta airport, right after she landed back in the US, to tell me a story.

Her presentation had a robust problem-centric opening, and in the meeting, while she was walking through this analysis of her customer's pain, the German executive she was meeting with took the unusual step of stopping the meeting. He stopped it so he could specifically make an observation, and I'm paraphrasing, but this is what he said: "I can't believe it. You're a US company but you didn't give me the PowerPoint company history lesson. You're talking about me? Thank you. I'm stunned!"

It's easy to miss what happened here. He didn't stop the meeting to talk about his problem, though Sue told me that a lively discussion around the problem did follow; rather, he stopped the meeting to comment specifically about the messaging approach. As the Lucy graphic depicts, it was truly a shock that the presentation was focused on him. I could see why Sue took the time to call me. The idea of anchoring a message in a customer problem makes logical sense when we teach in the classroom, but it's totally different when, out there in the field, the customer notices it enough to actually stop the meeting and comment on it.

By the way, in case you were wondering, she told me later that they got the deal.

Part 2: Insightfully Unpack the Problem

PRESENTER ACTION	AUDIENCE EFFECT
2. Deconstruct the problem. How many ways it's hurting them (hidden pain points)	**Reaction:** A) "Wow! You really understand my problem." B) "I need to act."

This is the most critical step. You will remember that in the initial research you did on the audience problem, you were looking for all the different manifestations and implications of that problem. Here is where you walk through them. In this part of the opening, you are helping the audience to see that their problem is bigger and more serious than they thought. If we revisit our hospital lighting example, you will recall that when lighting isn't done right, there can be downstream consequences for:

+ Clinical outcomes (from patients getting the wrong drug dosage)
+ Customer experience
+ Employee productivity

+ Patient satisfaction

+ Safety

+ Legal liability

All of which lead to:

+ Negative impact on the thing they most care about, which
is profitability

A skillful explanation of these various tendrils of the problem
impacts the audience in two significant ways.

1. Credibility

We always think that our wonderful credentials establish credibility, but in most cases they don't. While I hate goring sacred
cows, customers don't care how long you've been around, what
buildings you have, or how many people work in those buildings. What they do care about is whether you understand their
problem and can help them solve it. In their excellent book, *The
Challenger Sale*, Matthew Dixon and Brent Adamson (along
with their colleagues at CEB) explore this idea brilliantly. If
you can teach the customer something about their business,
especially with insights around their problem, that's a much
more valuable sales discussion. In short, that's credibility.

Will you eventually talk about your great capabilities and
credentials in the presentation? Absolutely, but not yet. Later
on you will almost certainly make a range of claims about what
you can do, and at those moments the relevant credentials will
be crucial to back those claims up. Just don't wheel them out on
slide one. A great rule to remember is: **credentials follow
claims**.

2. Driven to Act

The second reason you want to explore the audience's problem as fully as you can is that you are trying to plant a thought in their mind, which is, "This is serious. I need to do something about it."

In the hospital lighting example, if the problem is an electricity bill that's a bit higher than it needs to be, that can be easily ignored. But if the problem is a corrosion of clinical outcomes, patient satisfaction, staff productivity, and profitability, it isn't nearly so easy to brush that away.

For these two reasons, dwelling a little on your audience's problem is a smart thing to do.

That said, I'm aware that this idea of lingering on the problem makes some people uncomfortable. Are you wondering if this could be seen as "scaremongering" or "negative selling"? Personally, I've never seen that. People really do like talking about their problems as long as the environment is safe. In fact, salespeople have often told me about meetings that never got beyond the problem discussion—simply because the customer was engaged in a way they had never been when faced with the old "lead with credentials" approach. What's more, they always got the second meeting.

As for the fear of it being negative selling, no one is being criticized here, and you aren't blaming anyone for these problems, so this should not be a concern. Hospitals weren't foolish for installing fluorescent lighting; it was simply the best solution available at the time. But now there's a better way. Most presentations operate in a similar fashion. An audience problem is simply a "gap" or "tension" between the way things work now and the way we want them to work. There's no blame to be assigned.

THE MOTIVATION OF PAIN

If you're wondering whether highlighting the audience problem truly creates the motivation to act, as opposed to the motivation that arises from offering some gain or reward (or put another way, What is the relative power of pain versus gain?), a simple example will help us.

Imagine your all-time favorite band is coming to perform in your town. Tickets are incredibly scarce.

Scenario #1: You learn of a single ticket that is for sale. How much would you be willing to pay for that ticket? Keep that number in mind.

Scenario #2: Now imagine you already have a ticket to the concert, but a stranger offers to buy it from you. Knowing you cannot replace it, how much would you be willing to sell it for?

Here's the odd thing. The price you set in Scenario #2 to sell that precious ticket is almost certainly higher than your price in Scenario #1. For most people, the multiple is usually about three to five times, which is strange because the question is exactly the same in both scenarios: "What is the value of a ticket?"

The difference is that in one case there is a perceived loss involved — the pain of giving up the ticket. But in the other case, the driver of value is the perceived gain of getting the ticket. This is proof that we place a much higher value on avoiding loss than on obtaining a benefit. Weird, but true.

Part 3: Wave at the Solution

PRESENTER ACTION	AUDIENCE EFFECT

3. Allude to the solution.

We're here to solve it,
not to stare at it.
Give a "vision of the future."

Reaction:
"Wow! Maybe you can help."

In general, I always recommend closing out the problem discussion with a "wave" at the solution you're offering. You want to let your audience know that this problem can be solved, and that you know how to do it. As one of our team loves to say, "If you're going to burn down their house, at least show them the shiny castle on the hill."

While it is implicit in your presentation that you can solve this problem, it is helpful to make that explicit. People are motivated both by the avoidance of pain and the pursuit of gain. And while research shows that avoiding pain is about three to five times more powerful as a motivator to act, you don't actually need to choose between them. By presenting the problem but then ending with a positive vision of the future, you connect with both motivations. By showing the vision, the audience takes away an important message: "There is hope—this can be fixed."

The second reason to wave at the solution at the end of your opening is purely tactical. It almost certainly creates the bridge into the rest of the presentation, where that solution will be unpacked.

SUMMARY

Remember where this chapter started, because it explains why openings need to work this way. In today's society, people are overwhelmed with information, and they are seeking to disengage if they can. They filter based on relevance and they do it quickly, so your initial remarks must be highly relevant if you want to get through their barriers. Finally, as busy as people are, if your information solves a problem they have, that's your best chance of being seen as relevant.

The problem-centric opening will significantly support your efforts in three ways:

1. It secures initial engagement. People will lean in, and let you in, when you are there to talk about their problems.

2. It establishes credibility in a way credentials never can.

3. It drives action, because it helps them see that the problem is more serious than they had realized.

I cannot stress the importance of this final point enough. As I mentioned earlier, in most internal or external presentations, the battle we are fighting most often is with the "no decision." Change is hard, and it's always easier for the audience to do nothing. **Busy people like to leave meetings without a new project on their plate that they don't have time for and that hasn't been budgeted, so you have to take that "do nothing" option off the table. You must make the status quo an unacceptable option. When the problem narrative is well designed, it will do just that.**

Based on everything I've said here, the following two checklists may be helpful in structuring your presentation openings and closings. They contain all the elements you want to consider, and most of the presentations I make do conform to these structures.

ANATOMY OF AN ENGAGING OPENING

ELEMENT	RATIONALE
① Greeting (where relevant, give name/organization)	*Politeness: basic knowledge where it's not known*
② Thanks for time and promise to steward wisely	*Shows respect that their time is valuable; begins to allay their dominant fear of wasted time; alludes to audience-centricity*
③ "Why are we here?" – set up problem	*Huge moment of engagement: this really IS about them.*
④ **Briefly/insightfully unpack problem.** Dimensions and pain points; make problem as "intriguing" as possible (thorny, fascinating)	*HUGE: boosts credibility, deepens engagement (especially pain points), intrigue builds gap theory of curiosity*
⑤ Allude to solution – vision of future	*"Third leg" of engagement – potential of solution creates sustained engagement*
⑥ **Concluding benefit statement** ("At end of day, this is what you will have gained ...")	*Clarifies beyond doubt their reason to engage*
⑦ Only where really needed – BRIEF credentials	*Important in settings where credentials are truly needed for credibility (doctors, academics)*
⑧ Lay ground rules: • Phones off • Encourage debate • No sidebar discussion • Confidentiality where relevant • Timings (that will be met)	*Boosts engagement and establishes authority. **Your confidence to take authority will be noted.** Also, these rules set the meeting up for success.*
⑨ Where relevant: participant introductions; surface participant issues on a voluntary basis	*Basic socialization of room; boosts engagement by reinforcing problem orientation, and potential for solution*

While we are considering this opening checklist, this is a good place to present its sibling, a checklist for your close. Your presentation's close is another critical moment for engagement, and as you move toward your call to action, notice that several themes from your opening will reappear as you close some important loops.

ANATOMY OF AN ENGAGING CLOSE

ELEMENT	RATIONALE
① Thanks again for the time.	*However valuable the material, their time was still a gift - respect it*
② "Why were we here?" Clearly restate the problem, with particular emphasis on known and hidden pain points.	*Reconnect to audience problem - places audience back at the center, dials up the need for action, and creates urgency*
③ Summarize the INSIGHT LAYER - tie the key insights (NO data) tightly back to the problem.	*Reduces the argument to its lowest level of simplicity; establishes a clear, single proposition that the suggested action will solve the problem*
④ Clarify/request the desired action (**"ask for the sale"**) **defining specific next steps** where necessary.	*Ensures clear understanding of the required action and gives the opportunity for an immediate response*

CHAPTER TWELVE

WHOLE-PERSON ENGAGEMENT

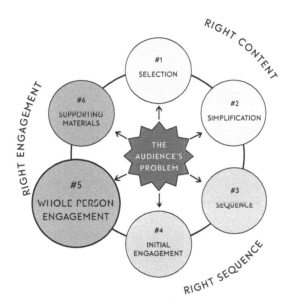

HAVE YOU EVER BEEN IN A MEETING, AND HOWEVER GOOD OR bad the content was, the one thing that really stuck in your brain was that one haunting or evocative image? There might have been dozens of slides and maybe hours of discussion, but out of all that, the single thing that endured—that "stuck"—was that one picture.

We are now entering the third and final phase of our overall design process and the piece that is arguably the most fun to do.

We call this phase "Right Engagement," which is a formal way of saying "stickiness" or memorability.

It's hard to declare any presentation a success if it's mostly forgotten, but as we've seen, that is the fate of most presentations. There are numerous studies that have shown typical presentations have a terrible retention rate, that anywhere from 70–80% of the information is gone within a day. So perhaps the most interesting question in presentation design is how to intentionally make your work sticky and memorable, even when the subject matter is dry and technical. The key word here is *intentional*. Lots of presentations are memorable but usually for all the wrong reasons.

I have fallen off a stage (twice) in my enthusiasm, and I've seen speakers destroy laptops, douse themselves in water, and even pass out. But these are nothing compared to the most memorable presentation I've ever been party to.

The Naked Man in New York

SEVERAL YEARS AGO I WAS IN NEW YORK TO DELIVER A LONG RESEARCH presentation to about sixty heads of marketing. It was a two-day meeting, and after a good first day, I got up to kick off the session the following morning. As I began, I immediately saw that no one was paying the slightest attention to me. They were all looking toward the left end of the back row of attendees. This was strange. What was even stranger was the man they were looking at.

Seated there in the back row was a completely naked man. I distinctly recall that while he had no clothes at all, he had a pen in his hand and was eagerly poised to take notes. Nude but enthusiastic. As it turned out, this quite senior executive was experiencing some kind of mental breakdown. We later learned that he had gone for an early-morning walk, and having been caught in the rain without an umbrella, he had simply removed his clothes and wrapped a tiny towel around his waist.

The audience looked at him and then, as one, they turned and looked at me, which is a point worth noting. It's an unspoken rule of presentations that the audience confers a certain authority on the speaker. Admittedly, this normally involves shutting down sidebar discussions or getting people back from a break on time, but occasionally it involves dealing with random nudity.

Mercifully, it ended uneventfully. I announced an unscheduled early break "while we get this gentleman the help he needs," and our team gently but firmly escorted him to the elevator. For some reason I can still picture his white bottom, peeking through the gap in his tiny towel, receding into the distance, though I don't summon the image consciously. (As funny as it seems now, it was disturbing at the time. After it was over, there was plenty of nervous, tension-relieving laughter. I recall asking the group, "Is everyone OK?" to which one attendee replied, "It's all right, Tim, at least we knew he didn't have a gun.")

This is a true story with an important point: Lots of presentations are memorable—you want yours to be memorable for the right reasons. **And what you want, of course, is stickiness of your big ideas**. If I'm presenting, I don't care if my audience doesn't retain much of my secondary data or supporting argument. And I certainly don't care if they forget me. But I care very passionately that they retain the big ideas I was trying to convey. Once again we return to our touchstone: "Powerfully land a small number of big ideas." This is what we are aiming for.

So how do you make those ideas truly sticky? The first thing to note is that much of what we've already done in our design work has contributed to a greater than average stickiness. When you fire-hose people, you will be forgotten; when you have a random structure, you will be forgotten; but the elegantly simple presentation, with a logical narrative, is markedly more memorable.

Stickiness, however, can go far beyond this. There are elements you can introduce to support and illustrate your argument, such as effective visuals, which may lead to a presentation embedding in people's memories for years or even decades. We simply have to understand what those elements are and how to use them correctly.

Facts and Data Matter

We are now descending from our high-level design questions and getting down into the details of how you actually make the points within your argument. As we do so, I want to lay a foundation stone. In any presentation, facts and data do matter. While statistics won't be your most memorable elements, it is essential that your argument be intellectually well supported. If you are proposing something that requires an investment, for example, you will certainly need data to quantify the relevant costs and benefits. Just remember, as we saw in the chapter on Simplification, the goal is to present the best data you have, not all the data you have.

What Is the Problem? Frequent Forgettability

AS IMPORTANT AS THEY ARE, FACTS AND DATA ALONE ARE NOT SUFFICIENT. If you look at almost any survey asking people to describe the presentations they see, the first word that shows up, almost without exception, is *boring*. Words like dull, colorless, and data dump are also usually on the list. So keep in mind that while data supports and proves our main ideas, it doesn't make them memorable. And if your ideas are forgotten, you have a problem.

To understand how to achieve deep memorability, once again we need to look into how the brain uses different types of information. Let's begin with a simple illustration. Imagine I am trying to convey the seriousness of the problem of world hunger, and to do that, I show you this chart on screen.

There are more than 800 million hungry people on earth

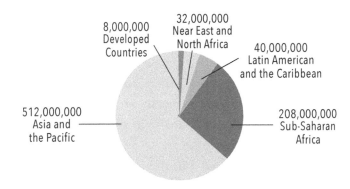

8,000,000
Developed
Countries

32,000,000
Near East and
North Africa

40,000,000
Latin American
and the Caribbean

512,000,000
Asia and
the Pacific

208,000,000
Sub-Saharan
Africa

It's a visual image, so it comes in through the eyes and is sent to the visual cortex. But it doesn't stay there. The visual cortex sends it to the part of the brain best suited to deal with it, and in this case, because it's data, it goes to the area of the left-brain where numbers and data are processed. There's nothing wrong with that, but it's not very sticky; unfortunately, we tend to forget left-brain data. (I should mention at this point that in this section there's an inevitable over-simplification of the brain's processes. While the "left-brain"/"right-brain" divide is quite real—in fact, several areas on both sides of the brain will get involved in almost anything the brain does—the simpler depiction will be helpful for the purposes of this illustration.)

Now, imagine that instead of the pie chart, I choose to convey the idea with this picture:

This image is communicating exactly the same idea, but the brain deals with it entirely differently. Once again, the image has gone into your visual cortex, but this time your brain has recognized it as a human face and sent it to that area where human faces are processed, which is over in the right-brain. In fact, your brain is so finely tuned that not only is there an area that recognizes faces, but there's an immediately adjacent area that recognizes human facial expressions. In this case, the pain and sadness of the suffering child and her anguished mother.

And, broadly speaking, information dealt with in the right-brain has more impact and therefore becomes stickier. You likely knew instinctively that this image was more memorable than the equivalent data. If you think about any advertising that relates to human or animal suffering, how does it communicate the problem? With visual images of suffering. The fact that you knew the answer proves the point: those images stuck.

This simple example serves to illustrate the opening idea. You have many choices for how to illustrate or demonstrate a point you wish to make. And because your brain does not deal with all information in the same way, some approaches will be more forgettable while others will be more memorable. If we can harness this understanding, radically improved stickiness is possible.

The Brain Violation: Western Rationalism

UNFORTUNATELY, MOST PRESENTERS TODAY MAKE ALMOST NO USE of the tools of right-brain engagement. If I grabbed twenty random presentation decks from the enormous stack in my office, I would find little effective use of story or visual in any of them. What I would find is an overwhelming preponderance of facts and data. Why? Because we tend to make our arguments purely "rationally," and the reason is that even though right-brain engagement is deeply wired within us, we operate in a left-brain culture.

Most Western organizations are highly rationalistic in nature, and in a left-brain, rationalist world, the unspoken rule is that facts and data are the only "legitimate" form of supporting argument. In fact, in many organizations today, if you were to present using pictures, you'd likely be branded some kind of New Age hippy, triggering a review of the firm's hiring processes. But if you stood up and presented an impenetrable mass of data, you would be applauded for each successive decimal place.

I'm exaggerating to make a point, but not much. Professionally, we live in a world dominated by business cases, ROI estimates, project plans, and good risk analyses. And let me restate: at one level there's nothing wrong with these, but if we limit ourselves to these tools, there's a whole half of the brain we aren't engaging.

People certainly are rational, but they are also highly emotional, and in fact, emotion plays the far larger role in human decision-making. **But as presenters, we generally steer clear of more emotional engagement because our organizations don't encourage or reward it. We are prisoners, if not victims, of a left-brain culture.**

There's a quote widely attributed to Albert Einstein, and though he didn't say it, it is brilliant nonetheless:

"The intuitive mind is a sacred gift, and the rational mind is a faithful servant. We have created a society that honors the servant but has forgotten the gift."

What a profound thought, and the reference here is essentially to left- and right-brain engagement. The intuitive (right) brain is a gift that, in Western organizations, we rarely unwrap.

The Essential Solution: Whole-Brain Engagement

THE WAY WE SOLVE THIS IS CONCEPTUALLY QUITE SIMPLE: WE NEED to intentionally engage the whole brain of our audience. And while that might send a shiver down the average rationalist's spine, even in the most formal business setting, it's both legitimate and absolutely acceptable to do so. But to understand how to do it well, we need to go one level deeper in terms of how the brain works.

Unlike every other organ in your body, your brain is profoundly functionally divided, and while it does perform different functions in different places, what's really going on is both more nuanced and more interesting than simply "the left-brain does math and the right-brain does music." In reality, most of the brain is involved in pretty much everything the brain does. As such, a better way of understanding the brain's functional division is that your left- and right-brain don't look at the world in the same way—they perceive reality differently.

The best way of explaining this is by using an illustration from the British psychologist Iain McGilchrist. His book *The Master and His Emissary* is a great read on this topic of the real distinction between left and right-brain.

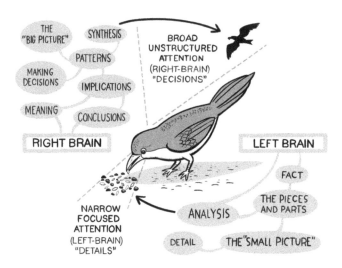

Imagine a bird that's feeding by pecking tiny seeds out of fine grit and gravel. In order to do this, it needs extremely narrow, focused attention. This is the left-brain on full display (and by the way, the bird and mammalian brains are highly similar). The left-brain is excellent at focus and details, so you can think of the left-brain as all about:

- Fact
- Detail
- The "small picture"
- The pieces and parts
- Analysis, in the sense of breaking things apart

If you like to use tools, knit or sew, or paint or build models, this is your left-brain in action. And whether you're left- or right-handed, tool use is always coded in the left-brain. **The left-brain is all about the details.** Now, if the seed in the gravel is all the bird is focused on, what's going to happen? It's going to get eaten or run over. So simultaneously, it needs a different kind of attention that's looking out at the bigger world, and McGilchrist calls this "broad, unstructured attention." This is the right-brain's area of excellence. You can think of the right-brain as being good at:

- Patterns
- Meaning
- The "big picture"
- Conclusions
- Implications
- Synthesis, in the sense of putting all the pieces together (the opposite of analysis)
- And of course, making decisions

And it makes sense that these things need to operate relatively independently of each other so the bird can both feed and be vigilant at the same time. So whether this development was Darwinian or Divine, the brain has these two hemispheres that are profoundly divided functionally. **The left-brain sees the parts; the right-brain sees the whole.**

There's a truly weird experiment that McGilchrist describes that shows just how real this separation is. In the 1970s, doctors developed a surgery to help patients who were severely epileptic. An epileptic seizure begins in one side of the brain, but there's a little "bridge" of tissue between the two hemispheres called the corpus callosum. Seizures will cross that bridge and propagate into the other hemisphere, and by doing so they can completely incapacitate a person.

Doctors realized that if you cut the bridge and severed the corpus callosum, you would contain the seizure in one hemisphere, which could help the patient immensely. So they tried it, and it worked.

Now, at this point, you're probably thinking that as helpful as the procedure might be, people who'd had this surgery would be pretty messed up. But the funny thing is that there was nothing discernibly different about them after having had this surgery. With one remarkable exception.

As you probably know, the left side of the brain controls the right side of the body, and vice versa, so doctors performed an interesting experiment. They took patients who had had this surgery and asked them to draw a cube in three dimensions with their left hand, which is controlled by the right-brain. And this is what they drew:

No problem, because the right-brain has no trouble seeing how everything fits together. However, when they asked the same patients to do the same thing with their right hand, which is controlled by their left-brain—but which can no longer reach across the bridge and ask the right-brain for help—this is what they drew:

It's quite remarkable, and it hammers home just how real this division is. The left-brain sees the pieces and parts but it truly can't see the big picture at all.

I suspect you can see where all this is going. When we present, we want to land big ideas, big conclusions. We want to be memorable, and these are all right-brain outcomes. And even more than that, we want action. We want a decision, and decision-making is also a thoroughly right-brain activity, because as you weigh all the different pros and cons, that is the very definition of synthesis. And as we just saw, putting the cube together is a uniquely right-brain function.

You see the problem.

> As Western presenters, we typically use left brain tools to create right-brain outcomes.

As one of our team members loves to say, "We're using a left-brain currency in a right-brain economy."

Of course, this doesn't mean that we can't get a decision if we make a purely left-brain, data-rich presentation. It happens all the time, and a healthy brain can easily do the work of moving the argument across the bridge. But by nature, decision-making is a more emotional, right-brain process, and there's great power in reaching out and "touching" that right-brain directly.

Before we dig into a set of specific "right-brain engagement" tools, I'm not in any way suggesting that we abandon the left-brain. For lots of reasons, that would be a mistake, not least because the rational data elements of your presentation will be important for your audience in terms of justifying their decision. In other words, it isn't a question of either/or. What you want to do is create both: a balance of left- and right-brain engagement, which actually multiplies the impact of your message, as demonstrated by the following example.

Imagine if you can, one of the Universal Studios parking lots in Orlando, Florida. Like all theme parks, Universal has a problem. Families show up expectantly every morning, park their cars, and head to the turnstiles. Universal is well known for providing an amazing, immersive entertainment experience that completely consumes those families on their day of vacation. So when they eventually emerge exhausted from the park, what commonly happens? They've forgotten where they parked. Easily done after such an engaging day.

Of course, like any provider of a great experience, Universal doesn't want the final piece of that experience to be frustrating. They want you to remember where you parked. One way they've helped solve this problem is to move away from alpha-numerics to a more visual system, which is smart. If you parked in "Jaws," it's certainly a lot easier to remember the Jaws image than "C17." But the second thing they did was brilliant. They also installed motion sensors in the lots, and when a family parks and begins walking away from their car, the sensor detects them, which triggers a tune being played. In the Jaws parking lot, it is, of course, the legendary *Jaws* theme (which is now playing in your head).

What happened when they did this? From what friends at Universal have told me, the number of lost cars plummeted. Why? Because they'd planted the idea in two places in the brain.

> This is the heart of what we need to understand about presenting to right- and/ or left-brain. We want to present to both.

An idea becomes more memorable when it is planted in more than one place in the brain, because your brain essentially creates a neural pathway between the two locations, and this wiring allows you to access the idea in two different ways. There's a great phrase from the book *The Brain That Changes Itself* that captures exactly how this works: "Neurons that fire together wire together."

An everyday example reveals this to be true. How easy is it to remember songs? Pretty easy, right? And one of the reasons is that they're stored in two places. If you care to try this, you will notice that you can recite the lyrics of "Happy Birthday to You" without the tune. You can also hum the tune without the lyrics. This demonstrates that even though you almost always retrieve them together, the two things are actually stored independently in your brain (lyrics in left, melody in right). This is why it's so much harder to recall poetry or Shakespeare—they are unidimensional instead of multidimensional. In other words, they have fewer hooks for your brain to latch onto.

Great presenters are multi-dimensional. Their material is more sticky because their big ideas light up more of the brain. If I verbalize an idea, support it with a powerful visual on screen, and you see that idea captured and highlighted in a handout, that multidimensional idea is far more likely to stick.

There are five ways to do this, each of which provides your audience with a different way of visualizing your big idea.

The Practical Tool: Five Methods of Visualization

1. Story

In recent years, the idea that story and storytelling are important in communication has been gathering momentum. We know that stories are great teaching devices, that they hold interest, and that they create context and meaning for points that would otherwise be purely intellectual.

Story has been a central teaching device in this book. In an earlier chapter, for example, I made the point that we need to strip out secondary material and focus on the primary. It's a great point, but it's very left-brain, and it's not that memorable. But then I told the story of the suicide-risk diagnosis presentation, and how the presentation based on three points shone like a diamond, but only when the seven secondary points had been left behind. The story brought the idea to life. (Do you remember what the three things were?)

As much as "storytelling" has become a hot trend for managers in recent years, it is only in the last ten years that developments in neuroscience have revealed just how important storytelling can be. It turns out that stories affect our brains in decidedly powerful ways; indeed, it's fair to say that stories are essentially the way we "code" a great deal of information. If I ask you about your summer, you won't give me a string of facts and data; you will tell me a series of stories. Cognitive scientist Mark Turner says, "Stories are easier to remember, because in many ways stories are *how* we remember. Story is the fundamental instrument of thought."

Stories really do grab hold of the brain. If you put a person in a functional MRI machine, or fMRI (an MRI machine that can identify which areas of the brain are active), and ask them to tell a story, you can see the multiple areas of the brain that are lighting up as they describe the various sights, sounds, and smells. However, what's interesting is that neuroscience has recently learned that if you later put a second person in the same fMRI machine and play them an audio recording of that story, guess what happens? Exactly the same areas of their brain light up.

We often think about trying to "connect" with our audience, or "get on the same page." In a surprisingly real way, story serves to do exactly this.

A second aspect of story is even more remarkable. I'd like to take you back to something I recounted earlier from Eva Kor, the Holocaust survivor, and I'll repeat here exactly what you read earlier:

> For example, she unfailingly tells the story of how, early on in her confinement, she got up one morning and went to the rudimentary latrine where, if the water was running, she could at least splash some on her face.
> As she tells the story, she describes stepping over the naked, dead bodies of other children in the washroom in order to get to the faucet. Children would often die in the night, she explained, and such was the harshness of the Auschwitz winter that it was a matter of life or death to recycle their clothes. So the children

would be stripped and placed in the latrine until morning when the bodies would be removed by the guards.

Here's my question, and I apologize in advance if it freaks you out. As you read that story, did you visualize that dirty latrine, the dead bodies, little Eva stepping over and around them to get to the water? Did you form an image of it in your mind?

You did. In fact, you couldn't help yourself. In every workshop, we always ask that same question about that same story, and every hand goes up. With any story you hear, your brain essentially makes a movie of it, filling in the picture either from the description, from your own past experience, or if you've never seen a picture of Auschwitz barracks, from your imagination. We often think we need to use visual aids in presentations, and we certainly should, but never underestimate the way in which stories create entire movies for your audience.

I now know Eva quite well, and I recently asked her why she doesn't use slides or project images of any kind. Once again, this dear lady revealed herself to be a communicator of unparalleled brilliance. She said, **"I think they're a distraction. I want the audience to form the pictures in their minds."** I sometimes think she should have written this book, except that her message is so much more important. (Her book, by the way, is *Surviving the Angel of Death: The Story of a Mengele Twin in Auschwitz*. I highly recommend it.)

As great as they are, when designing your stories be careful of one pitfall. While you want to provide enough color for the story to make sense, don't provide excessive details, especially where those details do not relate to or support your main point. As we discussed in the Simplification chapter, every element of your story is something that your audience can potentially be drawn into thinking about. The more details in the story, the more off-topic rabbit trails you may be creating. In short: tell tight stories.

2. Visual Images

The second tool of right-brain engagement is visuals. A great visual can powerfully complement any point or help an audience visualize your narrative. The starving child image we looked at a little earlier is a good example of this. Everyone understands the concept of world hunger, but the suffering seen on a human face lends the point additional depth.

We are all wired to relate to visuals. Research shows that your brain stores visual imagery twenty-two times more effectively than any other form of information. This is why if I asked you to visualize your childhood bedroom, or the Twin Towers on 9/11, you could do so with great detail, but if I asked you to remember your brother-in-law's phone number, you probably couldn't.

Used properly, visuals can add great impact to any presentation, and understanding this basic idea is why most people now try to make them a part of their presentation design. The problem here is that there are many ways to use them improperly, which is exactly what happens most of the time. And when you do get visuals wrong, it's a problem because they have a big effect on how your overall presentation is viewed. Projecting a barrage of complex slides is the all-too-common example of getting visuals wrong and bringing down your whole presentation as a result.

The topic of how to use visuals correctly is important enough to warrant separate treatment. In the next chapter, we will consider them in in detail, in relation to the presenter's other "supporting actor"—the handout.

3. Artifacts/Physical Experiences

The third core tool of right-brain engagement is the use of physical artifacts and other tactile/sensory experiences. While most presentations focus on the ear and the eye, humans assign particular value to the sense of touch. When we can touch and hold things, they become more "real" and more meaningful to us. The value of this "kinesthetic" connection is one reason why more and more companies have developed experience centers where their customers can physically interact with their products.

Used well, the right artifact can create an unusually lasting impression. And when you hear about a presentation that was vividly remembered decades later, it's surprising how often you find that some physical object was involved. At every workshop we teach, we go fishing for a memorable presentation where some physical object was used. The current record stands at around forty-four years, where an engineer in his early sixties reported remembering his high school graduation speech. Given that I barely remember what I had for breakfast this morning, that is pretty remarkable. When we asked him to recount the story, this is what he told us.

He was seated in a crowd of graduating high school seniors, listening to the commencement speech, when the speaker paused and said, "I want you to reach under your chair. You're going to find something taped there." All the kids duly obliged, and each one found a quarter. Holding his own quarter up, the speaker said, "Kids, I want you to take this quarter and put it in your pocket. This is the last free thing you're going to get. From now on you're going to have to earn it."

It wasn't the most uplifting message perhaps. (I jokingly suggested that he should have taped a screw there if he really wanted to illustrate what the future held.) But nonetheless, it stuck in an amazing way. **Over forty years later this engineer remembered the presentation as though it was yesterday—and note something crucial: He didn't merely remember the quarter; he remembered what the quarter had stood for. The big idea had been powerfully landed.**

I've seen this over and over again. When an audience can somehow touch or feel the idea, new levels of stickiness can be achieved. By extension, the highest form of this tool is the fully immersive experience, in which all the senses are simultaneously engaged. Obviously, in the majority of cases, you don't have this as an option, but when it happens it's pretty special.

Earlier this year, I had the great privilege of visiting and touring Auschwitz with Eva Kor. These were four of the richest but most difficult days of my life, and like most people, I've found it difficult to capture the experience in words. My best attempt at describing it would be to say that it's a place of unrelenting misery and evil.

There isn't a square inch where "the good stuff" happened, because there isn't any good stuff. There are only degrees of depravity that wash over you like waves as you walk from one location to another. It's sobering to say the least, but at the same time it's invaluable to be reminded of the dangers of unrestrained prejudice.

But hearing Eva speak there in Auschwitz provided me with a rare opportunity to compare the presentation I'd seen her make in the high school gym and the one she made inside the camp itself. To sit in a Montana high school auditorium, and listen to Eva describe the selection platform where she was torn from her mother's arms is one thing; to listen to her describe it, standing on the platform itself, in front of a red cattle truck and with the gas chambers painting a wretched, dreary backdrop, is wholly another.

Eva and the author in Auschwitz.
Perhaps there was one redemptive moment. In one of the Auschwitz museums is an enormous picture of children being liberated from the camp. The little girl at the head of the line is Eva, holding hands with her twin sister Miriam on the day of their liberation. Seventy years and one amazing lifetime separates the two Evas.

We've looked at the three core tools of right-brain engagement, which are story, visual, and artifact. However, to use them correctly you need to embrace one critical rule.

These must teach.

What do I mean by this? The reason you use these stories, visuals, or artifacts is to help you land an idea powerfully. Or put another way, to teach something important. That's why they're there. Think about the quarters under the chairs. Those quarters taught the idea the speaker was trying to convey, bleak as it was. Free golf balls are also artifacts, but they don't teach a point.

To ensure you're getting to the teaching, make sure that you:

A. Identify your point, getting it clear in your own mind.

B. Select the story, visual, or experience for its ability to teach that point.

C. Clearly deliver the lesson.

This might seem obvious, and yet it's extremely rare to see it done properly. Presenters insert stock pictures into their slides all the time, but those photos usually don't take anybody anywhere; they're merely there to liven things up. When I ask people why they use pictures, the most common answer is, "To make my presentations more interesting." The goal of being interesting is good, but that is not the primary purpose of your visuals.

Think about the various stories and images you've encountered in this book. It would be overkill to recount them all, but let me just highlight a few, noting three things in particular.

First, every story and visual was intentionally chosen to illustrate a specific point I was striving to get across. Second (though you'd have to go back and look at them to see this), that teaching point was always clearly made coming out of the story. Third, there should always be a relationship between the depth/scope of the story you tell and the importance of the point it teaches. A common mistake for speakers is "too much club," where they tell a lengthy, elaborate story (like a case study) to teach a barely significant point. As such, try to keep the two things in balance. There is nothing wrong with a big story, but you don't want to burn lots of pennies using a big story for a small idea. **Reserve big stories for teaching a big idea.**

THE STORY ...	WHICH WAS THERE TO TEACH ...
Ten-bullet CEO who sparkled but failed	*Delivery doesn't matter if there's a brain violation in the design*
Me being thrown into the presentation crucible	*You are being watched when you present – how you perform can accelerate or derail your career*
"These are not bad kids" – the key insight for the homeless shelter fundraising banquet	*The importance of really knowing your audience when developing insights*
There was a quarter under every chair	*The power of artifact to boost memorability*

Following on from our three core tools, there are two other, slightly more sophisticated tools of visualization that are worth noting: antithesis and allegory.

4. Antithesis: Harnessing the Power of Contrast

Antithesis is nothing more than a fancy word for contrast, and it simply means the setting of one idea against another. On the surface, it doesn't appear to be especially important to the presentation designer, but here's why it is: it's like catnip to the brain. **Our brains love to chew on contrasting ideas, which makes antithetical ideas incredibly sticky.**

Earlier, I mentioned that Johnnie Cochran's phrase "If it doesn't fit, you must acquit" presented an important contrast that he wanted the jury to wrestle with, and thanks in part to that antithesis, decades later we all remember it. As you start looking for antithesis, what you find, quite surprisingly, is that it keeps showing up in some of history's most memorable speeches and screenplays.

Almost everyone knows the line "get busy living or get busy dying" from the movie *The Shawshank Redemption*. But think about it: do you know any other single line from that movie? Whether it's "Give me liberty or give me death," or "Ask not what your country can do for you, ask what you can do for your country," it's the antithesis that causes these ideas to endure when everything around them fades.

If you want to get really fancy, a double antithesis sets two ideas against each other. Whether it's Muhammad Ali ("Float like a butterfly, sting like a bee") or Herman Melville ("It is better to fail in originality than succeed in imitation"), these are truly inspired. I actually made use of one of the most powerful of these earlier: "The designer has achieved perfection, not when there is nothing more to add, but when there's nothing left to take away."

And of course, how could the list be complete without the great master of rhetoric, Sir Winston Churchill, and perhaps his most remembered phrase, which I cited earlier from the "Battle of Britain" speech, delivered on August 20, 1940. In this one phrase he captures the gratitude of a nation to a small band of heroic fighter pilots who, despite being outnumbered four to one, fought and won a desperate aerial conflict with the German Air Force that would decide the fate of the war. And he does it with a masterful triple antithesis.

"Never in the field of human conflict, was so much owed by so many to so few."

Three contrasts, making for a wonderfully sticky phrase.

We teach our workshop primarily in the US, and yet seventy years later and three thousand miles removed, those US audiences can invariably finish Churchill's sentence perfectly.

Finally, I'm going to avoid going deep down the rabbit hole of Shakespeare, but can you guess what all the best remembered Shakespearean passages have in common?

+ "To be or not to be, that is the question."

+ "Now is the winter of our discontent made glorious summer by this son of York."

+ "Friends, Romans, countrymen, lend me your ears. I come to bury Caesar, not to praise him . . ."

+ "Once more unto the breach, dear friends, once more. Or close the walls up with our English dead . . ."[10]

AN UNIMAGINABLY BRILLIANT PHRASE

If you will permit me one seriously geeky Shakespeare moment, in the play *Richard II*, there's a candidate for my favorite, and possibly the most brilliantly constructed phrase in the English language. It's a double antithesis – but where both antithetical words have a double meaning. King Richard is in his later years, reflecting on frittering his life away, and he says,

"I wasted time, and now doth time waste me."

You really have to stare at this to apprehend how brilliant it is. The first use of waste means "squander," but the second use of waste means "decay" (as in "wasting disease"). The first use of time means an ordinary passage of time (as in the hours in a day), but the second use of time means time as an unstoppable force (as in time marches on).

I'm not just being geeky here. Shakespeare did this very deliberately. He fully intended his hearers to spot both double meanings and to enjoy the mental exercise of unraveling them.

---

[10] In fact, several of these speeches contain multiple antitheses. "To be or not to be" actually contains four, and two in the first few lines:

> To be, or not to be, that is the question:
> Whether 'tis Nobler in the mind to suffer
> The Slings and Arrows of outrageous Fortune,
> Or to take Arms against a Sea of troubles,
> And by opposing end them

It turns out that almost all of Shakespeare's most famous passages are deeply antithetical, and this is part of the reason why they are so sticky over 400 years later.

Whether *Shawshank* or Shakespeare, in simply reading these examples, I'm sure you "feel" how intriguingly sticky they are as your brain tries to wrestle with and untangle the oppositional ideas. The important question then becomes, how do we apply this in our own work? The following picture offers a clue:

This is an ad for the excellent workout system P90X. As you can see, it makes a highly intentional use of contrast, and in fact research has shown that contrast images like this play a significant role in the success of products in the diet and exercise industry. We see the before and after change, and we want it.

But do you see how what it's doing specifically applies to presentation design? The guy on the left has a problem. The guy on the right has had this problem solved. Does this sound familiar?

> In almost any presentation, you have the opportunity for the antithetical comparison between the audience's problem you are defining and the future solution you are proposing. That's where antithesis most powerfully fits.

An Antithetical Vision of the Future

When you are seeking to drive action, there is tremendous power in helping your audience visualize the result of that action—i.e., the "new state" that you are offering. Hence, a powerful strategy for a presentation designer is to describe the problem as the audience currently experiences it, often through story, and then describe a vision of the world as it could be if the solution were embraced and let the audience chew on the contrast. This is exactly what the P90X ad is doing. **In essence, you are using a vision of the future to motivate action in the present.**

Painting a picture of the new desired state is often nothing more than a word picture of the future you are proposing. In my pitch for the homeless shelter for those runaway teens, my scripting was something like: "Imagine that it's a bitter winter night next February, and there are thirty-five homeless teens roaming our streets. But instead of another potentially deadly night on a freezing park bench or in the clutches of a sexual predator, at 7 p.m. they walk into the new shelter, they take a towel and a sandwich, and they settle in for a night that's warm, dry, and safe."

This was a deliberate vision of the future that I was setting against the earlier description of today's problem. By painting these two pictures, I had set up the contrast that I needed: the world as it is now versus the world as it could be. In other words, paint a picture of the two states and let the brain's love of contrast do the rest. There's a phrase we use to summarize this idea, which is, **"Don't just tell them you can solve their problem. Give them a vision of the problem solved."**

I know this is a little more technical, but it is a powerful tool. Contrast deeply engages the right-brain, and interestingly, the place in your brain where you ponder contrast is actually only two synapses away from where you make decisions. In brain-science terms, that distance is nothing.

5. Metaphor and Allegory

The final weapon in our battle for right-brain engagement is the use of metaphor. Now before you assume this is difficult, let me assure you that presentation metaphor isn't complicated—it's simply a specific type of visualization, where your big idea is presented in a different "parallel" form.

The metaphorical visual is both powerful and easy to create. For example, imagine I want to communicate the idea, as I did earlier, that we tend to present too much information. I can describe that verbally and factually, and there's nothing wrong with that, but it's not very sticky. However, what if in addition to making the factual point, I show this image?

This picture is not literal. A picture of a starving child is literal. This picture is metaphorical: I'm clearly not suggesting you are actually a vomiting vegetable. The value of the metaphor hitting the screen lies in how the brain now deals with this unexpected turn of events. Your left-brain will be happily following along with my line of argument, but when this picture appears, it is completely thrown by the disconnect. And because it doesn't know how to put these apparently unrelated pieces together, it reaches over to the right-brain for help. Why? Because it's the right-brain's ability to discern patterns and meaning that sees the connection between the intellectual idea that "we present too much information" and the metaphorical treatment of that same idea that's in the image of the pumpkin. The right-brain recognizes that these are two representations of the same idea, and because you've now planted the idea in two places in the brain, it sticks more deeply.

As it happens, this particular image creates one of the most enduring moments from our two-day workshop, and an unusually high percentage of people recall it, even months after the class. (It probably helps that it's utterly gross.)

Beyond the allegorical visual, the allegorical story works in the same way, but is generally more powerful because it additionally leverages all the dimensions of story that we discussed earlier. This is best demonstrated by example.

Imagine the big idea that you want to land in your presentation is that "Overconfidence will be our downfall." You can make the point literally, but alternatively you could choose to tell the story of the Soviet ice hockey team coming into the 1980 Lake Placid Winter Olympics. This team was essentially unbeatable. Gold-medal winners in six of the last seven prior Olympics, they were the juggernaut of international ice hockey. But you probably know how the story ends. Somehow they are defeated by the ridiculously heroic efforts of an unlikely bunch of US college students.

So you tell the story, and this is how you end: "Guys, this is a great story, but why am I telling you this? Because we've had a great run, but if we think we can just show up and win, we're going to find ourselves crying on the ice like that Soviet hockey team. Over-confidence will be our downfall."

Because of the allegory, the big idea lands with far greater force.

Again, this is not difficult. Make sure you're clear what your big idea is, then look for a story from history or current affairs that teaches that big idea.

Here's your opportunity to practice. Can you think of five other stories that would teach that same "overconfidence" insight? See the box at the bottom of the page for some options.

SUMMARY

As you develop any presentation, you get to this point in the process where you are down in the details of the argument, figuring out how to make the big points you need to make, and in a way that will be remembered.

Western rationalism has led us to believe that facts and data are all we need, but while they are important, they primarily engage the left-brain. To create that rare, unforgettable presentation, we must touch the right-brain, and I've provided five tools that effectively facilitate that. And, as we've seen in these examples, when we create a balanced argument by combining great data with great illustration, we touch both sides of the brain. That's when real stickiness happens.

A few minutes' thought got me to:

- The "unsinkable" *Titanic*
- The British in 1776
- Microsoft Zune—their version of the iPod
- The Hare (as in *The Tortoise and . . .*)
- The fiery crash of the *Hindenburg*

These are all solid possibilities, but I suspect the Zune would have been best. The others are more clichéd, which you want to avoid.

CHAPTER THIRTEEN

❦

THE SUPPORTING CAST: THE CORRECT USE OF VISUALS AND HANDOUTS

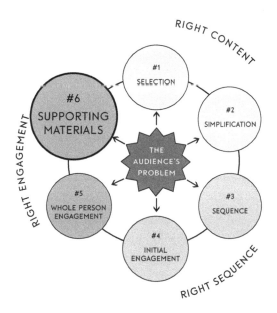

N THE PREVIOUS CHAPTER, I INTRODUCED THE IDEA OF VISUALS AS one of the core tools of right-brain engagement. However, the correct use of visuals and the relationship between visuals and handouts is worthy of a separate, focused discussion because it's something almost every presenter gets wrong.

What Is the Problem? You Can't Use a Tool Correctly if You Don't Know Why You're Using It

THE RELATIONSHIP BETWEEN VISUALS AND HANDOUTS IS ONE OF the most completely misunderstood areas of communication practice, and it stems from a general misunderstanding of the different purposes of the two tools. As we seek to untangle this, to the delight of many I'm sure, we are going to address one of the dumbest developments in corporate life. It's something that I've referenced earlier and that, in my view, has set the cause of communication back twenty years. It's the dreaded slide deck.

Let's back up for a moment. Whenever you present, you basically have three core tools at your disposal: your narrative comments (what people hear), your visuals (what people see), and your handout (what people read, and crucially, what they take away). Most presenters have the use of these thoroughly mixed up, which plays a big part in making them ineffective. Usually, the words that should be on the handout are up on the screen as slides, and the handout, or "deck," is simply a printout of these slides.

When it's done this way, neither visuals nor handout will be good; these slides are horrible visual aids, and the printed slide deck is about the worst form of take-home document you can build. Over the years, I've asked thousands of people to tell me—honestly—what they do with these brick-like handouts after the meeting, and while people are sometimes a little hesitant, eventually the truth comes out. At best they're filed away, but most people openly confess to throwing them in the trash. Either way, they almost never survive for long after the event. **Bottom line: If you want your message to be remembered, and especially if you want it to be retold by others, having your document thrown in the trash is probably not a good thing.**

As I've stated several times, the fundamental problem here is not PowerPoint, it's how PowerPoint is being used. But the fact that it's not the software's fault doesn't make the problem any less real. Wherever you look, people are becoming increasingly aware that today's PowerPoint habits are actually getting in the way of effective communication.

The final data from our executive survey is quite revealing. There are three simple statements here, and the bars are the percentage of respondents who agree or strongly agree with that statement.

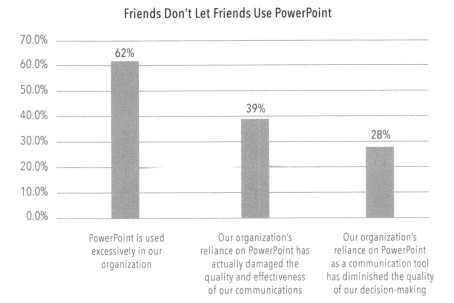

Friends Don't Let Friends Use PowerPoint

As you can see, at 62%, most people think that PowerPoint is being used too much in their organization. This is a surprisingly high number, and it reveals how widespread this problem has become. More surprising, however, and even more important, is the middle bar. Thirty-nine percent of people think that this Power-Point dependence is hurting them—that it has actually damaged the quality of communications in their organization. You must pause for a moment to see the irony in that number. The idea that for about four in ten people, the world's standard communication software tool has actually made communication worse is simply bizarre.

Finally, on the right, at almost 30%, a meaningful number believe that PowerPoint has damaged the quality of their organization's decision-making. This is a deeply troubling finding, and it likely relates to a complaint I hear frequently, which is that when a presenter is merely plowing through a mountain of slides, it tends to stifle debate and discussion. In fact, a friend of mine who runs a division of a Fortune 50 company claims they have a serious slide addiction, and he recently told me, "I hate it. The moment those damn slides go up, everybody stops talking."

Again, let's be clear. The problem isn't the tool, it's the user. I can take down a tree with a chainsaw, but I can also take off a couple of fingers. Whichever one I end up doing, it isn't the saw's fault. It's up to me to use my tools properly.

The good news here is that using PowerPoint correctly, and achieving exceptional results from it, is possibly the easiest thing this book discusses. In a moment we're going to get to the issue of whether slide decks make effective handouts, but let's start with the correct way to do visual aids.

Tool #1: The Correct Use of Visuals

First Principles: What Is a Visual Aid?

Visual aids are not crutches or teleprompters. They are not on screen so you can glance up there when you've forgotten what you were going to say and "unstick" yourself. I can't believe I need to say that, but I do, because it's shocking how many presenters use slides this way. Have you ever seen a presenter look at their screen and utter the immortal words, "So, what's next? . . . Oh, yes . . ." That's another rage moment for me.

> Slides are never an alternative to having proper notes and sufficient rehearsal. Visual aids aren't a safety net for the underprepared; they're there to help an audience learn. Period.

As such, visuals serve one of two specific purposes. You will use a visual:

1. Where the information is too complex to be expressed simply in words alone.

    There is some information that is simply too hard to grasp verbally. An organization chart is a perfect example; I could never explain an org chart in words, but on screen you would apprehend it in seconds. The key word here is "spatial." Spatial relationships (i.e., where we see the location of one object relative to another) will always be understood better as visuals. Hence, bar charts and pie charts are completely acceptable visuals.

2. Where you want to "imprint" a point visually.

    The earlier images of the starving child or vomiting pumpkin are examples of this. Here, the audience could understand the point verbally, but if I want it to land with more force than that, by adding the visual, I'm able to plant the idea in two places in your brain, which significantly increases retention.

If those are the two criteria for using a visual, then even a cursory look at the typical deck reveals that very few of these text-heavy slides meet either of these conditions. Most presenters put visuals on screen for some other reason (for example, as a teleprompter), and often only for the sake of having something up there to liven things up.

Long before you opened this book, you knew that visual aids were important, and that dense, bloated slide decks weren't the right way to do them. You've been a frustrated audience member enough times to know that. Everyone wants to be a visual aid "ninja," and the encouraging news here is that nothing could be easier. There are five simple rules of visual aids, and anyone can follow them.

The Five Rules of Visual Aids

Rule #1: Visuals Must Be . . . Visual

The purpose of visual aids is to visually reinforce the point being taught, not to restate the words the audience is already hearing. Hence, visual aids must be visual! You should be showing images, video (in moderation—videos can be visually overwhelming), diagrams/charts, pictures of people, places, and objects.

The obvious corollary of this is that you should not be putting the text of points that you are making up on screen, that you then read (often with little additional color). This "script on screen" is one of the worst of all presentation sins. The audience quickly learns that all they need to do is scan the slides for a few seconds to get what you're saying. And given they can read faster than you can speak, they end up either disconnected or distracted by guessing what bullet four might be.

Of course, giving your audience the text of your points is incredibly important. Just don't put it on screen. That's what handouts are for. We'll get to that in a moment.

This basic idea does not rule out putting any words on screen. There is no problem with:

+ Agenda
+ Table of Contents
+ Important quotes
+ Key Insights

Just be sure to keep this text to a minimum.

Rule #2: The Visual Must Teach

While visuals need to be visual, this doesn't mean we can merely throw in any old picture and be done, because as I stressed in the previous section, those visuals must also teach. There's a problem here that I'm seeing more and more frequently. Look at this slide.

- Leader in Cloud Deployment Software
- Focused Exclusively on Cloud and Connectivity
- Driving Agile, Metrics-Based, Cutting Edge Companies
- Global Data-Center Footprint
- Broadest Partner Network
- Fastest Growing Provider

This is a real slide (company name changed), and it's what many people are doing today. This slide designer knew that bullets alone were dull, so in an attempt to be more interesting, he or she added a stock picture to liven things up. But what ultimately is this slide at its core? It's still a bulleted slide.

> Simply adding a picture to a bulleted slide is like putting lipstick on a pig. It's still a pig. And while we're on the subject, animating the bullets doesn't make it a proper visual either. As exciting as whizzing bullets might be, that's just lipstick and eye shadow on the same pig.

Inserting a stock photo that vaguely connects to some point on your slide (I guess a racing car in some way ties to "fastest growing") is not using a visual to teach an insight; it simply creates the illusion of a visual. If I see one more picture of a happy, smiling, ethnically diverse group around a conference table on a slide about teamwork, or a pretty, smiling girl in a headset on a slide about customer service, I may lose it with the presenter.

What does getting it right look like? Look at this visual from an internal corporate presentation made by an IT director. The specific context isn't important, but the big idea here was: "What we are doing is dangerously outdated."

This is a stunningly effective visual. It's an image of a Polish cavalry officer, circa 1939. When the Nazis invaded Poland, triggering World War II, the heroic but hopelessly outdated Polish army had no choice but to send cavalry units against the oncoming divisions of Panzer tanks, with utterly tragic consequences. The image of the soldier shooting from behind his horse is simply heartbreaking. Indeed when I show this slide and explain it, it's sufficiently emotive that our workshop attendees often tear up.

With this image on screen, the executive quickly recounted the story of that brief and tragic Polish defense and concluded with the big idea: "This picture reflects exactly where we are today—what we are doing is dangerously outdated." The point landed with tremendous force.

Rule #3: One Idea Only

If the goal of a visual is to complement a key teaching point, then by definition the visual should be about that one idea only. Look at the Polish cavalry officer. One of the reasons this image is so powerful is that there's no distraction: nothing is interfering with the presenter's single idea. This is another reason why multiple bullets are unhelpful. Not only are they neither visual nor complementing a point, but by nature they contain several competing thoughts.

Data slides are a slight exception to the "one idea" rule. When presenting data, there will commonly be multiple conclusions/ideas within a single chart. This is no problem as long as you teach the points clearly and carefully. However, don't try to cover everything that the data teaches. Focus on your primary points. The more you try to cover "interesting" but largely secondary points, the more you will dilute the conclusions that matter.

Before we move on, let me show you a wonderful example that combines several of the principles I've covered. A company we work with has a sales presentation in which one of the critical ideas is: "We give you visibility." Their solution provides visibility into a business problem that costs their clients money, but where that cost is largely hidden. Here's the slide for that point:

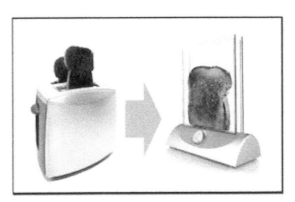

The story behind the picture is that toast often gets burned because you have no visibility inside the traditional toaster, and that's a problem. However, there is actually a new toaster under development, on the right here, that is completely transparent. As far as I can tell, it works on the power of witchcraft but it is nevertheless real.

This is a fabulous visual. It teaches one singular insight, which is: "You are getting burned today by a lack of visibility (pun intended). But with our solution, you will have perfect visibility."

However, in addition to landing a singular point, did you notice that this image is also antithetical, contrasting the old and new world? And because this company doesn't make toasters, they make data systems, it's also allegorical.

Insightful, antithetical, and allegorical. That's an impressive visual.

Rule #4: Take Them Down

Once your idea has been discussed, take down the visual. I'm sure you've been in rooms many times where the speaker has moved on to some new point while the slide on screen refers to a previous point. The image on screen now "clashes" intellectually with (and distracts from) the new point being made.

More importantly, remember that the screen should not be the center of attention in the presentation. That's the presenter's role. The way you prevent the screen from taking over is by making sure you do not have something on screen all the time, because if the screen is constantly "active," people will default to staring at it.

Show your visual, discuss it, make your point, and then take it down. And as you do so, you will notice that the attention automatically shifts right back to you. It's a great moment for the presenter, and it's not egotistical. You are trying to be at the center of a conversation, not to be the disembodied narrator of an hour of "slide-staring." In practical terms, in order to do this, you need to interweave a neutral "logo" slide between your visuals so that the screen shows only the logo slide while you continue speaking. After the first couple of times, the audience has fully figured out what's going on, and they like it.

An alternative is to make the screen go blank (in both Power-Point and Keynote, just press the letter "B"), but I do not recommend this. People's screen addiction is so strong that it will actually freak them out. Case in point: I recently heard a great story from someone we had trained. He was making a presentation and at one point, having finished discussing a visual, he made his screen go blank, which was the right thing to do. The audience, however, couldn't possibly conceive of a universe in which a blank screen could be deliberate, so they assumed the projector had broken. Before he could explain things, four people rushed up to the stage to help. Screen addiction is real, but you can help end it.

Rule #5: Not Too Many

How many visuals do you need? The basic answer is, "Not too many." Visuals are powerful and their overuse can easily cause dilution of impact as visual fatigue sets in. However, the more accurate answer is this: Since you only have a few big ideas, you probably need only a few supporting visuals—or you may need none at all, especially since you may choose to land your ideas with a story or physical artifact. Remember Eva Kor. A phenomenal speaker, but no visuals, only stories. It can be done.

There's no problem presenting data on slides where the visual treatment helps. But for the load bearing "insight support" visuals, don't overdo it. My working rule is no more than two or three of those in a one-hour presentation.

> The biggest overall takeaway here is this: You are not naked without something on the screen to talk to. You should be perfectly comfortable up there talking beside a blank screen because you don't need the screen to support your every point.

These are the fives rules of being a visual aid ninja:

+ Visuals Must Be . . . Visual
+ The Visual Must Teach
+ One Idea Only
+ Take Them Down
+ Not Too Many

There is nothing remotely hard in adhering to these—it's simply a matter of self-discipline. However, as easy as it is to get visuals right, this does have significant implications for your deck. In short, you aren't going to have one.

The Bear Trap: How Does the Presentation Live on After the Presentation?

THE APPROACH TO VISUALS I JUST DESCRIBED IS A REFRESHING RELEASE from the on-screen slide-bomb problem we all dislike so much. However, I'm sure you see the dilemma that's been created. You can no longer print those visuals to make a handout.

In almost all presentations today, the audience's handout, if one is provided, is a printout of the presenter's slides—this an important document, containing information that the audience needs for future reference. But if you now use visuals correctly, you can't simply print the slides, because the handout would be an agenda and pictures of cavalry officers and toasters. It would be useless to the audience. So what is the right way to do handouts?

First: Is it important to have a handout as a permanent takeaway from the meeting? Yes, absolutely! It's huge. I was at a conference recently where there was a speaker with great content, but he was using slides with no handout. Look at this photo I took of a man in front of me.

He was only one of dozens of people I saw trying to capture the information they needed. This tells us how important it is to supply listeners with a permanent document for future reference.

The handout is essential because no matter how sticky a presentation is, the human mind still has limits you can never overcome. No one can remember everything you want them to remember, but if the handout is this important, surely getting rid of the printed slide deck is a problem, right? No, it's not, because printing your visuals to make a deck was the wrong answer in the first place.

Freeing You from the "Deadly Default": The Handout and Visuals Are Not the Same

THE ISSUE HERE IS A SIMPLE LITTLE DEFAULT THAT MAKES THE presenter's life a lot easier, but that is completely flawed in its thinking. Here's the default process:

Step 1: Build a slide deck.

Step 2: Print it out to make the handout (six slides to the page for illegible good measure).

It feels smart and efficient—you now have your visual aids, and the audience has the essential handout they need. But just because it's efficient doesn't mean it works. In fact, if you follow the logic, you see that this default can only lead to disaster. **When presenters try to build something that is both an effective run of slides and a complete takeaway document, that approach inevitably compromises both elements.** How? By trying to combine both, and especially with the document in mind, presenters invariably end up with too many slides, all overloaded with information (and far too much text), while ironically, they still have a subpar handout because presentation software really doesn't shine when it comes to creating documents. These are the printed decks we all dislike so much.

The flaw is back in that seemingly innocent default that says your slides and handout can be the same. That is completely wrong. Visuals and handouts can never be the same, because they serve two fundamentally different purposes:

- ✦ Your visuals are there to visually complement your big ideas.

- ✦ Your handout is there to provide a crisp, clear documentary summary of the discussion.

These are completely different purposes, and the moment you try to make them the same, the compromise destroys the effectiveness of both. But if we uncouple handout design from slide design, everything finally clicks into place.

The Final Piece of the Puzzle: The Complementary Handout

IF YOU ARE BUILDING A PRESENTATION, YOU START WITH YOUR important architectural questions, using the pyramid to get to high-level design that you then storyboard into a logical sequence. You then build out the detail of the argument combining the best of your facts and data with the right stories and visuals. That's the whole book in five lines.

Now, let's come back to the handout and an important question. When you present, do you want the audience scribbling notes and burning dozens of pennies trying to capture what you are saying? Absolutely not, because A) it's exhausting, and B) every time they make a note, they are disconnected from the speaker. Have you ever been in a presentation where you hear something interesting, so you jot a quick note, and when you emerge you ask, "Where are we?" If an audience is constantly scribbling, those frequent disconnections mean they are missing much of what the speaker is saying. Lastly, C) it's a horrible record of the meeting. Those notes are usually illegible and make no sense when you go back to them six months later.

Tool #2: The Complementary Handout

The inevitable conclusion of this argument is that you must create a handout with the specific purpose of providing the critical information the audience needs to remember, so they don't get distracted by taking notes. It should contain your key ideas and all the pertinent information that supports those ideas, and while you might choose to embed some central graphics or images in it, it's absolutely not a printout of your slides. And to really integrate it properly into the presentation, as you present, you need to follow and frequently reference where you are in the handout, as I will discuss in the Epilogue on delivery.

For a typical one-hour business presentation, a simple one-page handout will usually suffice. You can create this in PowerPoint, but I'd not recommend that, as PowerPoint is not a good document creator. Other applications will build a better document. InDesign, for example, is exceptional, but Word is often perfectly adequate. It doesn't need to be flashy; it only needs to contain the important information.

To many of the people we work with, this doctrine of separating visuals and handouts is one of the most vital lessons they feel they've learned. The moment you abandon the idea of the printed slide deck and build a great handout, a whole new world opens up.

1. As the presenter, you are now liberated to have powerful, complementary visuals. You now have the flexibility to use whatever you want on screen because you are no longer tied to visuals as your handout.

2. Thanks to a good handout, your audience is liberated from note taking, which allows them to engage in the conversation at a completely different intellectual level. In many presentations the audience is taking notes, trying to capture what your presentation "is," but if you give them a great handout, they are free to think about what it all "means."

But most important:

3. You achieve "retellability," which is the gold standard of communication.

Early in the book, I made the argument that the presenter's highest standard of success, and the standard we should be shooting for, is "retellability." You want your story to stick so well that it can be retold.

Almost by definition, however well a meeting went, it's what happens afterward that really matters. The lights come up, handshakes are exchanged, and people leave. But did your audience truly retain what you told them? Will they act on it? Did your boss ultimately decide to back your project, or did your customer decide to select you in that decision meeting they had a week later? Every presentation needs to live on after the meeting adjourns.

That's a pretty high bar, because remember that less than 20% of most presentations is retained after a few hours, while those decision meetings might be a week away. The ability of your audience to retain and retell your story to others is extremely difficult when they try to do it unaided, but a good handout totally changes that.

> Under this model, the audience has a take-home document far superior to any slide deck, leading to vastly improved long-term retention and a much-heightened ability to retell your story.

At a recent workshop, this played out right in front of my eyes. We had covered the first morning session and were breaking for coffee. The CFO of this company had been delayed by an early meeting, and he joined the workshop at that coffee break. Despite the fact that the early run of content is fairly complex in its structure, I watched as right there in the break, Guillaume, the French CEO, opened up his handout and, tracing through it, retaught the core ideas from the first ninety minutes of content. **In fact, the "dirty little secret" of the handout is that as you work the audience through it during your presentation, you are implicitly training them to retell the story to those other decision-makers.**

The crisp, clean handout is unquestionably your greatest ally in the battle to achieve real long-term stickiness. A few years ago I delivered a keynote at a company's leadership conference. For this meeting I created a simple, laminated, one-page handout. Months and even years later, when I was visiting their offices, I still saw these handouts pinned on cubicle and office walls. You're never going to see a deck pinned to the wall, unless it's held there by darts.

How to Build a Great Handout

GIVEN OUR POWERPOINT DECK DEFAULT, FEW PEOPLE ARE EXPERIENCED in handout design, but have no fear—building an exceptional handout is simple when you follow three simple rules.

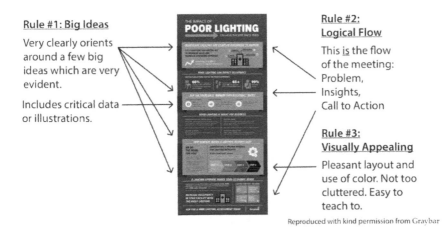

Rule #1: Big Ideas

Very clearly orients around a few big ideas which are very evident.

Includes critical data or illustrations.

Rule #2: Logical Flow

This is the flow of the meeting: Problem, Insights, Call to Action

Rule #3: Visually Appealing

Pleasant layout and use of color. Not too cluttered. Easy to teach to.

Reproduced with kind permission from Graybar

Rule #1: Big Ideas and Critical Data/Illustrations Only

A typical handout should contain only the more important ideas and data. It is essentially a summary of everything that mattered during the presentation. As you feel comfortable you can add more detail, but generally, the shorter, more succinct versions work best. Put additional information in an appendix, which can be as long, messy, and ugly as you like. In other words, don't over-invest design time in your appendix.

One last word on handout content: never do "fill-in-the-blanks" handouts. While popular in some settings (church in particular), they do not create engagement; rather, they create the illusion of engagement, while the audience is, in fact, intellectually disengaged while writing. Aside from fill-in-the-blanks being insulting to adults, deliberately withholding your teaching is not only counter to all logic, but it kills your ability to skip a section and weakens the take-home value of the document.

Rule #2: Logical Flow

By definition the handout should follow the flow of the design storyboard. Often it is helpful to include your transitions, especially when these are framed as audience questions.

Rule #3: Visually Appealing

You want a handout that is visually appealing, not visually over-whelming (another reason to obey Rule #1). Applications such as InDesign, or even Word, allow this. Using color and varying fonts and typefaces will boost visual appeal, as does the addition of a few select graphics. And for reasons no one understands, laminate it. **People think paper is pretty cheap, but if you laminate a handout, those same people will suddenly treat it like you've given them a Gutenberg Bible.**

By the way, always build your handout last. It's permanent, so you want your argument fully developed before you institutionalize it. It's frustrating to build a handout too early, and then scrap 200 copies as a key insight or sequence gets modified.

SUMMARY

Virtually all presenters understand that visual aids and handouts are both vital elements of most presentations.

However, thanks to the well-established cultural norm that is the slide deck, those presenters invariably fall into the trap of making their slides and their handouts the same. When we understand that these two tools serve a fundamentally different purpose, we realize that they can never be the same, and that each has to be designed to fulfill its specific purpose.

Visuals complement teaching points, handouts provide a documentary record, and separating them signifies the end of the slide deck. This change alone will yield one of the biggest improvements in your presentation's effectiveness.

CHAPTER FOURTEEN

THE DESIGN IS DONE:
GETTING TO GAME DAY

FIRST, CONGRATULATIONS! WE HAVE WALKED THROUGH THE entire model, and you have learned a proven process for effective presentation design. I want to finish by discussing briefly what happens next, and how this initial design is converted into the presentation itself.

Refine Your Design: Making Room for Iteration

IMAGINE YOU'VE DESIGNED A PRESENTATION BY USING THE MODEL presented in this book. As good as it is, you should also know that it's highly unlikely you have the whole thing exactly right the first time. This is not a criticism of your efforts; it's merely a reflection of reality. Because we stitch presentations together in pieces, it's hard enough to get any individual piece exactly right, and all but impossible to get the entire presentation right the first time. As you see it all coming together, various gaps and overlaps will reveal themselves. As such, the finished product will require some evolutionary "versioning" before it will be right.

Unfortunately, most people begin their preparation so late that they never give themselves the chance for any of the intellectual evolution that every argument needs. Thanks to procrastination, an alarming number of people go to the podium armed only with their first draft, which is tragic, given the enormous improvement that always comes from allowing a little evolution of thought. This point can be exquisitely demonstrated by an illustration from the art world.

Guernica

Collection Museo Nacional Centro de Arte Reina Sofía, Madrid

The painting above is titled *Guernica* by Pablo Picasso. It's regarded by many as his finest work, and it is certainly one of the most moving and powerful antiwar paintings in history. In preparation for World War II, the Nazis developed a range of military innovations, including dive bombing, and tested them on innocent Spanish villages during the Spanish Civil War. In one such action in April 1937, they bombed the village of Guernica with devastating effect. Picasso's legendary painting captures the horror and suffering of this carnage, and it lives today in the wonderful Reina Sofía gallery in Madrid. (This museum is a must-see, and my sincere thanks go out to them for their permission to reproduce this and the following image.)

I'm no art historian, but the painting's important elements can be clearly discerned. You can see the woman on the left clutching her dead child, the soldier at the lower left with the severed head, lying next to his broken sword. The bewildered onlookers on the right, observing in utter disbelief. And at the center of the painting is a horse, facing to the right, with his head turned back to the left, and with a huge gash in his side. To many art historians, this is the central message of the painting. The horse is the symbol of Spain, and at its core, the painting captures and mourns the death of Spain.[11]

At about twelve by twenty-five feet, it's an imposing piece of art. On a recent visit to Madrid, I stood in front of it for over an hour, trying to take it all in. It was a deeply moving experience.

However, close by, in the shadow of this great masterpiece on an adjacent wall to *Guernica*, humbly hangs another fascinating painting.

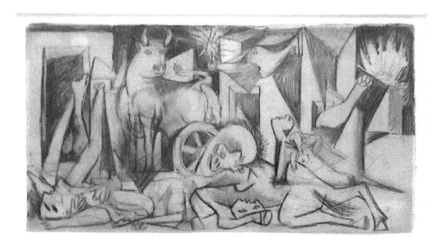

As you can see, it's an early draft of the masterpiece. It is a modest four feet wide, and it makes my point perfectly.

---

[11] It's clear that Picasso felt the pain of Guernica extremely deeply. During the war, he was questioned by a German Gestapo officer who, speaking about the painting, asked, "Did you do this?" To which Picasso replied, "No, you did."

> Wherever there is design, there is always an
> evolutionary process. Your first draft will never be
> your best. Your thinking needs to percolate.

In the case of *Guernica*, this little painting is a fascinating window into the evolution of Picasso's thinking, and perhaps two things are of note. First, the draft version is clearly more cluttered, while the finished version draws much starker attention to fewer elements. We can deduce from this that, consciously or unconsciously, Picasso was defoliating. He was jettisoning the secondary and highlighting the primary content. He clearly moved in the direction of more powerfully landing a small number of big ideas.

Second, do you notice what is essentially absent in the draft? The horse. Only barely visible, it is much less prominent in the draft painting. **I think it's fair to say that the process of refining the design allowed the bigger—and arguably most central—idea to surface in Picasso's mind.**

Studying the two paintings together, we can see that through this evolutionary process the artist is getting to a final understanding of A) what's really important, and B) how it all fits together. That's precisely what every presentation designer needs to do. I'm not saying we're building museum-quality art in our presentations, but we need to make at least a little room to figure out what's truly important and how it all fits together.

The Practical Tool: The Design Refinement Round

THE WAY YOU DO THIS IS SIMPLE. YOU NEED TO RUN THROUGH THE presentation a few times, purely to test and refine the design. At this stage, you are not working on delivery. This is not "rehearsal"; indeed, to even think about delivery at this stage is a distraction.

You will get to rehearsal a little later, and I will discuss this extensively in the Epilogue. At this stage, however, you do need to speak it out loud, because as you have probably noticed, you reprocess things differently when your ideas are spoken out loud than when saying them in your head.

This design refinement round will clearly reveal:

+ Is the problem you're addressing compelling? Have you "found the pain"?

+ Are the big ideas clear?

+ Is there too much information? Are you firehosing?

+ Is the proportion right? Where are the 100 pennies spent?

+ Is the presentation simple enough? Is anything confusing?

+ Does it have a clear, logical flow? Are the transitions clear and well stated?

+ Does it have the right level of data?

+ Are the illustrations strong and each teaching a point?

+ Is the call to action clear and specific?

As you can see, every element of your design is on full display the moment you speak it out loud, and spotting problems while there's time to fix them can save you a lot of heartache later. One thing you will especially notice is how your language improves. There's a real difference between weak, unimaginative, overused language and robust, stimulating language. And as you do a couple of design refinement rounds, you will increasingly find those perfect phrases that precisely capture your ideas. **If you would like a diagnostic tool that reflects these questions, and that you can use to evaluate the design of your presentation, you will find this in the Appendix, and it is also available for you to download.**

I've mentioned Winston Churchill's "Never in the field of human conflict . . ." phrase a couple of times. You may be interested to know that when traveling by car on the day of the speech, Winston was preparing. When he came to the famous sentence, it was "Never in the history of mankind have so many owed so much to so few." I think we can all agree that this version doesn't quite hit the mark. His companion in the car, General "Pug" Ismay, certainly noticed, and he gave him several reasons why it didn't work. Thanking his friend, Winston immediately changed the wording to "Never in the field of human conflict . . ." and the rest is history. This is the perfect example of evolutionary versioning.

Language is one of the great human distinctives, and when used powerfully it is a great asset. I like to suggest that language be "muscular." Be willing to use words that are less common, as long as they are still readily understood. Much of the impact of Shakespeare, Lincoln, Churchill, or Martin Luther King Jr., arises from their deliberate use of muscular language.

For purposes of demonstration, here are some completely random examples of common presentation terms, with some slightly more engaging, muscular equivalents.

WEAK WORDS	STRONG EQUIVALENTS
risky	hazardous
great	exceptional, exemplary
upcoming	looming, impending
went	limped, progressed
bad	troubling, disturbing
many	several, a myriad
nice	cordial, pleasant
happy	ecstatic, overjoyed
strong	durable, substantial, vigorous
grow	blossom, flourish
develop	cultivate, nurture

Time and Timelines

THIS STEP OF REFINING YOUR DESIGN SOUNDS GREAT (OR: VALUABLE, beneficial, worthwhile, profitable, fruitful), but you may be thinking that real life simply doesn't allow the time for it. In reality, the process I've laid out in this book consumes far less time than people are typically taking today, because it frontloads thinking, which avoids a lot of wasted time later. But, while designing a presentation this way will not take more time (and this includes a couple of quick rounds for refinement), it does require a different timeline. More specifically, you need to start earlier. Look at the two charts below.

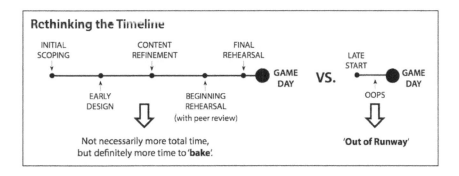

The typical presenter starts too late and runs out of time before they can get to any real design refinement. Obviously, no two presentations are the same, but for the typical presentation, if you are willing to start a few days earlier than you typically might, you will have the time to let the argument develop. This will be hugely beneficial, because the improvements that come at the refinement stage will be starkly noticeable. The frightening alternative? Discovering a horrible sequence problem while you are up there giving the presentation itself.

The Final Step: From Finished Design to Finished Materials

WITH THE DESIGN-REFINEMENT ROUND COMPLETED, YOU WILL HAVE a presentation design you are exceedingly happy with, and converting your finished design outline into the actual presentation is fairly straightforward. The proof of that is that you have already given a decent verbal version of the presentation, because that's exactly what you did in the design-refinement round.

Whether you've been doing this on paper or in the MAST software tool, you now have an outline that contains every element of the presentation:

+ The problem you're addressing and how you're going to unpack it

+ Your big ideas, or pyramid insights

+ How these insights are sequenced into the story, and what the transitions are between them

+ How each insight is supported with data

+ How each insight is supported with visuals or stories

+ What the action is that you are asking from the audience and how you will ask for it

The three items you physically need now are: your notes, your visuals loaded into PowerPoint/Keynote, and your handout tidied up and printed. And given that you've run through it a few times, you already have each of those elements in draft form—and the key points from your working set of notes are the basis of your handout.

Which only leaves delivery, and in the Epilogue of this book, I will outline the critical elements of delivery that will help ensure **precision**. You shouldn't worry too much about your eye contact with the audience, but you do need to make sure that what comes out on game day is precisely what you built here in this design phase.

But as we learned from Eva Kor and countless other examples: great presentations flow from great design. And you now have that great design under your belt. **You have built an argument that will powerfully land a small number of big ideas.**

CHAPTER FIFTEEN

CLOSING THOUGHTS

A T THE END OF OUR JOURNEY TOGETHER, I'D LIKE TO SHARE three simple conclusions.

Closing Thought #1: A Path Through the Maze

From the beginning of this book, I've stressed that the fundamental reason why most people communicate poorly is that they don't understand the "rules" or "natural laws" that govern how the human brain wants and needs to consume information. When we don't understand those rules, we are destined to break them. Firehosing, poor sequence, and a host of other mistakes are the result.

Well, that's now changed. You now have the rules, woven into a simple framework that will allow you to successfully navigate the maze of your audience's mind. The following graphic summarizes everything. The way things are presently is on the left, and the way things will be if you follow the model is on the right. (It's a little antithesis to close.)

AS THINGS ARE TODAY	AS THINGS WILL BE TOMORROW
Large amount of irrelevant material crowds out information that matters	Tightly focused on a few critical insights, intentionally selected to drive action
Material that's far more complex than you realize	Complexity simplified to fit within audience's processing capacity
No clear flow; rabbit trails; audience confusion	Logical sequence that answers the audience question
Leading with our credentials / all about us	Leading with the audience problem
Dry facts and data (and usually far too much detail)	Deeply engaging the left- and right-brain through visuals and stories
Your slides are the same as your handout	Great visuals and a complete handout that complement your narrative
Leads to: boring, confusing, forgettable, sender-centric, less likely to drive action	**Leads to: compelling, engaging, audience-centric teaching that leads to action**

Closing Thought #2: You Need to Get Started

The change captured in the table above is one that most people would dearly like to see in their own communications. But the sad truth of most business books is that if they are read at all, their readers often do little with the information presented to them, and therefore fail to benefit from anything valuable the book has to offer. This book is no different.

The principles laid out here have been proven to be effective in various environments from TEDx speaking engagements to industrial sales messaging, from sermon design to conference keynotes. **But for it to work in any of those places, the principles need to be adopted.** The good news is that once you do, you'll see such profound positive results that you'll wonder how you ever made it through using your old method—and how your audience managed to make it through with you.

So take the next presentation you are called to make, and design it using this process. If it seems a little overwhelming, simply break it down into manageable chunks (in the Appendix, I've provided a simple quick-start guide that takes all the tools of the book and lays them out for you. If you want a PDF copy of this to print out, go to Oratium.com/downloads, find the quick-start guide, and use the code chartwell99 to download it).

Of course, the software tool MAST is an easier and more comprehensive way to get started, because the tool walks you through the entire process. So if you're interested in using it and haven't already done so, the login details are on page 63. If you have any problems, simply email us at bookquestion@oratium.com. You can also email me with any questions or feedback at TimPollard@Oratium.com. I hope you do—I'd love to hear your stories.

Closing Thought #3: You Can Be the Communicator You've Always Wanted to Be

In any given year, we are all exposed to hundreds of presentations—from the huge ballroom to the "round-the-table," and thousands of other communications of every kind. As we've seen, the vast majority of these fail to connect with our brains and are quickly forgotten.

But in that vast sea of mediocrity, some shining islands rise up: Eva Kor teaching us to "never, ever give up"; therapist Aaron Sironi revealing the heart of suicide-risk diagnosis; Graybar solving the problem of hospital lighting; and even, hopefully, my banquet presentation conveying that those desperate homeless teenagers are "not bad kids."

These islands don't rise up on the superficial waves of sparkling delivery; they rise on the geologic force of great design.

Early in this book, I raised the question of whether great communication is the product of natural talent, because if it is, greatness truly is out of reach for most of us. Having read this far, you now know otherwise. We've seen that great communication is the product of disciplined, "brain-aligned" design. This is wonderful news because, if the key isn't talent, then it all comes down to self-discipline, and that means that greatness is within the reach of anyone willing to work at it.

> Think about it: you don't need "talent" to stop firehosing people or to sequence an argument properly or to find that perfect image. You simply need the self-discipline to do so.

I've seen this over and over again, watching average communicators become exceptional.

The Work Is Worth It

It's true that some presentations are not especially important, but taking them seriously and getting them right still matters because the audience always deserves your best. However, sitting above these are the numerous presentations we make that *are* important, where the outcome we want is critical to our plans and where we are being implicitly or explicitly evaluated—we want those presentations to stand out as shining islands in that sea of mediocrity.

But then, higher still are those presentations where we are placed, often uncomfortably, under the brightest spotlight—those moments that have the potential to change our future. These are certainly few, but perhaps not as rare as we might think.

You saw this quote earlier, but no matter how often I read it, I never grow tired of the way Shakespeare so perfectly captures the essence of these great moments:

There is a tide in the affairs of men.
Which, taken at the flood, leads on to fortune;
Omitted, all the voyage of their life
Is bound in shallows and in miseries.
On such a full sea are we now afloat,
And we must take the current when it serves,
Or lose our ventures.

In that moment, uncomfortably under the spotlight, be the amazing communicator you want to be. Take the current when it serves.

EPILOGUE

THE ESSENTIALS OF DELIVERY

Part 1: Rehearsal

A Tale of Two Engineers: The Tortoise and the Hare

ABOUT A YEAR AGO WE WERE WRAPPING UP A SALES MESSAGING project with the customary meeting where the new messages are presented to, and reviewed by, a "panel" of executives, prior to being tested out in the market.

We had two messages to review that day, and our coaches who had worked with the teams told me they were both going to be good. One team had chosen a sales guy to make the presentation, and the other team had chosen a brilliant design engineer, who understood the product perfectly but was a Chinese national with somewhat limited English language skills.

In these projects, we make sure the teams develop a script, because we want them to capture the best articulation of the new pitch. The sales guy (let's call him "Brian") was the first to present, and I noticed that while he was holding the script, he really wasn't looking at it. He launched in, and while he was supremely confident and comfortable, over the next 30 minutes he made one of the worst presentations I've ever seen. It failed to discuss the customer's problem adequately, the ideas were fuzzy, the sequence didn't make sense, and he never referred to the handout. I was leading the review that day, and this was a challenging moment.

As diplomatically as possible, I began to lead the room through a critique of this disastrous message, and within the first 30 seconds the cause of this train wreck was all too clear. I pointed out that the customer problem wasn't unpacked well, and the team responded in unison (and through gritted teeth) that "it was in there but Brian forgot to cover it." I discussed the lack of clarity of the insights, and the team again responded that "they were in there clearly but Brian didn't explain them properly." And the same with the sequence ... and on and on. The team was furious with Brian, and with good reason, because they had done some fabulous work that he had managed to completely destroy.

What happened here? Brian had looked at the script a few times, so he thought he had the presentation "down." But he was wrong, and he torpedoed himself and his whole team as a result. Ultimately, by rewinding the tape and working back through the script together, we saw all the great work that had been done, and it all ended well, except for Brian.

Our Chinese engineer went next, and lacking that comfort level provided by his first language, he simply read the script verbatim. It came out a bit wooden, but since we weren't concerned with delivery at this stage, this hardly mattered. Most importantly, the argument came out exactly as designed, and it was a strong argument. Everything about it was good, and with little modification it went on to achieve great success in the market. (As in fact, did the first pitch, once we finally found it.)

It's a simple story, but once again, the lesson is profound. **Brian had wildly overestimated his ability—in the moment—to articulate this presentation in exactly the way it was designed.** This was not the first time I've seen this happen, and curiously, it is often a salesperson who perpetrates this mistake. Something went badly wrong with the delivery here, and it sure wasn't eye contact.

Introduction

For the reasons we've already considered, the primary focus of this book is the mastery of presentation design, but that focus does not mean that delivery skills don't matter; far from it. Delivery absolutely matters, because it is critical that the presentation that's been designed is the presentation that is executed. But, of course, if the issue is precision, then the things that matter in delivery will be starkly different from the things you see emphasized in traditional training.

Delivery probably does merit its own (shorter) book and maybe one day that companion book will be written. But for now, I prefer to limit the discussion to only the essentials of delivery. In many ways, this might be the right answer anyway. In delivery, as with anything else, it will always be easier to focus on a small number of big ideas.

What Is the Problem? "Mind the Gap"

In this final section, the problem is obvious, because it jumps out of the Brian story: If we believe that audiences will be engaged, held, and moved to action by a compelling argument, then it's little short of tragic when a presenter builds that great argument, only to deliver something substantially different on game day. But it happens all the time. All too frequently there's a distinct gap between what the presenter intended to say and what they actually said. Big points get missed or misstated. Transitions fall by the wayside, data is mis-explained, and by far the most common problem: riffs that were tight and punchy in the mind become long, rambling, disjointed musings when they come out of the mouth.

The main cause of this gap lies in the way we prepare to deliver our material. We typically run though a presentation a few times, hearing it "in our head" and thinking that we know exactly what we are going to say and how we are going to say it—but we're wrong. We don't actually know either of those things at all. There's a world of difference between having a general idea of what we are going to say, and having grooved the specific language so well that this, and only this, is what comes out on game day. And by the time you discover you didn't know it, it's always too late. We've all lived that painful moment, where we realize it isn't as clear in our head as we thought it was, and there's a sea of puzzled faces in front of us who've realized exactly the same thing.

In order to solve this problem, we have to unearth the root issue, which in this case is something we've already discussed. It's the difference between recognition and retrieval, and it's a deadly trap. **Have you ever leafed through your slides, preparing for a presentation, and, recognizing everything on them, said, "OK—I'm good, I've got this," only to discover that when you stood up to actually deliver them, that crisp clean narrative wasn't there at all?** If so, you fell into the recognition versus retrieval trap. You knew the material well enough for your brain to recognize it, but not well enough to fully recall it. You recognized the penny, but you couldn't draw it.

Compounding this problem is the fact that when you stand up to present, at the very moment when you need your brain to be on its best game and find that perfect articulation, you are usually nervous, and you are certainly distracted by the other aspects of being in the spotlight ("Is Mike texting? Should I ask him to stop? Do these pants make me look fat?"). And the higher stakes the setting, the more this will be true. Nervous, distracted minds do strange things. They will often blurt out unintended phrases or freeze up altogether. Case in point: in one presentation not long ago, I actually saw a speaker unable to spontaneously name all four of his kids.

> Every one of us has a friend we love dearly, but who's completely unreliable. That's the brain you have when you present. If you don't know the material well enough, and you are relying on your brain to rescue the situation, be warned – he's probably not showing up.

I recently helped a nonprofit leader put a fund-raising banquet presentation together, in which he was going to talk about a water sanitation program for the extreme poor in Indonesia. This was a lighter involvement than our usual consulting, and I had simply helped him identify the three main points he would present. I attended the banquet, and unfortunately, while the three points were in the presentation, owing to his less than adequate preparation and compounded by his evident nerves, those points were so obscured by eddies, minor details, and personal anecdotes that they were almost completely lost on the audience. Given that the points had been clear in his mind just a few days earlier, all I can attribute this to is the fact that he was asking his mind to create the argument— clearly—in the moment, and that was simply too big an ask. It was a good presentation, but it was a long way from what it could have been.

Like It or Not, the Key to Precision Is ... Rehearsal

As you seek this high level of precision, don't underestimate how much good design has already helped you. If you have confusing, illogical, and dense material, it's a hundred times harder to get that all straight in your head, and you'll be wrestling with it on game day just as much as your audience is. But if you have crisp, clean, logical material, it won't be fighting you nearly as much, and you are already well on the way to it coming out right.

As important as the design is, however, the main way you get there is through rehearsal. Exceptional communicators invariably use rehearsal to achieve complete mastery of their material, which not only gives them the clarity and precision they need in the presentation itself, but also frees them up to be much more "present" in the room. This allows them to be far more effective in other important aspects of delivery, such as reading and responding to the signals the audience is sending, managing the clock, and dealing with unexpected disruptions.

Rehearsal gives us the fluency we need, and the "presence" we want. And let me be very clear on one thing, because it is a question we are asked in every workshop. **Rehearsal gives us the fluency we need, not because we have *memorized* our material, but because we have *learned* it.** Most people can't memorize material, but in truth, they don't need to try. Rehearsal is about learning, not memorization. When you've truly learned your material, having safely tucked it away in your long-term memory, you are now free to simply talk naturally and conversationally, and enjoy the day.

"Mom ... He's Doing It Again"

There are lots of reasons why we don't rehearse, and it's a lively discussion in our workshops.

- ✦ I don't have time.
- ✦ It feels weird/people are watching ("Mom, he's doing it again").
- ✦ I think I've got it.
- ✦ I don't want to sound wooden.
- ✦ I don't want to hear how bad it is (seriously, when I first heard that in a workshop, I laughed because I knew it was a joke, and that I'd never hear it again. I was wrong. It actually shows up about one in three times).
- ✦ I've given it before.
- ✦ I don't know how to do rehearsal.

To some extent, these reasons are legitimate (with the exception of "I don't want to hear how bad it is," which is just plain crazy. Do you really want to hear how bad it is when you're up there giving it?). But the real reason is hiding behind this list. Knowing that people always manage to make time for the things that are truly important, the real reason is that they don't think it's going to make that much difference. That's the mistake people make—they simply have no idea how much better rehearsal is going to make it; if they did, they'd make the time and get over the weirdness.

So let me make the case by outlining four big things that rehearsal does.

1. Final content refinement.

Do you remember the story of Winston Churchill and how his rehearsal in the car led to the completely unimpressive phrase "Never in the history of mankind have so many owed so much to so few" becoming the legendary "never in the field of human conflict was so much owed by so many to so few"? The amazing thing about rehearsal is that these are the moments where you do some of your clearest thinking regarding the argument you are trying to make. The refinements you make during rehearsal are often some of the best you will discover. You won't be doing any radical rework at this stage, because you will have done that in your design refinement round, but the small changes you make here, particularly in language, will be making your argument noticeably better.

The reason this happens is interesting. As the presentation moves into your long-term memory, your own working memory is freed up to re-engage with the argument, which always leads to big improvement.

2. The language gets locked in.

The second big thing rehearsal does is cement that final language you have just found, making sure that those perfect words are what actually come out of your mouth on the day. Even the most powerful idea can be robbed of all its strength through sloppy, imprecise (or overused) language. We need the right words, precisely because words matter.

The problem in view here is something we rarely think about, which is the enormous complexity of spoken language. How many different ways are there of wording even this one simple paragraph? If you think about all the possible permutations of syntax and vocabulary, mathematically speaking, there's an almost infinite number of ways it could be expressed, and it's the same with any idea you are trying to convey. So here's the question:

> If you only have a "pretty good" idea of what you want to say, what are the chances that your brain is going to pull the single cleanest and most perfect phrasing from an infinite range of possibilities? Not a chance.

And yet, that's what the unprepared speaker is asking their brain to do. If you only have a vague idea of what you want to say, the chances of getting it exactly right in the moment are almost zero.

Of course, this doesn't mean you will merely stand up there with a silly grin on your face if you are less than fully prepared. No—your brain can still pull good, solid, workmanlike language out of the ether in the moment. But is that what you want? **Of the infinite number of ways I can say something, many will be weak, some will be good, but only a few, maybe even only one, will be fabulous, and that's the one you want to make sure you say. Only practice and rehearsal get you to those.**

It's what I call "muscle memory of the mouth." When you have grooved those key phrases through repetition, they are much more likely to come out in the moment, especially if your brain has merrily wandered off into the briar patch of wondering whether that odd draft you're feeling is the legendary unbuttoned fly you were warned about in that traditional training.

3. **It stops you from saying that thing you really shouldn't have said.**

All speakers embellish. They add in phrases, words, and thoughts they hadn't planned. And with the exception of speakers who are delivering from a script, every speaker does it in every presentation. The question is, how far off-plan are you going, and how much damage are you doing? The risk here is very real, as I can demonstrate with two questions:

Question 1: In a presentation, have you ever said something you didn't plan to say? Of course.

Question 2 is similar but subtly different: In a presentation, have you ever said something you planned *not* to say? Yes!

In other words, there was something that you explicitly decided to stay away from in the design room, but then you said it up on stage. This again reveals that our on-stage brains are not to be trusted. **Back in your office, you had a sound reason for deciding to leave out that horribly off-color joke, but up on stage, your brain suddenly decides that this is the funniest thing ever. It's not.**

The value of rehearsal as a way to combat this problem cannot be overstated. The less-rehearsed speaker is asking their mind to find the words in the moment to a much greater extent than the highly-rehearsed speaker, and this is extremely dangerous. In addition to the problem of imprecise and sloppy language we've already discussed, this degree of ad libbing opens the door to undisciplined embellishment, which causes three dangerous things to happen:

+ **Blowing up your time.** If you planned a tight 30 minutes but start embellishing content back in, you are inviting back the problem of firehosing. Embellishing can easily kick a tight 100 pennies back up to an overwhelming 137, and I can prove this. How many speakers run long, especially at conferences? Almost all of them. How many speakers rehearsed to run long? None of them. What happened? They embellished the extra content in. What's the point in building a presentation that stays within your audience's limited working memory if you're going to blow yourself up on game day?

+ **Blowing up your flow.** Imagine you've designed exactly the kind of logical narrative flow that is a huge help to audience comprehension and retention. What happens if you're up on stage and you utter the immortal words, "now, I know this is a little off topic, but let me quickly ..." No! By introducing your own rabbit trail, you destroy the flow you worked so hard to create. Whenever I hear a speaker utter the phrase "OK, where were we?" as he or she seeks to find their way back from some self-inflicted briar patch, that's another rage-inducing moment for me. If you don't know where we are, how am I supposed to? The less-rehearsed speaker is always more prone to introduce these flow-destroying eddies.

+ **Blowing up yourself.** This point is an odd combination of seriously funny and deadly serious. Your brain is a connection engine and whenever you are presenting, in some dark back room behind the scenes of your conscious mind, it is constantly making connections. Some of these are inappropriate, rude, or brutally hurtful. And here's the scary thing: they are trying to get out of your mouth. You've probably heard of a Freudian slip. That's what we're talking about here.

   The stories of this happening are as terrifying as they are funny. Here's my worst transgression:

   Many years ago in a previous job, I was making a presentation to a leadership group at Disney. I was presenting a case study as a possible direction they might take to improve sales effectiveness and they were pushing back pretty hard. I was saying that it would work for them and they were saying that it wouldn't. The discussion got pretty animated in a perfectly good-natured way, when I, for reasons known only to my subconscious, uttered the immortal words, "Guys, I don't see why you're not getting it! This is not a Mickey Mouse idea." There was a dull thud as the words landed, and after a pause, a dear friend, Randy Garfield, said, "You know, Tim, we don't say that around here."

"I'm sure you don't" was my timid reply.

It's a funny story, but within it lies a serious point. To my knowledge, I've never used that phrase in conversation before or since. But there I was, surrounded by the legendary Mouse, and his name was trying to get out of my mouth. Executives at Disney are genuinely the most gracious (and as it turns out, forgiving!) people you will ever meet, and the culture of Disney truly seems to infuse everything they do, but can you imagine how bad this gaffe could have been?

You don't have to, because I can show you what that looks like. I know of one US company where a top executive went to visit their German subsidiary, partly with the goal of getting them to comply with some new internal policy. He was pressing them in the meeting, while they were expressing their dislike for this change, and in the heat of that moment he said, "Look guys, I don't want to be a Nazi about it, but we really need you to adopt this policy." There's nothing funny about this story, because that thud was heard a continent away. There really is such a thing as a career-ending comment, and this came awfully close. That executive is still not permitted to travel outside the US, and I suspect his upward mobility is likely also in question. Once again, I am quite certain that he had no intention whatsoever of summoning that phrase, but when you're in Germany, surrounded by all things German, **don't underestimate what interesting things your little connection engine is doing, and just how much these gremlins are trying to get out of your mouth.**

It all comes back to rehearsal. The clearer you are on what you want to say, the less you are ad libbing in the moment—and the less likely one of these three dangerous problems is going to show up.

When it comes to fighting embellishment specifically, there are two rules that will really help you:

1. **Trust your instincts on leave-outs.**

   Through rehearsal, as a matter of discipline, if you planned NOT to say something, under no circumstances say it. You had a reason for leaving it out during your preparation. You must trust that instinct, because your mind on stage makes decisions about as well as a teenage boy.

2. **Stick to the plan.**

   Plan what you're going to say, and then — within reason — say only what you planned to say. With sufficient rehearsal, you will know when you are deviating from the plan; you will hear yourself doing it, which is half the battle. The other half is having the self-discipline to stop.

4. It's the key to recovering when a presentation gets derailed.

If you think about it, 100% of presentations get derailed in some way. It may not be a naked man, but there's always something like a late start, or an unexpectedly long discussion, or a temperamental projector, or any one of a thousand things that can snip ten minutes off your time. The under-rehearsed presenter is much more likely to be thrown off by these, and he or she usually tries to solve the problem by speaking fast and banning questions, which is a horrible solution. The prepared presenter simply knows how to trim that 10 minutes out and seamlessly stitch it all back together.

Taken together, these four reasons (plus the fact that rehearsal is a wonderful cure for nerves) create an overwhelmingly compelling argument to rehearse to a much greater extent than we normally do. Rehearsal makes a huge difference. If that's true, how much do we need and how do we do it?

The How of Rehearsal

"Just Do It" is a good rule of thumb. The good news about rehearsal is that it isn't intellectually hard; it's simply a matter of self-discipline. However boring or unnatural, the discipline to turn back to the first page and start again is a marker of greatness. That said, the rules of rehearsal are worth knowing.

1. **Conditions:** As far as you can, you should physically replicate "game conditions"—if you will be presenting standing up, you must rehearse standing up, as this will mirror the lung capacity you will have on the day. This will help you develop your actual breathing/speaking cadence as well as the inflection, modulation, and hand and body movements you will use on the day. You want "show time" to feel exactly like rehearsal so your mind easily slips into it.

   Typically, I do not rehearse in front of others, because I generally already know what I'm looking for and they don't. Admittedly, that's a personal view, but I think it's true for many speakers. That said, if you have someone you truly trust, and you want those untainted eyes, then go right ahead, as long as they know how to pitch their comments at the right level. You can end up in an asylum if your helpful dummy audience either aims too high as in, "maybe you can lose that whole first half," or too low as in, "you said 'and' where I think you meant 'but.'" (True confession: in a long-ago consulting role, I actually had a junior analyst removed from a rehearsal for saying that.)

   Regardless of whether you choose to work solo or with a dummy audience, always do your last rounds alone. You don't want any external distractions in your final preparation.

The one exception to going it alone is humor: try that on everyone. It is never quite as funny in rehearsal as it is on the day, because testing it is artificial, but that's OK. If it's fairly funny, it will generally be good in front of an audience. But if you are about to drop a career-ending bomb, it's best for someone to tell you, and they probably will.

> And finally, if you decide to leave that joke out, I'm begging you: *Under no circumstances whatsoever* change your mind on stage. I have never, in my life, seen that decision turn out well.

2. **Amount:** There is no single, right number here, because it depends on the setting. The right amount for you will depend on length, complexity, familiarity, and most important: stakes. However, as a working rule, I recommend 3–4 full run-throughs of any new material where you are reasonably familiar with it, and when it's a moderately important setting. But if you are less familiar and the stakes are high, don't hesitate to do more. When we coach TEDx speakers, it's not uncommon for them to do 15–20 run-throughs, and that mirrors my own experience for critical keynotes I've given. Clearly, this heavy rehearsal is for those rare, high-stakes moments when you sincerely need your best game.

   The idea of rehearsing that much probably feels like bad news, but here's the good news ...

3. **Focus:** Is all your material equally important? No. You don't need to get everything perfect, and remembering that small delivery glitches are readily forgiven, what you really want to do is make sure you are flawless on your most critical

content. I call this "proportional preparation." Within any presentation there are a small number of critical moments that you expressly want to get right, which are:

+ Opening
+ Close
+ Critical insights
+ Transitions
+ Complex points or explanations
+ Humor
+ Planned questions to the audience

If you truly nail these, but have a few minor misspeaks on the rest, you're probably fine, and given this subset is probably only about 20% of your total content, this is pretty good news. Focus the extra rehearsal on those key moments, but remember that anywhere you are trusting your mind to find the words in the moment, you run the risk of stepping on any of the three land mines of embellishment, which is why you always rehearse the whole thing a few times.

You may be wondering, within this 20%, what is the most important? Clearly your insights are right up there, but topping the chart is your opening. It is the moment when you are being most carefully scrutinized (although don't forget that in the majority of cases your audience wants you to do well), and it's also the moment when your brain is most fuzzy and most likely to freeze on you. **No matter what the setting, I will always rehearse my opening the most and it's always the thing I do last. Right up to the moment when I stand up, I will be silently mouthing those first few sentences.**

Other Game-Day Prep

As we think about this preparation for the big moment, there are a few other things you want to do, if you can. In particular, try to get into the room ahead of time, preferably when it's empty. There are several aspects of room setup that can help or hurt you, and the safest assumption is that the room is not going to be set up right. In fact, hotels almost seem to specialize in messing this up. So:

+ Be willing to move tables, affording everyone the best possible view of podium and screen

+ Bring people in as close as you can. In a rectangular room, speak from the wide wall. There's nothing worse than a long thin room where the back row can only be seen with binoculars. If the room is a tennis court, present from the net post.

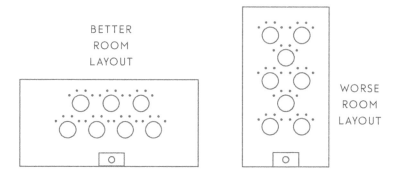

+ Check whether the lighting is bright enough for the audience to read the handout. If it is, are the lights too bright and washing out your screen? Getting this balance right can be tricky. Many, many times I've pulled light bulbs to make my screen clear.

+ Temperature: Make it cold. Seriously. People work much better in cooler rooms. You don't want hypothermia, but close to it is OK. If people complain on the day, sincerely listen to their complaints and then ignore them. If necessary, pretend to fiddle with the thermostat. I'm only partly joking. If it's after lunch and you or someone turns it up to 75 degrees, it doesn't matter how good you are, you've lost (68 degrees is optimal).

+ Pre-test all your technology. Nothing will unravel someone faster than them taking the stage and plugging in their laptop, only to discover that it isn't talking to the projector. There's almost no worse start than a frantic, panicked ten minutes of hunting for those mysterious laptop settings that will make it all work. I've never understood why, but perhaps it's because we've become so dependent on our technology that those kinds of failures can be utterly devastating to a speaker.

+ In higher-stakes settings, back your technology up. At the very least, have your visuals on a flash drive kept apart from your laptop. In super high-stakes settings, I carry two laptops that are mirrors of each other. Is that excessively geeky? Yes. Have I needed it? Once. By the way, I didn't discuss this, but one of the best additional benefits of using a handout is that it is impervious to an irrecoverable technology failure, like a blown projector. That has happened to me more than once. I missed not showing my visuals (although I was able to sketch some diagrams on the flip chart), but at the end of the day, it was only me and my handout and we were just fine. What's more, the audience noticed it, because a speaker who can function independent of their technology is an increasingly rare animal. It's a bigger deal than you might think. I've seen presenters reduced to a pile of smoking rubble when their technology crutches got pulled away.

From a logistical standpoint, there are real benefits to getting into the room ahead of time and getting it set up just right, but there's an intangible benefit beyond that. As any athlete will tell you, seeing the big arena ahead of time makes a huge difference with nerves. You don't want the first time you walk out on stage to be when five hundred pairs of eyes are watching you.

Closing Thought: "No Guarantees"

The arguments for thorough rehearsal are overwhelmingly compelling. If the first time the words come out of your mouth is on game day, then your chances of getting it right—exactly the way you designed it—are extremely slim. But does all this preparation *guarantee* that everything will go the way you want? No, because however well prepared you may be, there are still numerous elements that remain out of your control. That's just life. So here's the rule:

"Control everything you can control and leave the rest in the hands of ...."
(fill in your own preferred higher power)

Part 2: Communication Mechanics

The Top Ten of Communication Mechanics

If you get everything right up to this point, you are going to be far beyond "fine"; you are going to be amazing. You will have exceptional material, and it is going to come out exactly the way you have planned it. However, it is true that there are a few aspects of speaking mechanics you want to get right, and it can cause a bit of a distraction to your audience if you get them wrong. Now that you are finally up on stage, what are the few important things you need to know about that moment?

1. Be Yourself

Some people seem to adopt a completely different persona when they speak in public, as if they are trying to be some larger, better version of themselves (even sometimes to the point of adopting a fake British accent—please don't do that!). This makes no sense at all. Don't try to be someone you're not; be yourself, because you are perfect just as you are. As Oscar Wilde once said, "Be yourself, everyone else is taken."

Your speaking style should be the normal *you* in a usual conversational setting. Think of it as a "conversational coffee shop" tone, or a relaxed talk between friends. However many people there are in the crowd, they should all feel that you are talking to them personally.

2. Speaking Clarity

Many people have been told they speak too fast, but if that's you, that's probably not what's going on. The more likely issue is that you don't speak clearly enough (as evidenced by the fact that people can listen to podcasts quite easily at 1.5x normal speed). A speaking clarity problem distracts your audience, and it can become quite serious if you are speaking to a group where English is a second language for some, or in any room with poor acoustics. Whenever you present, you must enunciate clearly. **One excellent way to improve your diction is to consciously think of forming your words at the very front of the mouth, with your lips, teeth, and tongue.** You will be surprised when you see that you can consciously do this and how much of a difference it makes. In addition to improving your enunciation, if you truly do feel you speak too fast, write "SLOW" over your notes.

3. "Ums" and "Ahs"

The issue of verbal "tics" gets a lot of airtime in traditional training, but it actually isn't an issue very often. Even if you do have some of this in your speech, unless it's excessive, people aren't noticing. The important point here is that most of the time, "ums" and "ahs" are what your mouth does while your brain is figuring out what to say next. The reason we know this is that these tics rarely show up in ordinary conversation. The best cure for that is, therefore, rehearsal! When you really know your material and it's coming out of long-term memory, most of this problem will go away.

4. Eye Contact

Yes, have some. Seriously, way too much has been written on this. Eye contact is good, so look at your audience, no differently than you would look at someone in any everyday conversation—and that's the rule. Don't look over their heads. Some speakers do that, and it actually is annoying, as is fixing them with such a creepy, hawk-like stare that it screams "psychopath."

5. Body Language and Movement

Again, this topic is absurdly overdiscussed. When it comes to body language, basically everything is OK, as long as you aren't doing anything weird or distracting. One hand in the pocket is fine, indeed I often think that makes you look thoughtful. Churchill did that all the time.

That said, one posture to avoid is where you are "closed-off" with your arms folded low across your body in an obviously defensive way. Protecting your body organs from impending spears does not exactly exude confidence. Other than that, you are your best visual aid, so err on being expressive: use your arms and hands liberally. (Yes, empty your pockets of keys and change if you feel strongly about it. Check that your fly is closed.)

Movement is generally positive, and stepping away from the podium shows confidence; it also adds a little energy to the proceedings, but don't walk out into the crowd as some speakers like to do. The audience doesn't like it.

One important thing to say about movement is that, as good as it is, it can separate you from your notes. As a general principle, even if you know the material very well, you want to stay close to your notes because they are an invaluable ally in your battle to stay precisely on-message.

> There's nothing worse than wandering off to make one point, only to have to scamper back to the podium because you've completely forgotten what you were going to say next.

"Congruence"

The key word to remember regarding eye contact and body language is "congruence," which means that your general body language should match your words. If your point is serious or grave, (think of a funeral eulogy), then your body language should be still and sober. However, if your point is fun and upbeat, then your body language can be far more animated, expressive, and buoyant.

Interestingly, only once in all of Shakespeare's plays do we ever get his view on how they should be acted. Within the play *Hamlet*, a play is put on, and the character Hamlet is directing it. He gives advice to the players about how it should be performed, and this is widely regarded as the only time Shakespeare makes his views on acting known, which makes it fascinating. In addition to telling them that they need to learn their parts rather than simply memorize them, he also says, "Suit the action to the word and the word to the action." Congruence.

6. Teaching to the Handout

This will be the unexpected item on the list. Teaching to the handout simply means referencing where you are in the handout at all times, and tying your presentation to it. This is not as foreign an idea as you might first think, because almost all presenters already know how to "teach to the screen," as in "OK, look at bullet 3," or "look at this chart." This is no different; you're merely doing it in reference to the handout ("OK, look at that graphic on the lower left …"). Remember that the audience is processing everything for the first time, and anchoring them in the handout helps to keep them in the flow of the argument. It preserves their mental energy by minimizing their note taking, but by far the most important is that it is boosting both their retention and their ability to retell the story. Teaching to the handout is an important practical skill, with three simple rules:

+ Rule #1: In your opening, explain that you will be walking through the handout, and that this will save them from making notes as well as give them a useful takeaway.

+ Rule #2: Teach to it diligently (just as you would currently teach "to" the screen). Reference it often, indicate where you are, and be crystal clear when you are moving between sections.

+ Rule #3: Draw special attention to the critical words, phrases, and ideas that you most want them to remember (and which should therefore be prominent in the handout). Do not be afraid to read these verbatim—this actually rewards your hard work of designing precise language for the handout.

7. Managing the Clock

The clock is ticking, and it is not your friend. The right mindset to have is that you are in a life-or-death battle with the clock and only one of you will prevail, which is why you need to be managing the time from the first moment. A big mistake that almost all presenters make is to be much too relaxed and moving too slowly at the beginning, when all their time is stretching out before them and they sense no pressure. That's a recipe for disaster. Every minute is equally precious, so don't waste a single one. **If you squander time early, by the time you realize what you've done, it's almost impossible to get it back.** The key to finishing at 11:30 isn't what's happening at 11:25, it is what was happening back at 9:45 when you closed down that unnecessary discussion.

8. Energy

Simple fact: your audience will never be more excited about the material than you are. They will rise or sink to *your* level of enthusiasm, so you need to set that bright and buoyant tone. The good thing about enthusiasm is that it's infectious and people like passionate presenters. Hopefully you don't have to fake that enthusiasm, but if you aren't energized by the presentation, nobody else will be. Some good tactics here are:

+ Keep the room cool.

+ Good speakers can usually carry the early afternoon slot, but that is tougher sledding. If that makes you nervous, try to get the presentation scheduled for morning or late afternoon. (By the way, never say, "I know I'm the only thing standing between you and lunch/cocktails . . . yuk, yuk, yuk . . ." Trust me, its not as funny as you think it is. And do you really want to introduce that kind of negative idea?)

+ Eat light or not at all. I will never eat any kind of big meal before I speak. Healthy snacks are best. Eat the biggest steak you can afford afterwards.

+ An old friend of mine taught me a brilliant trick many years ago. Before you get up to speak, visualize yourself up there being lively, witty, and sparkling. There's good brain science behind this, because the brain actually does visualize most things before it does them. As strange as it sounds, it's easier to stand up and sparkle if you've visualized it.

+ But remember . . . **a presentation's design is where the energy really comes from.** Not firehosing adds energy, and that phenomenal story or visual is the greatest energy injector. Design the energy in.

9. Humor

When properly used, humor will make almost any presentation better. It unites people, it puts them at ease, and it adds energy to the room. But be careful. It is much trickier to use than it looks, and when it goes wrong, it goes spectacularly wrong. The key is to use the humor that works for you, run it by other people, and re-hearse the heck out of it.

> Unless you have spectacularly good humor instincts, never, ever trust spontaneous humor, unless you feel like spending a night in the county jail.

There are numerous articles written by comedians from Woody Allen to Jerry Seinfeld, and all say the same thing. When it comes to humor, the difference between not funny, funny, and hysterical can come down to one word, or a heartbeat's difference in timing. However spontaneous it may appear to be, the best humor is excruciatingly carefully planned and rehearsed. This lesson is well understood by professionals, and it is something that every speaker needs to learn.

10. Responding to the Unexpected

In the fall of 1989, I was presenting in Germany, teaching a marketing planning seminar on a rainy Thursday in Heidelberg. I was somewhere in the morning session when a woman burst through the door sobbing uncontrollably. It was evident that this wasn't grief or despair, but through her tears, and with much waving of the arms, she addressed the room loudly in German, at which point everyone else in the room started crying. Of course, I'm the idiot at the front who has no idea what's going on (a role I specialize in), so the senior manager in the room turned to me, admittedly a bit stunned, and said, in perfect English, "The Berlin wall has come down." I have hardly ever worked in Germany, so it was incredibly unlikely that I would have the honor to be there on that particular day, but there I was. People were pouring across the border from East Berlin, grabbing the nearest phone, and suddenly everyone in the West was receiving calls from much-loved but long-estranged relatives. I thought about it for about ten seconds and said, "Class dismissed. We can come back and do this another time." And that was that. I guess if you speak frequently enough, eventually you see everything.

Normally it's not that dramatic, but the unexpected event or mistake is always going to happen. Sooner or later, every speaker faces the annoyingly loud lunch setup, or knocks over their water glass, drops their notes, or trips over a mic cable. Whether it was some external distraction or something you did, how you respond in those moments sends huge signals about who you really are on the inside. **If, instead of folding up like a cheap suit, you are calm and collected, people will see that you are the person you have presented yourself as being, and that this wasn't all merely a big act.**

The thing to remember about mistakes is that they look much bigger to us as presenters than they do to the audience, so when you make one, simply relax and laugh it off, because it's funny and the audience doesn't expect you to be perfect anyway. They know you're human just like they are, so this isn't such a big deal. Laugh, and your audience will laugh with you . . . and their confidence in you will grow.

With this deep dive on design and a look at the essentials of delivery, you are ready to go. I sincerely hope you will find that it was a valuable investment of your time. Do tell me how it all works out at:

timpollard@oratium.com

APPENDIX

REVIEW & REFINE

Once your communication or presentation is complete, ask yourself these questions:

Am I leading with a **problem** my customer/audience has?
Is the problem compelling and insightful – does it "find the pain"?
Do I have a clear summary statement of the problem?

Have I landed the key **insights** that will lead to engagement and action?
Have I stated those clearly and memorably before transitioning to the next section?

Is the **sequence** right?
Does it flow with the questions my customer/audience would ask?
Are my **transitions** natural and logical?

Is the argument supported intellectually?
Have I backed up key points with **sufficient and compelling data/facts**?

Am I engaging the customer/audience **beyond intellect alone** (e.g. story, visuals, and artifacts)?
Is it multidimensional and memorable?
Have I moved from "fact telling" to "story telling"?

Is it **simple enough**?
Is the quantity and complexity manageable?

Is the summary strong with a **clear and compelling call to action**?

Is the **handout/collateral at the right level of detail** and layout?
Do I have the right — and right number of — projected visuals?

When rehearsing, ask:

Do I **signal the customer/audience** when to pay attention?
Does it sound like spoken English?
Am I matching my tone and emotion to my words?

Grade yourself: A, B, C or F. Fix the lower grades first.

WWW.ORATIUM.COM
406.272.6556
info@oratium.com

You can visit oratium.com/downloads for a copy of this checklist using the code chartwell99.

INDEX

ACKNOWLEDGMENTS

In a very real sense, every workshop attendee we meet pushes our thinking with their questions and observations. Every single class makes the content better.

Special appreciation to Eli Murphy, Jerry Wall, and Stacey Aaronson, our extraordinary book consultant, whose tireless efforts helped so much to bring this book to fruition.

I particularly want to thank some specific individuals at certain clients who, in addition to embracing what we do, never cease to challenge us to innovate and improve both our content and the way that we fit that content to the real-life challenges of organizational change. Saumil Shah and Jodie Schroeder of Rockwell Automation; Suzanne Lynn-Duncan of State Street; Michelle Ellis, Amy Linsenmayer, Amanda Bjerkan Hennessy, and Michelle Reynolds of Disney; Sven-Ake Damgaard of Ericsson; Sue Graham of Elantas; Bill Mansfield and Dave Moeller of Graybar; Candace Thornton, Rick Johnson, and Glen Brooks of Verisk; Mike Edmonds, Tim Qualheim, Andrew Jones, Gary Wetzel, and Chris McCarthy of S&C Electric; Emi Hofmeister and Madi Shove of LinkedIn; and of course, Mitch Jones and Don Fletcher of R E Mason/Emerson. What's so humbling is that you have also offered so much friendship and encouragement to a young company.

As I look back on the years I spent at the Corporate Executive Board, developing and refining this thinking, there's a handful of extraordinary communicators with whom I've been blessed to share this journey. We were a Band of Brothers in the true Shakespearean sense. John Roberts, Dave Willis, Michael Hubble, Andrew Abela, Dan Currell, Jessica Sweeney-Platt, Martha Piper, Caren Gordon Cohen, and the recently departed and sorely missed Jerry Sorkin. Rest in peace, my friend.

And in a similar vein, the most gifted communications coach I've ever seen, Tamsen Webster. If you ever need coaching on a TED-style talk, visit her site at www.tamsenwebster.com.

Also from my time at CEB, I'm especially grateful to those individuals who pushed my thinking as we wrestled to turn complex content into exceptional presentations. You helped lay the groundwork for Oratium. Jay McGonigle, Pope Ward, Haniel Lynn, Derek Van Bever, Molly Maycock, Tom Monahan, Pete Buer, and the legendary Mike Klein.

I've had the privilege of enjoying the best formal and informal mentorship of some of the finest business leaders and thinkers in the world. I'd particularly like to thank the three who have invested most selflessly and deeply: Brian Hodous, Drew Pace, and Chris Curtis.

Finally, there's a short list of individuals who have done nothing to help me be a better communicator, but who through friendship and accountability have done everything to help me be a better husband, father, and son. You are better friends than I deserve. Crull Chambless, Joe Halligan, Deri Jones, Jason Ludwick, Brock and Jen Lutz, Ashok Nachnani, Paul Thomson, Jacob and Michelle Troyer, Mark Williams, and Pastor Steve. I hope I can grow up to be like any one of you.

ABOUT THE AUTHOR

TIM POLLARD is the founder and CEO of Oratium. Throughout the course of designing and delivering approximately 1,000 complex presentations to boards, national conferences, and executive committees, while working for companies as diverse as Unilever, Barclays Bank, and the Corporate Executive Board, Tim never stopped seeking to understand and capture the underlying "science" of extraordinary communication. The result of this journey has been the development of a unique set of tools and processes, and a remarkable ability to teach and coach others on their journey toward exceptional communication. As a result, Tim is one of the world's leading thinkers and writers in the field of advanced communication skills. He is a sought-after speaker, particularly on the topics of executive communications, sales messaging, and donor messaging.

Tim and his wife Ruth are British by birth but now reside in Montana where they're raising their four wonderful kids—three in college and one in high school. Tim is passionate about his family, fly fishing, and his church.

You can contact Tim at
TimPollard@Oratium.com

ABOUT ORATIUM

Oratium is a consulting and training company where tools and processes are brought to bear, solving their clients' particular communications challenges. Many organizations have included the Oratium program as a module in their leadership academies, training senior and future leaders in advanced communication skills. Additionally, many companies have applied the Oratium model to their sales messaging, frequently seeing a transformation of their sales outcomes as a result.

Through Oratium's unique, brain-based approach to communications, organizations from the largest corporations to the smallest nonprofits have seen a renaissance in their executive, sales, or donor communications.

Learn more at www.oratium.com
or contact us at
info@oratium.com

CPSIA information can be obtained
at www.ICGtesting.com
Printed in the USA
FSHW012351080919

9 780998 237312